MAKING
AUSTRALIA

John Thornhill, a Marist Priest, has
earned a reputation as one of Australia's
foremost lecturers and authors. A
philosopher and theologian, he has been
a member of the International
Theological Commission and is
president of the Australian Catholic
Theological Association.

MAKING
AUSTRALIA

Exploring our National Conversation

John Thornhill

MILLENNIUM
BOOKS

First Published in 1992 by
Millennium Books
an imprint of E.J. Dwyer (Australia) Pty Ltd
3/32-72 Alice Street
Newtown NSW 2042
Australia

National Library of Australia
Cataloguing-in-Publication data

Thornhill, John, 1929– .
Making Australia: exploring our national conversation.

Includes bibliographical references and index.
ISBN 0 85574 899 0.

1. National characteristics, Australian, 2. Christianity – Australia.
3. Australia – Civilization. I. Title

994

Cover designed by Robert Enemark
Typeset in 11/12pt Sabon by Graphicraft Typesetters, Hong Kong
Printed by SRM Production Services Sdn. Bhd., Malaysia

Dedication

To Aaron, my nephew,
Who was a true Australian,
and to his generation.

ACKNOWLEDGMENTS

The author gratefully acknowledges the use of material from the following works. Every effort has been made to locate the sources of quoted material and to obtain authority for its use.

A Short History of Australia by Manning Clark. Copyright © 1962 by Manning Clark. Renewed © 1980, 1987, by Manning Clark. Used by permission of New American Library, a division of Penguin Books USA Inc.

In Search of Henry Lawson, Manning Clark, South Melbourne, Macmillan Company of Australia, 1978.

A Discovery of Australia, Manning Clark, Crows Nest, NSW, A.B.C. Enterprises, 1976.

The Shape of Belief: Christianity in Australia Today, Dorothy Harris *et al*, editors, Flemington Markets, NSW, ANZEA Publications, 1982.

"Equanimity" and "The Quality of Sprawl", *Collected Poems*, Les Murray, North Ryde, NSW, Collins/Angus and Robertson Publishers, 1991.

"Australia", *Collected Poems 1930–70*, A.D. Hope, North Ryde, NSW, Collins/Angus and Robertson Publishers, 1971.

Gallipoli to the Somme, Dudley McCarthy, Surry Hills, NSW, John Ferguson Publishers, 1983.

Australia, John Rickard, Harlow, Essex, Longman Group UK, 1988.

Australia, W.K. Hancock, London, Ernest Benn, 1945.

Voss, Patrick White, London, Jonathan Cape, 1968.

After the Dreaming, W.E.H. Stanner, Crows Nest, NSW, A.B.C. Enterprises, 1968.

Australia: The Daedalus Symposium, Stephen Graubard, ed., Cambridge, MA., American Academy of Arts and Sciences, 1985.

A Crucible of Prophets, Veronica Brady, Sydney, Theological Explorations, 1981.

Kangaroo, D.H. Lawrence, Laurence Pollinger Ltd. and the Estate of Frieda Lawrence Ravagli, Harmondsworth, Middlesex, Penguin Books, 1977.

The Penguin New Literary History of Australia, Laurie Hergenhan, ed., Ringwood, Victoria, Penguin Books, 1988.

The Landscape of Australian Poetry, Brian Elliott, South Melbourne, Vic., Longman Cheshire Pty Limited, 1967.

The Australian Legend, Russel Ward, South Melbourne, Vic., Oxford University Press, 1989.

Preoccupations in Australian Poetry, Judith Wright, South Melbourne, Oxford University Press, 1966.

CONTENTS

PREFACE

This book is the outcome of a period of study-leave taken in 1990. As an academic, I seem to have spent a large part of my life on the outskirts of discussions carried on in Europe and North America. The opportunity to take up the study of Australian issues met an increasingly felt personal need to understand what we Australians share as a people and the realistic hopes we can have for our young country.

The world-building processes of the cultural conversation in which Australians have been engaged for the past two hundred years have involved a number of identifiable assumptions or options. These are, for the most part, little reflected upon. However, they have shaped our shared understanding of what it means to be human. The chapters which follow are an exploration of this shared experience and the ethos it has produced.

In this discussion of the assumptions and options we have made, the terms 'myth' and 'ideology' will be used in a carefully defined sense. Though it may come as a surprise to them, white Australians, like Aboriginal Australians, have had assumptions which can be described as 'mythological'—numinous meanings seen as establishing the context in which the common project of being human is to be taken up. Various ideological visions have given coherence and direction to our common endeavour. The experiences we have shared in a continent different in so many ways from other lands have left their mark on the distinctive outlook which we have come to share.

Today many Australians struggle, whether or not they recognise it, with the radical option implied in a disillusionment with the mythologies and ideologies which sustained the formative period of our history. This fact has a fundamental importance in this inquiry.

The interpreters and representative Australians who feature in the following chapters—such people as Judith Wright, Manning Clark, Les Murray, Patrick O'Farrell, Patrick White, Henry Lawson and C. E. W. Bean—are those I have found persuasive and significant. Others, no doubt, would have made different choices. For my part, I am grateful for what they have helped me to discover about all we share as Australians.

A comment made to me by the poet Noel Rowe, when my project was in its early stages, helps to define its scope. Concerning the controlling metaphor indicated in the sub-title, Noel pointed to the subtleties which belong to a living conversation: 'a process which works its evasions as well as its affirmations, its silences as well as its words, its absences as well as its presences, a process where the unifying impulse is often in tension with the pluralist instinct... in any genuine conversation, we do not always tell the whole truth, we do not always make sense (somehow the irrational needs to be accommodated as a major dynamic in culture). There are elements of determinism and cynicism which, precisely because they are "absences", are reminders that the conversation (culture) is not entirely free, nor even coherent'. Coming from the poet's sense of 'wholespeak', as Les Murray calls it, these comments reminded me that the analysis I was undertaking was being made, in large part, in the 'narrowspeak' of philosophy. As such it can provide some of the signposts which point out the way for those wishing to explore other aspects of the conversation which makes Australia.

As a theologian, I feel another of Noel Rowe's comments is worth quoting in these introductory remarks. If the ongoing process of Australian culture can be likened to a conversation, that conversation must take place between equal partners. Having for so long assumed a privileged position, theology may be surprised at being asked to relinquish it. In the end, however, theology must find a voice which is no longer that of a 'privileged participant'. As Noel Rowe puts it in a comment quoted in the final chapter, we find in the story of Jesus of Nazareth, not a 'higher' but a 'deeper' authority.

The first seven chapters of this work have no explicit theological reference. They do, however, provide the material which sets us on the threshold of what European theologians have come to call a 'political theology': an encounter between an Australian culture becoming critically aware of itself, and the challenge to human existence given to the world in the Christian tradition.

The writer is greatly indebted to the friends and colleagues who have commented upon the text in its formative stages: Veronica Brady, John Eddy, Robert Gascoigne, Cyril Halley, Rosa McGinley, Patrick O'Farrell, Noel Rowe and Tom Ryan. Shortly before his death, Manning Clark gave a word of encouragement. While they cannot be held responsible for the text as it is now published, their criticisms and suggestions have contributed in important ways to its improvement.

Special thanks are due to my brother-in-law Peter Robinson, who provided much valuable material, to Mary Ann Mortimer for providing the art work, and to Gai Smith, the librarian of Catholic Theological Union, whose generous assistance proved invaluable.

Words cannot express my indebtedness to John Sweeney and the Greystanes community of the Society of St Gerard Majella for their generous hospitality during the months in which this book first took shape.

1.

MY COUNTRY, MY PEOPLE

In these days of international travel many Australians know what it means to come back 'home'. It is an experience accentuated by the vast distances which make ours one of the most isolated countries in the world, and by the sense of contrast with what has been left behind. Australia is an island-continent, set beyond those islands with which the southern sweep of the Asian land mass peters out. It has little in common with its northern neighbours. To the east and the west it looks out on the vastness of the Pacific and Indian Oceans. Nothing lies to the south except the great Southern Ocean and the emptiness of Antarctica. The final leg of the journey takes several hours. There is no question of slipping over a frontier and suddenly finding oneself back home.

I shall never forget my first experience of coming home to Australia. After five years of study in Europe, circumstances made it necessary for me to return at short notice. In 1958 a passage by sea was still the normal way of travel between Europe and Australia; it was arranged, however, that I should come by air. The journey, in one of the last generation of propeller-driven aircraft, took much longer than it does today. Its last stage was a long flight across the continental interior from Darwin to Sydney.

During my years overseas I had never been nostalgic for Australia. Making contact with places and institutions which were the sources of our Western tradition made my years in Europe a rich and satisfying experience. I would have been glad to extend my stay, often recalling the advice given to me as I was leaving Sydney: 'Don't let study interfere with your education!' I was in no way prepared for the overwhelming impression which the red-ochre landscape of Australia's interior was to make on me that April day.

In those days lower altitude made it possible to see what lay below the flight path in much greater detail. What I saw is still imprinted on my memory: the vastness and emptiness of the outback, the thin lines of grey-green trees which marked out the tracery of empty river beds against the prevailing ochres, the remote homesteads linked with the outside world by a tiny yellow ribbon of road.

Eventually the suburbs of Sydney shimmered below us in the midday haze. The harbour came in sight. We were soon on the ground. Customs officers in white socks and navy shorts—strange after the covered legs of Europe—strode through the cabin with insecticide cans held aloft. I listened to the distinctive accent and matter-of-fact greetings of the men who attended to immigration and customs procedures. I had come back to my own country and my own people. Somehow, it bore in upon me, my life and my future was one with theirs.

Many times since that day I have had the experience of coming home. I have seen others sharing it in their own way. More and more of them, as the years have passed, have been migrant families returning to Australia after travel overseas.

1. The question of an Australian identity

It is only in recent years that I have begun to ask myself what it was that I was identifying with, in owning Australia as my own country and in owning Australians as my own people. This question is one of the central concerns of the chapters which follow. A brief look at some of the ways in which Australians have attempted to answer it may serve as an introduction to our discussion.

The question of a cultural identity was of no great concern to most Australians in 1958, the year of my return to this country. This was soon to change. Within a few years publications which took up the question were to attract a widespread interest.

In 1958 J. D. Pringle—a gifted journalist who had been brought from the United Kingdom to edit *The Sydney Morning Herald* and who had just returned to England—published a small volume entitled *Australian Accent*[1]. Pringle wrote as 'a British migrant who lived there for five years and nearly settled there for ever'. He sensed the time was ripe for Britain to take more seriously 'this young and vigorous nation to which she gave indifferent birth' one hundred and seventy years before, and that Australians who, like others, disliked criticism were 'now mature enough to take it'.

Although he hesitated to agree with their view, Pringle found that most Australians saw their country as 'still very English'. He summed up the absence of reflection he found among the Australians he had encountered by quoting D. H. Lawrence's words 'The vast continent is really void of speech'. In his judgment, Lawrence's *Kangaroo* was the 'one profound book' written about Australia.

In a footnote, Pringle had second thoughts. He had overlooked, he said, Sir Keith Hancock's 1930 publication *Australia*, which he judged 'certainly the best general account of Australian history and politics ever written'. The value of Hancock's work has long been recognised; even today its seminal ideas are of real value to those who seek to interpret the Australian experience. Hancock himself, however, began his brief Preface to a 1945 reprint of his work by warning the reader that his book was 'in many respects out of date'.

The book which Pringle could praise in such high terms in 1958 speaks to today's reader of an Australia which has long since disappeared. Hancock judged that 'the Australian people had not come of age'. The 'exuberant, egotistical, idealistic nationalism' at the turn of the century 'was a sign, not that Australians had already become a nation, but that they wished to become one'. Hancock was on sound ground when he challenged Australians to recognise that 'nationality consists, not merely in political unity, but in spiritual achievement'[2]. His view, however, that the essential source of this achievement was found in the resources of British race and stock would make many contemporary Australians smile. 'Among Australians', he wrote, 'pride of race counted for more than love of country... Defining themselves as "independent Australian Britons" they believed each word essential and exact, but laid most stress upon the last'[3].

On the surface, at least, it seemed that things had not changed all that much in the thirty years between Hancock's *Australia* and Pringle's *Australian Accent*. Hancock wrote of a nation of 'independent Australian Britons'; Pringle wrote of an Australia in which 90 per cent were of British stock and which had adopted a migration policy favouring the maintaining of this preponderance. In the end, however, Australia of 1958 puzzled Pringle. He saw it as 'an Anglo-Saxon nation', but he also found it 'almost as different from Britain as the United States, with its own standards, its own culture, its own traditions'. No doubt the Celtic influence, to which Pringle pays little attention, provides one of the keys to an understanding of the characteristics which puzzle him.

Today it is not difficult to recognise that Hancock and Pringle were too close to the events to appreciate in full the effects of two world wars and a worldwide economic depression on the Australia they wanted to interpret. Being caught up in these conflicts, and the disillusionment they brought to the Western world, could only have a profoundly unsettling effect on the Australian self-awareness beginning to express itself at the end of the nineteenth century in the 'exuberant nationalism' which Hancock dismissed too easily. What Pringle saw as a lack of reflection may have derived in large measure from the uncertainty with which Australians faced the question of what their involvement in these conflicts had achieved. The economic depression which overtook the world for a large part of the period between the world wars made survival the dominant concern of most Australians, leaving little energy for such things as the exploration of national identity.

The fact that Donald Horne's *The Lucky Country: Australia in the Sixties*, published a few years later in 1964, could immediately become a best-seller makes it clear that beneath the numbness to which we have referred, Australians were indeed concerned to understand themselves and were waiting for someone to articulate this understanding for them. Horne's interpretation pulled no punches. Concluding his book, he makes it clear that his title is ironical: 'Australia is a lucky country run mainly by second-rate people who share its luck... Australia has had gambler's luck... The saving Australian characteristic—and this has something of the gambler's coolness about it—is the ability to change course quickly, even at the last moment, and seek a quiet, easy way out'[4].

The country Horne challenged was beginning to know the unprecedented affluence of the 1960s and the buoyant mood such affluence brought. Australia had become one of the world's most urbanised nations in the nineteenth century; in the twentieth century, he suggested, it could become 'the first *suburban* nation'[5]. Australians, he argued, should explore the positive potential of suburban life, rather than destroy themselves by falling in with the bohemian fashion of the moment which made suburban life a target for ridicule. For Horne, 'The image of Australia is of a man in an open-necked shirt solemnly enjoying an ice-cream. His kiddy is beside him'[6]. It is significant that, as Donald Horne urged Australians to face the challenges of emerging nationhood, the argument of his book saw no place for a Christian contribution to the country's future.

Craig McGregor's *Profile of Australia*[7], which appeared a couple of years later, expressed similar concerns. McGregor saw Australia as having 'lost most of its radical inspiration', and as giving itself up to 'the pursuit of contentment'[8]. If Australia had been 'a backwater of late Victorian culture for so long', now it had 'suddenly become part of the Western world' and knew the beginnings of a new awareness[9]. For McGregor, the problem Australia faced was 'whether an intellectual, artistic, educated tradition can be built up which will modify and direct the materialism' of the culture which was emerging[10]. He saw no place, however, for religion in these efforts to counter a growing materialism; he portrayed the Christian tradition as having been essentially obstructionist. Like Horne's work, McGregor's volume had a wide readership. Many Australians were eager to understand what being an Australian entailed. Horne and McGregor essayed a description of Australia as it was in the 1960s. Other thinkers had already begun to seek an interpretation of the national ethos which looked to its roots in our previous history. In 1943 Vance Palmer, writing in *Meanjin*, urged Australians facing the threat of a Japanese invasion to ask themselves whether they 'deserve to survive': 'there is an Australia of the spirit', he argued, 'submerged and not very articulate...the Australia of all who truly belong here'[11].

Eleven years later, in *The Legend of the Nineties*[12], Palmer explained more fully the 'Australia of the spirit' to which he had appealed. He pointed back to the developments in Australian awareness during the last decade of the nineteenth century mentioned by Hancock. These he saw as establishing a distinctive identity whereby Australia 'carries its past history in its bones'. While acknowledging the naivety and shallowness pointed to by Hancock, Palmer considered that there was 'an intensity about the spirit of the early nineties that created images and ideas having a continuous force' for the Australian people[13].

The year after Palmer's book appeared, historian R. M. Crawford[14] drew attention to Russel Ward's suggestion that the 'nomad tribe' of bush workers—a phrase coined by the novelist, Anthony Trollope in his account of travels in Australia, published in the 1870s—had left their mark on the Australian character. This 'bush ethos' was taken up 'as distinctively Australian by the writers and journalists who were creating an aggressively Australian literature towards the close of the century'. As a consequence 'it entered the consciousness of Australians as a national myth or legend, enshrining values and attitudes they took to be essentially Australian'. According to this idealised Australian ethos, Crawford wrote, 'respect is given, not to wealth or rank or display but to those qualities regarded as the common qualities of the genuine bushman. A man is expected to display independence and courage in the face of danger or adversity, but not to be different from his fellows...he must stand by his mates through thick and thin'.

In 1958, the year Pringle published *Australian Accent*, Russel Ward developed this idea more fully in a work entitled *The Australian Legend*[15]. As he wrote in the Foreword, he attempted in this work 'to trace the historical origins and development of the Australian legend or national *mystique*'. Through this legend, the bush workers as a group 'had an influence, completely disproportionate to...numerical and economic strength, on the attitudes of the whole Australian community'. Few books in the field of

Australian history have been so widely commented upon. As we shall see, not all agree with the case argued by Ward, but few will deny that, with Palmer, he has put his finger on something of great importance in an understanding of the distinctive outlook of Australians.

The question of a distinctive identity and ethos assumed a new form in popular awareness in response to the massive immigration program adopted by Australia in the decades following the Second World War. In that period, Australians found themselves forced to come to terms with the upheaval brought by the war—in particular, with the fact that the British connection had been greatly modified; tentatively, they were entering on a new phase of self-understanding and self-criticism.

It is not surprising that the initial reaction of the established Anglo-Celtic community was essentially defensive. Assimilation to the Australian way of life became the official policy. It was equally understandable that the migrants themselves, as Richard White points out, saw this policy as 'a useful tool of intolerance'[16]. In so far as it took recognisable shape, this 'Australian way of life' seemed to be identified with the life-style and respectability associated with the new suburban affluence. Immigration Minister Arthur Calwell, for instance, argued that 'proper housing and other amenities' were necessary to help migrants 'fit themselves quickly into the Australian way of life'[17].

The work of Richard White I have just quoted, published in 1981 under the title *Inventing Australia*, is a fitting one with which to conclude this section. White surveys the search for an Australian identity within a historical perspective. He explains his rationale in his Introduction. In his judgment 'There is no "real" Australia waiting to be uncovered'. National identities are 'inventions'. One is not 'truer than another because they are all intellectual constructs, neat, tidy, comprehensible—and necessarily false'.

Under the influence of the nineteenth century European idea of national identity, something distinctive in the experience of the Australian people is interpreted in a way which reflects the changing intellectual needs and fashions of Western culture. These interpretations serve a social function, often related to the interests of those groups in society wielding economic power. Using this Marxist rationale, White makes an illuminating analysis of the images of Australia which have been operative in the various periods of our history, from the 'Hell upon Earth' of early penal days to the 'Everyman and his Holden' of the suburban Australia which received our postwar immigrants. The challenging approach of this work, used as a text in many tertiary courses, provides a suitable starting point for our own discussion of what constitutes the *real* Australia.

2. Australia as a project

There are few things more important in any inquiry than asking the right questions. Questions about 'identity', 'image', 'ethos' and 'legend' will certainly shed light on important aspects of Australian culture, but they can only give us part of the answer to the question of what makes the real Australia.

Henry Lawson—for all the inadequacies of his tragic life, one of the greatest of Australians—hits the mark far more truly in the yarn in which he portrays an Australian, in a New Zealand coach, grumbling about his country. 'Why, it's only a mongrel desert... The worst, dried up, God-forsaken country I was ever in... I was born there. That's the main thing I've got against the darned country...' An English fellow traveller who is inclined to agree with him soon finds his mistake. The story's title—'His Country —After All'—sums up the paradox of the situation. In fact, the Australian is on his way home!

Patrick White makes the same point when he describes the ambiguity of the relationship to her country of Laura Trevelyan, the young woman who, in a mysterious and tragic way, was to share in the journey into the Australian interior of Voss, the explorer. Too young to remember coming here, she owned that she was somewhat fearful of the adopted land 'which, for lack of any other, she supposed was hers'[18].

Before all else, being an Australian is *being here* and being willing to make something of it. Not all those who have found themselves here were here by choice. Most of the first white settlers came against their will; many of those who have since migrated to these shores came because the land they loved most was closed to them. They all became Australians, however, in the measure in which they took up a share in the project of trying to make this a place where existence was bearable for themselves and their children.

As might be expected, this common human project of making an existence which is at least bearable, and if possible fruitful and even joyful, has produced its different moods of shared ethos. Its experience has given rise to a crop of images and legends expressing the way in which Australians would like to see themselves. Being an Australian, however, takes us beyond these things; it is a matter of the will, of the making of a choice like that made by the character in Lawson's story, for all its ambiguity[19].

We cannot understand human history, nor the story of any people, except by coming to terms with the whole breadth and mystery of human existence and of the human choices which give expression to that existence. That is where the reductionism of Richard White's too exclusively Marxist interpretation falls down. We have much to learn from what Marx brought to light in his understanding of the influences which help to shape history. But if Richard White's study pretends to reduce the ultimate meaning of the two hundred years of struggle and hope, joy and suffering, achievement and failure which constitute our history to no more than the interplay of successive power groups and the intellectual constructs which have supported their vested interests, we can only protest that we do not recognise ourselves.

Vance Palmer was closer to the mark with his understanding of Australians as those who 'deserve to survive' because of the contribution they are ready to make in carrying forward the common project, and with his 'Australia of the spirit... the Australia of all who truly belong here'. What leaves us uneasy is the seemingly implied demand that all should conform to some predetermined ethos. It calls up fearful memories of the repressive rationale which produced the Fascist and Nazi regimes and the nightmares they let loose in our century in the name of a pretended nationhood. On what terms, then, can we understand the real Australia as a common project?

3. Australia as a conversation

The real Australia is constituted by those willing to take part in the project of achieving a way of being human together. As a typical contemporary democratic community, we come together with a wide range of resources and many different points of view as to how this project may be carried through successfully. John Courtney Murray, the Jesuit theologian who successfully championed the cause of religious freedom at the Second Vatican Council, took his stand upon the wisdom embodied in the Anglo-Saxon tradition of legislation and jurisprudence. He conceived the modern democratic community as made up by 'citizens locked in argument'. The direction taken by the project they share is not determined by the imposition of any one point of view, but by the outcome of a public debate of the issues involved. Professor Manning Clark could be interpreted as adopting a similar point of view when, in his 1976 Boyer Lectures, he said of the historical process as a whole 'All history is about conflict'[20].

But how are the various points of view arising in a democratic society to meet and contend with one another? Reflecting critically upon the 'powerful pressures to conform' which were present in Australia prior to the Second World War, John Rickard writes 'A culture should be identified not so much by any sense of shared values, which may be artificially induced, as by the means it develops to reconcile or at least to accommodate the dissonant forces within it'[21].

B. Nesbitt takes up this same line of thought in his discussion of the debate in the *Bulletin* between Henry Lawson and Banjo Paterson, which, as we shall see, has great importance for anyone seeking to understand the experience which has shaped Australian history. He cites the view of R. W. B. Lewis that as a culture advances towards maturity 'it seems to produce its own determining debate over the ideas that preoccupy it', and that this debate 'may be said to *be* the culture, at least on its loftiest level; for a culture achieves identity not so much through the ascendancy of a particular set of convictions as through the emergence of its peculiar and distinctive dialogue'[22].

J. C. Murray speaks of 'argument'; Clark speaks of 'conflict'; Rickard speaks of 'reconciliation' and 'accommodation'; Lewis speaks of a 'determining debate' and a 'distinctive dialogue'. These thinkers all express themselves in a way which suggests the moments and moods which contribute to a *conversation*. Whether we have seen it clearly or not, the soul of the project which has made Australians one people has always been the conversation to which we brought our various points of view as we sought the way forward together.

It is a sad fact of our history, like all others, that differences in outlook have more often than not given rise to bitter conflict. These same differences, if they are taken up in a spirit of honesty and respect, *can* give rise not to conflict, but to a productive dialogue. It is of the nature of a wholesome conversation that each party enters into it expecting to be enriched by coming to appreciate more fully those things to which their partners in dialogue are deeply committed.

Professor Manning Clark often returns to the 'three different visions of God and man' which we Australians have brought to our conversation, 'Catholic Christendom, Protestant Christianity and the Enlightenment'[23]. The manner of their meeting has been, for the most part, a savage and uncompromising confrontation. How much more productive would it have been for all parties if a respectful dialogue had taken place, in which those involved really expected to have their own point of view enlarged by coming to appreciate the concerns of the other parties. Such attitudes were probably impossible, it must be conceded, for the men and women of nineteenth century Australia. Our appreciation today of the rights and freedoms essential to a just democratic order provide a framework within which such a conversation becomes possible. Today, of course, the presence of non-Christian traditions in our Australian society calls for an enlarging of our conversation which could never have been anticipated in the nineteenth century.

What this discussion is bringing to light is the real nature of the common good, or 'common weal', which should unite a wholesome human community. In the last analysis, the common good is the ordered collaboration of the citizens, a collaboration through which they share in a common culture and strive towards a fulfilled human existence. The common good of a human community shapes the common endeavour of the participants. If it is authentic, it looks beyond material efficiency and benefits to a maintaining of the inalienable rights of each human person. The essential function of legislation and jurisprudence is a serving and maintaining of this order without which a full human existence is not possible. The achievement essential to the common good belongs, not to government, but to the community as a whole. The more genuine the conversation entered into by the community, the more fruitful will be their common achievement[24].

Conceiving the real Australia as the outcome of an ongoing conversation will prove a valuable tool in the discussion we are about to undertake.

4. From a provincial conversation to one that is multicultural

I propose to reflect upon some of the fundamental implications of the conversation that has carried forward our Australian project. Before doing so, however, it is necessary to discuss Australia's peculiar cultural situation, a situation which only came to an end with the Second World War. Through most of the decades which make up our short history, our culture has been, in its basic elements, derivative. If, as we shall see, the conversation which animated the Australian project was developing a distinctive tone of its own, it was still a remote corner of the larger conversation of the British imperial project and its cultural complexity.

When W. K. Hancock wrote his *Australia*, the British connection was still firmly in place: we were 'independent Australian Britons'. Pringle began his *Australian Accent* with the remark 'most Englishmen who go to Australia expect to find it a replica of England'. Though he warned them that this would not be the case—that they would find a country 'with its own standards, its own culture, its own traditions'—Pringle's Australia was 'an Anglo-Saxon nation certainly'; Australians, he found, still preferred to see themselves as 'a very English country'.

Though it is evident to us today that the very nature of things demanded that Australia should ultimately assume an identity clearly independent of Britain, it took a century and a half for such an independence to emerge. We had our origins as a group of colonies, creatures of Britain. The American colonies settled the question of their independence decisively and unambiguously by a dramatic declaration; our relationship with Britain, by way of contrast, was to become one of the most complex issues in our shared experience. It is not surprising that it troubled us in a way that had much in common with the confused self-consciousness of an adolescent seeking independence and selfhood beyond the constrictions of outgrown family relationships.

This underlying confusion was evidenced in an incident which took place on the morning of 11 June 1849 when, despite continuous rain, a crowd of four or five thousand Sydney citizens gathered at Circular Quay to protest against the disembarking of convicts from the recently arrived ship *Hashemy*. The ambiguities of the Australian situation were clear enough. Mr Lamb, the member for Sydney, was the principal speaker and moved a formal motion of protest. Echoing the sentiments already expressed by Mr Robert Campbell who had introduced him, he appealed immediately to 'the British character of the community' of New South Wales, threatened with compromise, he said, by the resumption of transportation. The formal protest the community was urged to make was an expression of its 'spirit of loyalty to the Queen', of 'the highest and holiest patriotism that could animate them as citizens', of 'their loyalty to Great Britain'. The words of the petition to be sent were read out. They expressed similar views: 'we greatly fear that the perpetration of so stupendous an act... will go far towards alienating the affections of the people of this colony from the mother country'; the protest was made 'in the strength of our loyalty to Great Britain'. Mr Lowe, who seconded Lamb's motion, did not hesitate to point to the outcome of similar protests on the part of the American colonies: 'in America, oppression was the parent of independence, so would it be in this country'[25].

On the one hand the people of Sydney felt that it was unjust that a decision of such importance in the life of the colony should be made in complete disregard of their views. On the other hand they took their stand as Britishers, loyal to the Crown and appealing to the values proper to the British tradition in which they shared. Their relationship with the metropolitan culture was paradoxical. Their cultural identity itself depended upon the maintaining of British traditions. At the same time they wanted to assume responsibility for a social project which had become distinctively their own. Within a few years, the discovery of gold was to bring a rapid population growth and the increased prosperity which gave them a greater measure of confidence. The slogan they adopted during the second half of the nineteenth century was 'Australia for Australians'.

Despite the slogans, however, Australian culture during this period remained a provincial expression of British culture. As S. Glynn points out, a good case could be made that during a large part of our history 'the cultural differences between London and Cornwall, or London and Yorkshire, were greater than the differences between London and Australia'[26]. Rickard makes the same point in another way: 'often the ties between "Home" (as Britain was called) and colony could be stronger than between, say, Victoria and New South Wales'[27].

It was not easy for adolescent Australia to settle for such a modest self-appraisal. For this, I suppose, we can be grateful, because the young country's yearning to express something of the originality of the Australian culture gave rise in the last decade of the century to developments of great importance in our ongoing Australian conversation. These developments found expression in the literature to which reference has already been made, literature which found a notable expression in the work of such writers as Henry Lawson.

From an early date, native-born Australians could not but be aware that they were different. The stock which had been transplanted to Australia from the British Isles soon developed physical characteristics remarked upon by those visiting the colony. A government report in 1822, for instance, found the children of convicts 'a remarkable exception to the moral and physical character of their parents'. In 1827 P. Cunningham, who had spent two years in Australia, described the currency lads and lasses as 'a fine interesting race'.

Those who almost a century later saw Australian troops embarking for Gallipoli were extravagant in their praise. 'For physical beauty and nobility of bearing', wrote John Masefield, 'they surpassed any men I have ever seen; they walked and looked like kings in old poems'. According to Compton Mackenzie 'Their beauty, for it was really heroic, should have been celebrated in hexameters not headlines. There was not one of those glorious young men I saw that day who might not himself have been Ajax or Achilles. Their almost complete nudity, their tallness and majestic simplicity of line, their rose-brown flesh burnt by the sun and purged of all grossness by the ordeal through which they were passing, all these united to create something as near to absolute beauty as I shall ever hope to see in this world'[28]. D. H. Lawrence was obviously struck by the robust physique of Australians; more than once in his novel *Kangaroo*, published in 1923 after a brief sojourn in this country, he remarks upon the well developed limbs of Australian youths.

How is this extraordinary impression to be explained? In the British army, at that time, it was common for officers to be considerably taller than men in the ranks. Among the Anzacs, however, no such difference existed. Hancock attributed the new physical type which had developed in Australia during the nineteenth century—taller and slimmer, more pointed in features, having typical colouring of hair and eyes—to a blending of the genetic pool, something which did not take place, except in the upper classes, in the highly regionalised life which prevailed in Britain, and to the nourishment and exercise enjoyed by Australian youths. He concluded whimsically, 'if such a creature as the average Briton exists anywhere upon the earth, he may well be found in Australia'[29]. In our day, of course, a further pooling of genetic resources has once more modified the typical Australian.

If the Australian project was really a provincial corner of the great British enterprise, those who saw themselves as more identified with the metropolitan culture did not hesitate to remind Australians of their provincial status. The first generation of white Australians born in Australia were called 'currency lads and lasses'. The name was a none too subtle put-down. There were two types of legal tender in New South Wales after Governor Macquarie remedied a currency shortage by introducing the 'holey dollar': a coin produced by stamping out the centre of a Spanish dollar. These two currencies were called 'sterling' and 'currency'. If the locally born were likened to the makeshift coinage, 'currency', British stock was 'sterling'.

As the nineteenth century progressed, many Australians came to resent the name 'colonial' with its patronising overtones. Disparagement of Australians as second-rate Britishers continued well into the twentieth century, and came from even the highest level. In 1931 King George V resisted the appointment of Sir Isaac Isaacs as the first native-born Governor-General. When our government refused to reconsider, he pointedly omitted the customary reference to his being 'pleased' in his announcing of the appointment. Not long ago a reviewer of one of David Malouf's novels noted with regret the following jibe in a column of *The Times*: 'I hear that the Australian Broadcasting Corporation and the *Australian Book Review* are to complete a list of the ten greatest Australian works since the war. Nominations on a postage stamp please'. There was certainly a British side to the development of the 'cultural cringe'.

D. H. Lawrence wrestled with the puzzling ambiguity of Australia's cultural situation during his visit to this country. Somers, the character in *Kangaroo* through which Lawrence explores his own reactions, finds Australians uncouth, even barbarians: 'The most loutish Neapolitan was nearer to him in pulse than these British Australians with their aggressive familiarity'[30]. Describing outback life in his *On the Wool Track*, first published in 1910, C. E. W. Bean tells of a boundary rider who had worked for about twenty years on the same run. One day he astounded the property owner: 'I see they reckon the King's goin' to be crowned next year... I guess I must go and see 'im'[31].

It was still customary for the Australians I remember from my Brisbane childhood to refer to the British Isles, which they had never seen, as 'home' or 'the home country'. Bernard Shaw found this attitude baffling. 'You Australasians', he commented, 'are extraordinary really. Every year thousands of you... journey to see an inferior country which you persist in calling Home in spite of the fact that its people ignore you and are scarcely aware of your existence. I wish I could persuade you that THIS is your home, that these lands should be the centre of your art, your culture, your drama'[32].

One after another, our most gifted writers, artists and scholars, from Henry Lawson and Percy Grainger to Christina Stead, Sidney Nolan and Patrick White, reacted to Australia's provincial situation by living abroad, for varying periods of time[33]. Robert Menzies's words gave expression, no doubt, to what many Australians experienced: 'At last we are in England. Our journey to Mecca has ended, and our minds abandoned to those reflections which can so strangely (unless you remember our tradition and upbringing) move the soul of those who go "home" to a land they have never seen'[34]. John Rickard comments 'Mecca indeed:... the first beholding of England could have almost a religious awe to it'[35].

But the relationship of dependence and patronage was also resented. Victor Daley's poem 'When London Calls' captures the bitterness which Australia's relationship with Britain, the 'haggard-eyed Imperatrix', could engender:

They leave us—artists, singers all—
When London calls aloud,
Commanding to her Festival
The gifted crowd...

Sad, weary, cruel, grand;
Her crown imperial gleams with gems
From many a land...

Sad, sad is she, and yearns for mirth;
With voice of golden guile
She lures men from the ends of the earth
To make her smile[36].

It was inevitable that the patronage of the parent culture should make itself felt through a British control of Australian affairs. Reaction to this was not long in appearing. In 1832, Horatio Wills established a paper entitled *The Currency Lad* 'to campaign against all the plums in the colonies falling into the baskets of Englishmen'. In his first issue, Wills wrote: 'Look, Australians, to the high salaried foreigners around you. Behold those men lolling in their coaches—rioting in the sweat of your brow'[37].

It was not easy, however, for provincial Australians to make headway against the many forms of British establishment. A century later G. H. Cowling, an Englishman who was professor of English literature at the University of Melbourne, wrote an article published in the Melbourne *Age* in which he found the prospects for an Australian literature very bleak indeed. He provoked a stinging response from an Australian scholar, P. R. Stephensen: 'is this the kind of anti-Australian nonsense', he asked, 'these professors are imported from England to teach to teachers of our Australian youth?' Stephensen agreed that Australia's intellectual life was anything but flourishing, that the arts were 'stultified, smug, puerile', that literary gifts were little appreciated and seldom fostered. 'In what, at present, can an Australian take pride? In our cricketers, merino sheep, soldiers, vast open spaces—and what then? Until we have a culture, a quiet strength of intellectual achievement, we have nothing except our soldiers to be proud of!' Gifted Australians had taken flight, he wrote, 'driven out by the intolerable hegemony of the second-rate in positions of authority here'[38].

In arguing his case, Stephensen identified with admirable clarity the problems peculiar to a provincial culture, and stated clearly the place an authentically Australian culture must find for itself within the broader conversation of the cultures of the world. 'Art and literature are at first nationally created, but become internationally appreciated... Each nation contributes ideas to the culture of every other nation... every contribution to world-culture... must be instinct with the colour of its place of origin... There is a universal concept of humanity and world culture, but it does not destroy individuality, either of persons or places or nations ...cultures must remain local in creation and universal in appreciation'.

Nothing but our soldiers to be proud of! It is ironical that it was ultimately through military involvement in the broader world that Australia began to move towards assuming responsibility for its own cultural conversation. But this development was the outcome of a long and tragic experience. There is something remarkable in the fact that, despite the antagonism Australians felt towards the parent culture and its establishment, Australia made a massive contribution to Britain's wars. At the turn of the century, more than sixteen thousand Australians went to the Boer War, as compared with about six thousand Canadians. The Australian response to Britain's war with Germany in 1914 was immediate and generous. There was no separate declaration of war. The Governor-General of the time spoke of Australia's 'indescribable enthusiasm'. By the end of 1914 more than fifty thousand had enlisted; Prime Minister Fisher promised that Australia would defend Britain 'to our last man and our last shilling'. As historian Dudley McCarthy points out, nobody seemed to question the assumptions which led the Australian government to seek British approval for the appointment of an Australian commander for Australian volunteers[39].

The prospects of an adventure on the other side of the world must have played a large part in the decision of many young men to enlist, but there can be little doubt that for large numbers of them the response was also animated by the sense of patriotism which had been absorbed with the British nationalism and imperialism fundamental to Australia's provincial culture—something to which I shall return in a later chapter. No doubt the ambiguity of our provincial situation also asserted itself: adolescent Australia was fired by the prospect of giving an ultimate proof of national worth on the field of battle[40].

The dubious nature, in the end, of the European conflict, and the massive character of Australia's involvement—her casualties were relatively heavier than those of Britain herself!—made a subsequent disillusionment inevitable. The fact that Australian troops won admiration for their contribution to the conflict, and the formation of the new legend of Anzac, however, only served to complicate the working out of this disillusionment. John Rickard notes how the old antagonism to the parent culture came to find its place in the Anzac legend itself. 'Gallipoli . . . was not only a defeat, but, in the end, an irrelevant sideshow. This, however, allowed for a subtle anti-Britishness to intrude itself into the saga. The defeat could not be laid at the feet of the heroic Anzacs: the failure of Gallipoli was a failure of British strategy. Hidden in the Anzac myth is a feeling that the Anzacs had been sent on a fool's errand. But the sense in which Gallipoli was a sideshow also had the effect of giving the Anzacs a slightly proprietorial attitude to the campaign, ignoring the fact the British soldiers were in the majority'[41].

Twice during the course of the war those who wished to increase Australia's commitment to the conflict by the introduction of conscription were narrowly defeated. Loyal imperialists were shaken to find that many of their fellow citizens did not fully share their views; the attitudes and values of the Australia which was emerging were far more complex than they had assumed them to be.

It is not surprising that Australia lapsed into a state of numbness in the period following the war. It was not uncommon for the homes I visited as a child to give pride of place to the recently acquired maroon volumes of C. E. W. Bean's *Official History of Australia during the War of 1914–1918*. Their countless photographs portrayed in horrifying detail the nightmare which was supposed to be a war to end all wars. The Australians who had bought them must have asked themselves what had been achieved by a conflict which had unleashed carnage and destruction such as the world had never known. It was a question to which a nation which had made such a massive and unhesitating commitment could not easily give the straightforward answer it deserved. The great economic depression of the 1930s pushed Australia into even greater uncertainty. And then, almost immediately, new war clouds began to gather in Europe and Australia found itself caught in another worldwide conflict. It was significant, however, that this time Australia made its own declaration of war.

The poet A. D. Hope returned to Australia from studies in Oxford in 1931. The poem 'Australia', composed in the years following his return, expressed a reflective mood of Australian awareness. Hope looked with the eyes of a returning exile at this strange old land, and was reminded of the long struggle we had had to come to terms with it:

They call her a young country, but they lie:
She is the last of lands, the emptiest,
A woman beyond her change of life, a breast
Still tender but within the womb is dry.

With a merciless eye, he recognised how far the country was from finding its true destiny:

Her rivers of water drown among inland sands,
The river of her immense stupidity
Floods her monotonous tribes from Cairns to Perth.

The Australia he found seemed, as yet, no more than a place

Where second-hand Europeans pullulate
Timidly on the edge of alien shores.

A sense of hopelessness in the future of European civilisation tempted him to think that Australia too had no hope, that we were condemned to be a people

Whose boast is not 'We live' but 'We survive',
The type who will inhabit the dying earth.

But no, he dared to hope that we could find our true independence from Europe, and make a worthy future, a contribution to the human story:

Yet there are some like me turn gladly home
From the lush jungle of modern thought, to find
The Arabian desert of the human mind,
Hoping, if still from the deserts the prophets come,

Such savage and scarlet as no green hills dare
Springs in that waste, some spirit which escapes
The learned doubt, the chatter of cultured apes
Which is called civilisation over there.

With the Second World War and its aftermath, the provincial phase of the conversation which had shaped Australia for so long moved towards its end. Before the war, Australians were convinced that, whether they liked it or not, protection from possible aggression on the part of an Asian power made the maintaining of the British connection essential. In 1931, the British parliament's Statute of Westminster granted Australia complete autonomy of government. 'The new statute', writes Geoffrey Blainey, 'was seen as being of little practical consequence and even as slightly subversive to the spirit of empire, and it was not adopted by the Australian parliament until 1942'[42].

The events of the Second World War made it clear that Britain was not able to ensure Australia's security. Prime Minister John Curtin's 1942 declaration was a historical turning point: 'Without any inhibitions of any kind, I make it quite clear that Australia looks to America, free of any pangs as to our traditional links or kinship with the United Kingdom'. Old attitudes still asserted themselves however: Winston Churchill, angered by the independent line taken by the Australian government at that time, is supposed to have burst out with a comment that 'the Australians are from bad stock'.

The full implications of Australia's new self-reliance took time to sink in. I have suggested already that the lack of reflectiveness Pringle regretted in the Australia he wrote about in 1958 was the last moment of a numbness which resulted from the traumatic upheaval experienced by an adolescent Australia's involvement in the two world conflicts, and by the impact of worldwide economic depression. The large influx of migrants in recent decades has given a new multicultural configuration to the Australian conversation.

The statistics of immigration speak for themselves. On the eve of the Second World War, 98 per cent of Australia's population were born in Australia itself or in the British Isles. Immigration policy has favoured immigrants from the United Kingdom and New Zealand, and throughout the whole immigration program they have been the largest single source of migrants. When the original policy did not achieve the ambitious targets which had been set, however, migrants were sought from elsewhere. The pattern of postwar immigration from these other countries falls roughly into three phases. From 1945–1954, northern Europe (Germany and Holland) were a major source; from 1955–1974 the Mediterranean countries (Italy, Greece, Yugoslavia, Malta) provided large numbers; from 1975 onwards South-East Asia (Vietnam, Indonesia, Malaysia) provided many of our immigrants, a large number of them being refugees.

During this period, a development of first importance took place in the awareness of white Australians. As they became less threatened by the cultural diversity developing in their midst, they were able to acknowledge once more the existence of the Aboriginal people and their culture—after a long period during which the majority of white Australians more or less unconsciously chose to act as if they did not exist. During the period 1961–1971 Australia's Aboriginal population more than doubled (from 79 300 to 160 900).

Throughout the present century, the section of our population born outside Australia has ranged between 15 per cent and 25 per cent. In other words, those in the population who were born overseas have been at least one in seven and at times as many as one in four. In 1981 the figure was one in five. Comparing these figures with those of other advanced industrialised countries, we find that our proportional intake is considerably greater than any of them—including such countries as the United States and West Germany, which during this same period relied heavily on the intake of foreign workers and their families[43].

Australia, we are told, is entering upon a new phase of multicultural development. In a certain sense, of course, the white Australian community has been multicultural from a very early date. From the arrival of the first fleet in 1788, the colony had an Irish component. In 1791 their number was substantially increased, when the ship *Queen* brought Irish convicts directly from Cork. From the first the colony began to reflect the cultural complexity of the British Isles. The community which developed in this country during the nineteenth century was one in which there coexisted distinct cultural traditions. The interchange between these cultures—those of England, Ireland and Scotland—in the first phase of Australian history, was an interchange which in all its diverse moods, ranging from common cause to distrust and antagonism, was grounded in the symbiotic relationship which had been produced by centuries of European cohabitation. Today's multiculturalism, in which juxtaposed cultural traditions enter into a new and unprecedented relationship, is of course, very different.

The antipodean transplant of the cultural interaction of the British Isles had, of course, its own distinctive features. For one thing, the Scots were no longer up in Scotland and the Irish were no longer across the Irish Sea, but these two groups were dispersed throughout the colonies, rubbing shoulders with fellow citizens of Anglo-Saxon extraction. There was also a considerable increase in the Irish component.

In the introductory chapter of his *The Irish in Australia*, the historian Patrick O'Farrell gathers together the conclusions to which he has been led in his long study of the part the Irish have played in our history. Not all will be in unqualified agreement, perhaps, with his claim that until the recent past, 'the Irish have been the dynamic factor in Australian history, that is, the galvanising force at the centre of the evolution of our national character'[44]; but he has clearly put his finger on something of fundamental importance in our history. O'Farrell argues that the version of our history which has tended to establish itself—the view reflected in the works of Hancock and Pringle to which I have made reference—has really been 'the story of the ruling classes', a view which promoted 'a consoling sense of unity in national experience and endeavour'. In O'Farrell's judgment, this view is open to the criticism that 'it avoids, disguises and minimises' a fundamental dynamic of our history: 'that it was composed from the beginning of diverse peoples; and that its major internal formative force was tension and conflict, ultimately of a most creative kind, between minority and majority groups'.[45]

The cultural interaction to which O'Farrell refers deserves more study than it has received from those seeking to understand our national character. My own personal experience over the past fifty years makes it possible for me to reflect upon a very limited segment of the cultural exchange to which O'Farrell refers. If he emphasises the challenge the Irish brought to an Australian establishment, my own experience makes me aware of other ways in which the Irish made their contribution to the emerging Australian ethos.

Patrick Morgan, in reviewing O'Farrell's recent publication *Vanished Kingdoms*, remarks that because Gaelic Ireland 'had been largely obliterated during the eighteenth century...families of Irish descent here passed little on, not through any fault of their own, but because they had little to pass on'[46]. Surely a distinction is called for. If the Irish who came to Australia had few resources of 'high' culture to pass on, at a more fundamental level of cultural community they had a living tradition with very ancient roots, deeply established attitudes, and distinctive shared values through which they made their contribution to the ongoing Australian experience.

These qualities were very evident, I can now recognise, in my country cousins of southern Queensland—families with names such as Cavanagh, Skelly and Byrne. As a child, my visits to their homes were memorable experiences, enlivened by their characteristic good humour and sense of fun, generous hospitality and strong sense of kinship. The verses of P. J. Hartigan ('John O'Brien') were loved by the people of the cultural tradition in which I was brought up because they held up the mirror to qualities they recognised as their own. As a young man, I was to find these same qualities in my Irish relatives in County Cork. I found Stan Arneil's war diary—intended originally as a personal document, but ultimately published as *One Man's War*[47]—very moving when I read it recently for the first time. Its sense of family and the robust values it expressed so unashamedly put me in touch once again with the experience of early childhood. With countless subtle variations, these attitudes derived from Irish culture must have been an important factor in the development of Australian culture. In *The Australian Legend*, Russel Ward has drawn attention to this contribution[48].

Because my paternal grandmother was of English Protestant stock, that other important strand of the cultural traditions which coexisted in Australia in the mid-twentieth century was also a familiar part of my experience. My Protestant relatives were fine people by any standard; their qualities, however, were different from those of the Irish side of the family. They were townspeople: my father used to recall that his grandfather, as a 'mechanic' in London—in today's parlance, it seems, he was a high class joiner—wore a top hat and had an apprentice to carry the fine tools which were later to rust under his bed in colonial Brisbane. The Frith family were warm-hearted and generous, but in a more reserved way. More than once, in serious moments of family conversations I can recall from my childhood, it was owned that in their quiet, predictable goodness they had the edge on the Irish side of the family. At the same time they did not have the sense of fun and the capacity to laugh at themselves which were so evident in our Irish tradition.

Recently, a passage in the biography of C. E. W. Bean, the war historian whose writings we will consider in later chapters, brought vividly to mind the qualities of my Protestant relatives. 'Bean had had, not only the precepts of his parents but the examples of their lives always before him. In these precepts there was nothing of religious dogma or of stark puritanism, despite their undeviating moral tone. The morality of them was rather that of Christianity in its simplest forms: of love, of the goodness of life and humanity, of simple duty, of what was owed from man to man, and of the need for the cultivation of the mind and the spirit'[49].

As I look back on this experience I am led to reflect upon the nature of my own cultural alignment during those formative years. No doubt it has something to tell us about many of my generation. Both Catholic and Protestant branches of my family had been in Queensland since about 1870. Any sense of identification with a tradition that was peculiarly Irish was very submerged in my awareness. Such things as St Patrick's Day celebrations left me mildly embarrassed, even as a child. I had no appreciation of the fact that the warm qualities that made visiting my country cousins such fun had an Irish provenance.

On the other hand, it was a very real, though unreflecting, sense of Australian identity that made visits to my father's Uncle Reuben on the outskirts of Brisbane so attractive. The husband of my father's Protestant aunt was a truly remarkable man who, despite the loss of an arm in the First World War, operated his own work-shop as a mechanical engineer single-handed—literally! Many years before, as a young self-taught geologist and botanist, he had journeyed throughout Queensland, and he had a fund of wonderful reminiscences. Many a happy Sunday morning, my father and I were taken through his gardens and listened to his yarns. Those conversations are for me a kind of symbol of the community of Australian life shared by the two strands of culture we represented. This experience must have had countless parallels, in the work-place, in the armed forces, in the pub.

My concrete experience, as an Australian sharing in that strand of our culture which had its roots in the traditions of Ireland, leads me to identify with another observation of Patrick O'Farrell in the summary chapter to which I have referred: 'Irish-Australian self-assertion was directed towards a resolution of its identity in Australia, a quest ... which was so close to a local exploration as to lose its Irish character in its Australian context'[50]. O'Farrell's study of Australian history has led him to the conclusion 'that it was the condition of constant abrasion between minority and majority that gradually changed both, to their mutual improvement and the creation, by way of compromise, of a tolerant Australian charac-ter'[51]. That too I can identify with, though my recollections of the meeting between the majority of English descent and the minority from an Irish background which took place in the conversations my father and I had with his Uncle Reuben make me add that this meeting was not always an abrasive one.

There was a difference, of course, the religious one which was never referred to. There were also other subtle differences coming from our distinct cultural traditions, of which we were scarcely aware; but our sharing in a common Australian cultural experience to which these two traditions were contributing was beyond question.

Growing up in Australia, I felt that the religious difference which separated me from fellow Australians who were not Catholics was a considerable one. As I analyse my attitude at that time, however, I recognise that it had little conscious connection with Ireland. The adversarial attitude I had to the Protestant tradition identified rather with English Catholicism, with such figures as G. K. Chesterton, Ronald Knox and Evelyn Waugh. It is a measure of the cultural identity which had been engendered in me by my Australian upbringing that when I travelled to Europe in 1953, the journey's end to which I looked forward, and finally reached in the summer of 1956, was London. A visit to Ireland, made during that same summer, was to me at the time a family affair, with little sense of being a return to the source of a cultural tradition to which I belonged.

One of my main concerns in this work is a critical consideration of the content and themes which have shaped our Australian conversation. It has been necessary by way of introduction to emphasise the important historical development which has taken place within our culture. Previously a provincial component of that conversation which had its centre in the British Isles, it has now achieved a relative independence.

The challenge contained in this development can hardly be exaggerated. If the Australian project is to be carried forward successfully, we must find ways in which the conversation which maps our way into the future is truly multicultural. It must include, in the first place, Australia's Aboriginal people. It must include also those who have brought with them outlooks and values other than those of the Anglo-Saxon and Celtic cultures which have shaped most of our history. As Judith Wright reminds us—making use of the phrase which was common when she was writing—'all of us, to some extent, are new Australians'.

Because we, possessing a derivative culture, carry on a conversation animated by the values and wisdom brought from other lands, our cultural self-expression will have an element of nostalgia. If we reject our past, Judith Wright says, 'we fail to understand something important about ourselves, and we will not be able to set about making Australia into our real spiritual home. In the same way, if we accept it too wholeheartedly, and take too seriously the notion that we are a transplanted community, we deny the second aspect of our situation as Australians—the opportunity that is given us to make our loss into gain, to turn Australia into a reality, to become something new in the world'[52].

No one would agree more heartily than Judith Wright with the observation that among us there are those who cannot be called 'new Australians', whose nostalgia is not for a past lived beyond these shores but for this land itself which was cruelly taken from them. Eugene Stockton transposes Judith Wright's thought into a more recent idiom which does include them: 'We are all boat people'. For even the Aborigines, long before we did, travelled to this land by a courageous journey across the sea. Long before us, they came to know and love the land and to identify their existence with it. They, certainly, must have an honoured place in our Australian project and conversation.

Judith Wright's thought has an important extension. Not only must we bring to our project the memory of the traditions from which we white Australians derived our culture, we must not neglect the experience which shaped something peculiarly Australian during our formative decades. The multicultural nature of the Australian project from now on brings a considerable challenge. We are setting out on a path which has already been travelled by the United States of America. We will look critically at this American model in the next chapter. One thing is certain, however, namely that the legends and precedents of the formative period of American society before the massive intake of population which began during the nineteenth century have been of fundamental importance for American people in the later search for identity within a multicultural society. We may well expect that our earlier experience and the outlook it engendered will also have an enduring importance in the phase of our national conversation which is about to begin.

The analysis of the cultural development of the United States made in the next chapter may well lead us to the conclusion that the cohesion which has been an important feature of the formative period of Australian history has provided us with a cultural resource more resilient than that produced by the American experience.

[1]   London (Chatto and Windus) 1958.
[2]   London (Ernest Benn) 1945, p.235.
[3]   ibid., pp.56–57.
[4]   Penguin, 1965, p.209.
[5]   ibid., p.21.
[6]   ibid., p.16.
[7]   Sydney (Hodder and Stoughton) 1966.
[8]   ibid., p.22.
[9]   ibid., p.22
[10]   loc. cit.
[11]   Cited, John Rickard, *Australia* (Longmans) 1988, p.251.
[12]   Melbourne, 1980 (first published in 1954).
[13]   ibid., p.167.
[14]   'The Australian National Character: Myth and Reality', *Jour. of World Hist.*, 2 (1955) 704–18.
[15]   Melbourne (Oxford U.P.) 1958.
[16]   *Inventing Australia*, Sydney (Geo. Allen and Unwin) 1981, p.160.
[17]   Cited, White, loc. cit.
[18]   *Voss*, Penguin 1968, p.11.
[19]   Various contributors to John Carroll (ed.), *Intruders in the Bush: the Australian Quest for Identity*, Melbourne, 1982 (Oxford U.P.) discuss these ambiguities.
[20]   1976 Boyer Lectures, p.47.
[21]   *Australia*, p.192.
[22]   'Literary Nationalism and the 1890s', *Aust. Lit. Studies*, 5 (1971) pp.3–17, citing Lewis, *The American Adam*, Chicago, 1955, pp.1–2.

[23] 1976 Boyer Lectures, p.47.

[24] This understanding of the common good as the basis of human society is fully developed in my work *The Person and the Group: A Study in the Tradition of Aristotelian Realism of the Meaning of Human Society*, Milwaukee (Bruce) 1967.

[25] Cf. Manning Clark (ed.), *Sources of Australian History*, Melbourne, (Oxford U.P.) 1982, pp.243–53.

[26] *Urbanisation in Australian History 1788–1900*, Melbourne (Nelson) 1975, p.73.

[27] *Australia*, p.100.

[28] Cited, D. McCarthy, *Gallipoli to the Somme: The Story of C. E. W. Bean*, Sydney (John Ferguson) 1983, p.155.

[29] *Australia*, p.46.

[30] *Kangaroo*, Melbourne (Penguin) 1963, p.15.

[31] Sydney, 1925, p.55.

[32] Cited, Geoffrey Serle, *The Creative Spirit in Australia*, Richmond, Vic. (William Heinemann) 1987, p.130.

[33] Cf. Helen Bourke, 'Intellectuals for Export: Australia in the 1920s', pp.95–108, in S. L. Goldberg and F. B. Smith (eds), *Australian Cultural History*, Cambridge, 1988.

[34] Cited, Rickard, *Australia*, p.136.

[35] loc. cit.

[36] In Leon Cantrell, *Writings of the 1890s*, St Lucia (Univ. of Q. Press) 1988, p.13.

[37] Cf. Manning Clark, Duhig Memorial Lecture, *The Catholic Leader*, 26 Aug 1979, p.3.

[38] P. R. Stephensen, 'The Foundation of Culture in Australia: An Essay towards National Self-respect', in J. Barnes (ed.), *The Writer in Australia*, Melbourne (Oxford U.P.) 1969, pp.204–44.

[39] Cf. McCarthy, *Gallipoli to the Somme*, p.157.

[40] Cf. Bill Gammage, 'Anzac', in J. Carroll (ed.), *Intruders in the Bush*, 1989, pp.54–66.

[41] *Australia*, pp.119–20. The suggestion that the campaign suffered from British mismanagement is not without foundation. C. E. W. Bean, than whom there was no more staunch Australian upholder of things British, was disillusioned by his experience at Gallipoli, cf. McCarthy, *Gallipoli to the Somme*, pp.108, 142, 144, 182, 185, 210.

[42] In Stephen R. Graubard (ed.), *Australia: The Daedalus Symposium*, Nth Ryde, N.S.W. (Angus and Robertson) 1985, p.16.

[43] These statistics have been taken from W. G. Coppell, *Australia in Figures*, Penguin, 1981.

[44] *The Irish in Australia*, Kensington, N.S.W. (Univ, of N.S.W.) 1987, p.10.

[45] *The Irish in Australia*, loc. cit. Cf. also *Vanished Kingdoms: Irish in Australia and New Zealand: A Personal Excursion*, Kensington, N.S.W., 1990.

[46] Review of *Vanished Kingdoms*, *Quadrant* March 1991, p.74.

[47] South Melbourne (Sun Books) 1983 (1st ed., 1980).

[48] Cf. ch.3, 'Celts and Currency'.

[49] Dudley McCarthy, *Gallipoli to the Somme: The Story of C. E. W. Bean*, Sydney, 1983, p.55.

[50] *The Irish in Australia*, p.15.

[51] ibid., p.117.

[52] *Preoccupations in Australian Poetry*, Melbourne (Oxford U.P.) 1966, p.xix.

2.

FINDING THE TOOLS OF SELF-APPRAISAL

As pointed out, the new form of multiculturalism which has emerged in the Australian community since the Second World War may well lead to a development having something in common with what has already taken place in the United States. We have much to gain, therefore, from a consideration of the American model. Complex as it is, it deserves careful and prolonged study by those who are responsible for Australia's future.

1. The example of the United States: a plea for national modesty

The S. S. *Orontes*, on which I travelled to Europe in 1953, had among its passengers many young Indians on their way to tertiary studies in the United Kingdom. Conversations I had with them brought to light the astounding fact that a few years after the end of British colonial rule in India Britain's standing in that country was much higher than the standing of the United States. Indians saw the Americans as guilty of a crude self-interest in their attempts to influence the affairs and policies of their emerging nation. I recalled this immense irony when I later found extended visits to the United States a discomforting experience.

More than once, such visits have left me with a sense of disillusionment and even betrayal. The fact that the Americans are a generous and friendly people only made my discomfort all the more acute. The United States had been so successful in projecting an image as the homeland of freedom and the country of the future that, as a young man, America seemed to me a kind of promised land. If Europe made possible a living contact with the past, America seemed the place that would reveal the future.

But what most disappointed me when I came to know the United States at first hand, was not so much that the reality did not match the image projected, but that the self-appraisal of Americans never seemed to go deep enough to come to grips with the problem which lay at the heart of the identity they projected with such zeal and assurance. They seemed unable to acknowledge that the social experiment which produced the most powerful nation the world has ever seen had given rise to an unprecedented cultural situation.

Many Americans would be surprised and puzzled by this assessment. As a nation they possess great cultural wealth. They are capable, to a certain level, of a self-criticism which is more earnest than that found in most cultural traditions. It is probably true to say that few nations today would be capable of an appraisal of their identity comparable with that undertaken by Robert N. Bellah and his associates in their remarkable book *Habits of the Heart*. This work makes no concessions in its criticism of the individualism which has emerged as a dominant trait of American culture: tracing its historical development, challenging contemporary Americans not to evade the moral issues it raises, and urging them to reappropriate the resources in their national tradition with which they can take up the issue. And the American public was prepared to take up the challenge—*Habits of the Heart* became a national best-seller and gave rise to wide ranging debate[1].

Ironically, however, *Habits of the Heart* confirms the point we are making. Bellah and his associates have little to say about the problem fundamental to the American social experiment, to which I wish to call attention because it has importance for Australia as it enters its new phase of multiculturalism: the problem deriving from the fact that, because they have come together from a great variety of cultural backgrounds, Americans do not share in any single age-old cultural tradition. The union they have achieved, as the analysis carried out in *Habits of the Heart* makes clear, belongs to another level, that of an American ideal, a way of life that has been more or less deliberately created from biblical, republican and utilitarian elements. At the level of popular awareness, Americans have found their identity in the American 'dream', as it has been called, something far less robust and far more open to self-serving and deception than the cultural traditions in which the people of the old world find their identity.

The attitude in 1953 of people from India to Britain and the United States, to which I referred earlier, illustrates my point. Like those of other European powers, Britain's imperial exploits disregarded the fundamental rights of the peoples of her colonies; in the end her dealings with them were motivated by a self-interest never clearly acknowledged and often skilfully concealed. The paradoxical fact remains, however, that Britain won the respect of these people and, one after another, they paid her the supreme compliment of modelling their basic institutions upon hers. The institutions these emerging nations had come to admire were the outcome of the age-old tradition which had united and sustained the British people throughout their history.

There was no denying that this had its shortcomings. The remarkable system of parliamentary government, founded upon the fundamental rights of citizenship, was entangled in structures of class and privilege inherited from the past. In modern times, the British had shared in the exaggerated nationalism which possessed the peoples of Europe. But for all this, theirs remained a tradition with deep roots in values and ideals long nurtured in folk memory, which were symbolised in countless historical events, in national ritual, in literature, art and architecture. It was this cultural tradition which won the respect of the colonial peoples when they gained their independence.

The very nature of the social experiment which produced the United States made it impossible for Americans to share in a comparable cultural tradition. In the space of a century or so, wave after wave of Europeans streamed across the Atlantic to begin a new life; they pulled up their roots and threw in their lot with their adopted country. The cultural dislocation involved cost them a great deal. Their identity with the traditions which had nurtured them—as Germans, Irish, Jews, Poles, Italians etc.—was greatly modified as they struggled to maintain such beliefs and customs as would give them a social location and identity in the bewildering pluralism of American society. In Europe, what had united them with the people of their countries had been age-old traditions such as that of Britain; what united them in the United States was the American ideal, America's interpretation of itself as the ultimate home of freedom, the greatest democracy the world had ever seen.

Once more, *Habits of the Heart* bears out our point. Its authors recognise the importance of *tradition* as a bearer of the values which must be called upon if the American people are to take up the moral challenges of their present cultural development. The traditions to which they appeal, however, are not those of an old cultural heritage, but the teachings of those who crossed the Atlantic to escape religious oppression and of those who helped establish the American republic. In fact, the authors recognise that many of those they interviewed doubted that the American people have enough in common to be able 'mutually to discuss' their 'central aspirations and fears'[2]. 'Leaving tradition behind', it is acknowledged, 'runs all the way through our tradition'[3]. As they conclude their study, they look somewhat wistfully towards the heritage in traditions other than their own. 'Perhaps the truth lies in what most of the world outside the modern West has always believed, namely that there are practices of life, good in themselves, that are inherently fulfilling... We have imagined ourselves a special creation, set apart from other humans. In the late twentieth century, we see that our poverty is as absolute as that of the poorest of nations'[4].

The long established traditions of European peoples, such as the British, provide them with a resource which enables them to appreciate the complexities and subtleties of historical situations, the meaning of politics as the art of the humanly possible. The common ethos of the United States, on the other hand, gives rise to paradoxical shortcomings. American idealism often perceives international situations and relationships in very black and white terms, so that when policies are articulated they seem to be made on the premise that politics should aim at some universal implementation of the American ideal. At the same time, because they are serving the very recognisable social need of unifying the American people, the international policies of the United States easily become self-serving, so that America's own interests are rationalised as the carrying forward of the nation's great mission. The fears and tensions produced by the cold war, and the enormous responsibility of the United States in the events which have shaped the history of the twentieth century, have only served to accentuate these tendencies.

Avery Dulles, one of America's most respected theologians, essays an interpretation of the various stages in the development of American culture which is in substantial agreement with that made in *Habits of the Heart*[5]. His survey points to something which is important for our discussion: throughout its complex development, American culture has been shot through with a sense of God-given purpose. If the Calvinistic Puritanism brought across the Atlantic by the Pilgrim Fathers came to be greatly modified, Dulles writes, it has remained a living memory for later generations of Americans. 'It fuelled many 19th century exhortations about the "Manifest Destiny" of the United States, and it continues to reappear in Thanksgiving Day proclamations, in campaign oratory and in anniversary celebrations of the Declaration of Independence or the Constitution. Because of this vibrant tradition, it is still possible to speak of the United States, with Chesterton, as "a nation with the soul of a church" "[6].

In the secular order, as Dulles points out, once more in agreement with the authors of *Habits of the Heart*, the American outlook knew 'a major incursion of individualistic utilitarian philosophy in the 19th century'. 'The common good was reconceived as the net result of a balancing of contrary interests. The pursuit of private gain by individuals and groups was seen as contributing, in the long run, to the prosperity of all... The role of the Government was seen as that of an arbiter, laying down the conditions under which competition could be fairly conducted'[7].

It is clear that the group ethos which has sustained the American project has been something different from the cultural traditions of the old world, where similar influences were modified by the many checks and balances of complex cultural traditions.

Is it conceivable that, in the future, humanity will come to recognise the worth of such a thing as corporate and national modesty, the capacity on the part of political groups to acknowledge the limitations of their corporate endeavours which are the inevitable outcome of their historical situation, and to pass beyond the arrogance which is so often an expression of insecurity to a more realistic self-appraisal? The insights we have today into the follies of human history must surely point us in that direction. The publication of *Habits of the Heart*, and the response it evoked, would seem to indicate that such an attitude is not outside the realms of possibility.

Our concern here, of course, is with the cultural conversation which animates our Australian project. The analysis we have made of the situation of the United States is useful to us for various reasons. In the first place, our development is entering into a new multicultural phase which seems certain to have something in common with the American experience. A critical evaluation of the factors which have shaped the American ideal—which I will pursue further in the next section—can help us, perhaps, to find the path we should follow and to identify the dangers to be avoided.

It must be recognised that our situation contrasts in many ways with that which we have just been considering. In the first place, the experience we have shared as Australians has been very different from that of the United States. It has rarely given rise, for instance, to a temptation to self-aggrandisement. It may well be, moreover, that the long period of cultural homogeneity which produced our common ethos has given us a resource which will prove its resilience in the phase of our history we are now entering. It is for the reader to make his or her own judgment as we explore further what we have shared as Australians.

2. Culture as a world-building process

The comparison we have just made, between the United States and European nations such as Britain, was really a comparison of two very complex processes of world-building. The objective realities of the human situation do not vary essentially from culture to culture: the self and the others with whom life means collaboration or contestation; being woman or being man; an environment of land, sea and sky with its flora and fauna and changing seasons; work and play; health and sickness; love, hatred and indifference in ourselves and in others; hope and despair, success and failure; life and death. Being human means coming to terms with these realities of existence. We do not do this alone; being human also means sharing in a culture, participating in a project of putting these realities together to constitute a human world that is meaningful and bearable.

Through this process, a great variety of cultures have emerged, as creative insights have been shared and tested, values have been affirmed and pursued, procedures of symbolisation, articulation and transmission have been established or discarded. The project of world-building is one of the principal challenges faced by a new-world country like Australia. As Veronica Brady remarks, 'By definition the primary question posed by new societies like Australia is not, as in more traditional societies, "what role must I assume?" but rather, "what world am I to possess?" '[8]. The development of the culture of white Australians has unique features deriving from the geographical isolation which has prevailed for most of our history. Australian society was a kind of remote seedbed in which identifiable cultural elements brought from the old world found a life of their own, and in which indigenous growths eventually made their appearance.

As the pioneer Australian anthropologist A. P. Elkin notes, whether we recognise it or not we are all involved in the process of world-building: the fact that 'we spend our days without conscious reference to any systematised view of the universe, of man and nature, of life and consciousness, and of the processes of history... does not mean that we are not guided by some view of life, which is expressed in our daily conduct, in ritual and belief, and in times of individual and social crisis'[9]. Elkin makes a comparison between the 'philosophy' of Australia's Aboriginal people and the philosophies of white Australians, finding comparable world-building process at work in each culture.

W. E. H. Stanner, another anthropologist who has made an important contribution to our understanding of the Aboriginal people, makes a similar observation. 'The Dreaming is a proof that the blackfellow shares with us two abilities which have largely made human history what it is. The first of these we might call "the metaphysical gift". I mean the ability to transcend oneself, to make acts of imagination so that one can stand "outside" or "away from" oneself, and turn the universe, oneself and one's fellows into objects of contemplation. The second ability is a "drive" to try to "make sense" out of human experience and to find some "principle" in the whole human situation. This "drive" is, in some way, built into the constitution of the human mind. No one who has real knowledge of Aboriginal life can have any doubt that they possess, and use, both abilities very much as we do'[10].

As we gain a detailed knowledge of the great variety of cultures which have emerged in the course of human history and of their development, comparisons such as those made by the Australian anthropologists I have cited make it possible to identify certain factors which have been universally operative in humanity's world-building processes. The analysis we are to make of our Australian culture, in the following chapters, will look particularly at two such factors—probably the most fundamental of all from a socio- logical point of view—the mythological factor and the ideological factor. Let me explain what is meant by these. The American model I have described can help us to understand their relevance to contemporary cultural communities.

Few words are so loosely used today as the term 'myth'. Quot- ations included in the previous chapter made it the equivalent of 'legend'. In the discussion which follows, however, the two will be clearly distinguished. A legend is a story about human agents, transformed so as to endow it with a symbolic function in the life of a community. As Erich Auerbach writes, 'Legend arranges its material in a simple and straightforward way; it detaches it from its contemporary historical context, so that the latter will not confuse it; it knows only clearly outlined men who act from few and simple motives and the continuity of whose feelings and actions remains uninterrupted'. Interpreting the endless complexity of historical events is so difficult, Auerbach notes, 'that most historians are forced to make concessions to the technique of legend'[11]. It is clear legend plays an important part in the world-building process of Australian culture. I have already referred to the bush legend; the Anzac legend as we shall see has also had an important place in our awareness.

As a 'numinous story' (Alan W. Watts)[12], myth is essentially different from legend; it tells of actions which transcend the realm of human agency, actions which, however, have enduring con- sequences as far as human existence is concerned. Theologian John Knox spells out the essential characteristics of the myth in this proper sense. It is a story or imaginative narrative portraying 'a cosmologically significant act of God (or of some superhuman being)', which is of 'decisive importance for the world, particularly the world of men, whose response to it may be an essential part of the story'. The mythological narrative finds its source in the shared experience of a human community, so that it bears 'the marks of its culture' and persists over the generations 'as a part of its tradition'. It is revered by the community which possesses it, 'because it suggests, or answers to, and is believed actually to explain or account for, something distinctive and important in human existence, and particularly in its own'. The myth, therefore, becomes inseparable from the very existence of the community, having 'become itself an inseparable and indispensable part of the community's life and, for those sharing in that life, an irreplaceable symbol, an actual carrier of its power'[13].

While they may hesitate to use the term, interpreters of our Australian experience such as Judith Wright and Manning Clark are concerned with the mythological dimension we have described. Judith Wright writes of 'belief in a meaning in the human world, a direction that governs the flow and eddy of events, an underlying and overriding destiny that is not confined to man's own purpose and knowledge'[14].

'Manning Clark's five-volume *History of Australia*', writes Hugh Collins, 'can be read as a sustained attempt to tell his country's story outside the constraints of triumphant utilitarianism... Clark's prophetic judgment upon such tendencies in the nation's experience seeks to redeem from it the heroic witnesses to a larger spirit... Clark's rejection can be total because his categories are no longer the individual and the state, but the individual and eternity'[15]. For Clark, Australia's history has involved a confrontation between 'three different views of the nature of God and man transplanted overseas to an alien environment'—that of the Enlightenment, that of Protestant Christianity and that of Catholicism. He sees the fundamental dialogue of the Australian conversation today as being 'between those who hold a religious view of the world, who believe in the mystery at the heart of things, and those who believe in applying the principles of the book-keeper to the subject of human happiness and behaviour'[16].

What is affirmed through the mythological factor is beyond proof or disproof in the ordinary sense of the term. Concerning as it does the most basic level of human commitment and personhood, it confronts us with an order of option that Western self-awareness has come to call 'existential'. Of its nature, mythology —in the sense in which we are using the term—speaks of an order which is *given* prior to any human agency. For this reason, the mythological factor lies beyond rational demonstration: the measure of its worth is gauged from the authenticity and human fulfilment it brings at the 'existential' level—the ultimate level, as we have said, of human subjectivity.

Ideology is another factor which is universally operative in the world-building processes of a great variety of cultures. It is impossible to understand the ongoing development of our Australian conversation if the workings of the ideological factor are not recognised and critically evaluated. Perhaps Karl Marx's greatest contribution to our understanding of the historical process was his recognition of the part played by ideology in its development. His discussion of the function of ideology was concerned before all else with the socio-economic order, and the way in which the outlooks of different groups contributing to and benefiting from the process of production and exchange are shaped by group interest. Marx's insight has far broader applications however.

The solidarity of any social group is achieved through a *consensus*, in which the group identifies itself through the taking up of shared ideals and a common cause. In the sense in which we are using the term, 'ideology' refers to such a shared outlook as a system of ideas, symbols and imaginings which serves the needs of a particular historical group in the achieving of an identity. This consensus and its characteristic emphases come inevitably to reflect the experience of the group and the challenges it has had to overcome in the pursuit of its common purpose. To be effective, this consensus must translate the subtleties and complexities of the actual situation into a coherent outlook accessible to the rank and file members of the group. This interpretation is selective, even distorted. The formation and maintaining of such a shared outlook is a function, not so much of the ideas in themselves, but of the manner in which the ideas meet the felt needs of the group[17].

The more effectively an ideology establishes itself, the more important become the identity and security it has brought to the group, so that the group will instinctively resist whatever threatens the consensus which unites it. What was discussed in the last chapter, concerning Australian experience while our national conversation was a remote corner of the ongoing conversation of British imperialism, clearly involved the workings of the ideological factor. It is not difficult to recognise that the formation of legends has much in common with the process Marx emphasised. As Bill Gammage points out, legends 'take hold not because they are true, but because they appeal to a consensus about the present'[18]. In an essay entitled 'Countrymindedness', Don Aitkin gives a definition which summarises the points we have been making:

> I take ideology to be a system of values and ideas that among other things presents a more or less extensive

picture of the good society, and of the policies and programmes necessary to achieve it; distinguishes goodies from baddies; accounts for the historical experience of a group; and appears as "truth" to that group while being at least plausible to outsiders. Ideologies, unlike philosophies, obtain their force very much from social experience; they cannot be proved wrong, partly because they are sufficiently elastic to accommodate awkward facts[19].

W. K. Hancock has provided an illustration of the ideological factor at work while at the same time pointing to the imaginative focus which is fundamental to its effectiveness. Concerning the Australian gold rushes, he wrote 'Australians have loved to look upon them as a time of new and true beginnings... They have acclaimed the diggers as their Pilgrim Fathers, the first authentic Australians, the founders of their self-respecting, strenuous national life, the fathers of their soldiers... for respect for ancestry is a spiritual necessity in every nation, even the youngest, and the legend is more important than the fact'[20]. Hancock recognises the working of the ideological factor. Ironically, however, he also provides an unconscious illustration of the way in which it can lead to a selective consciousness. In 1930, when he was writing, Australians were unable to acknowledge the fundamental importance of the part played by the 168 000 convicts transported to this country in the formation of our national ethos. In the decades since, these inhibitions have disappeared.

The American model we discussed clearly illustrates the working of the mythological and ideological factors in a contemporary political community. We only have to reread Knox's detailed analysis of the place of mythology in the life of a community to recognise its equivalent in the sense of God-given purpose which has characterised the distinctive ethos of the United States. The rationalised self-interest which shows itself in America's international policies—the United States, of course, are not alone in this— illustrates the ideological factor. The American example alerts us to the care with which the workings of these factors must be scrutinised in the self-criticism we are about to make. Since an ideological consensus is necessary to any community in its finding of historical identity, there can be no question of renouncing the process; a healthy community, however, must become critically aware of the distortions and self-serving which so easily characterise the ideological consensus fundamental to its existence.

In the following chapters, I shall discuss three orders of assumption which have helped to shape an emerging Australian self-awareness: mythological assumptions, ideological assumptions (using these terms in the sense we have defined), and shared attitudes reflecting the unique experience of our life together in our island-continent. As we embark upon this discussion, it is important to recall that the cultural community in which we share as we take up our Australian project, far from being monolithic, has always involved the interaction of different strands of tradition. I refer in the last chapter to the contributions made by the very different cultural traditions brought to this country from the British Isles. Our controlling metaphor, that of a 'conversation', implies this interchange of various points of view.

On the other hand, conversations revolve around specific themes, and take place on the basis of certain shared assumptions. Not all participants in our national conversation will have had the same view of the topics taken up in our conversation, nor have they owned the assumptions which made the conversations possible in the same terms. Anglo-Saxon Australians and Australians of Irish descent, for example, would have had very different points of view as far as the project of British imperialism was concerned, and this example has countless parallels. That acknowledged, it is true to say that these common themes and assumptions have given the Australian conversation its fundamental shape. For this reason they deserve to be considered in themselves, as a first step towards a critical awareness of what we share as Australians.

Let us conclude this chapter with some brief remarks about the literature and the arts which, reflecting and exploring the world which our culture is creating, play an important part in its world-building process[21].

Georg Lukacs points to the cultural significance of the distinction within literature between epics or sagas and novels. Epics he interprets as 'literary products of integrated ages of faith'; novels, on the other hand, he sees as 'the expression in literary form of "problematic" ages of doubt'. 'The novel is the epic of a world that has been abandoned by God'[22]. It may well be argued that the cultural transition noted by Lukacs is open to a positive evaluation. If his distinction is not made too unyielding, however, it can be an illuminating one when related to the framework I have been discussing.

The strong direction taken by the story line of the epic is the literary expression of a culture in which faith is securely integrated into the world it has established. To use the terminology we have adopted, the epic is an affirmation and celebration of mythological truth, meeting the existential needs experienced by the members of a historical culture. In fact, the epic has had little place in Australian literature[23]. Like the body of modern Western literature, whether in the form of novel, poetry or drama, our literature gives expression to a moment in the world-building process which must explore the ambiguities and uncertainties of being human, and

which calls into question the mythological and ideological presuppositions at work in contemporary Western society. The same
may be said, by way of analogy, of the visual arts and the cinema.
Some examples from our literature may serve to illustrate what
has been said. In Joseph Furphy's novel *Such Is Life*, we meet the
ambiguities of Australian experience and Australian hopes at
the turn of the century. George Johnston's novel *My Brother Jack*
reflects Australian disillusionment in the period between the wars.
The novels *Coonardoo*, by Katherine Susannah Prichard, *Poor
Fellow My Country*, by Xavier Herbert, and *To the Islands*, by
Randolf Stow, confront us with the tragedy of the meeting between
the very different cultures of black and white Australians, opening
the door on a part of our Australian world filled with darkness,
fear and shame. Les Murray's novel sequence *The Boys Who Stole
the Funeral* invites the reader to evaluate the mythological and
ideological presuppositions of contemporary Australian society
through imagined reactions to the bizarre enterprise of two youths
who hijack the body of an old digger to give him a fitting country
funeral.

Patrick White's novels have something of the parable form. The
parable stands between mythology and other forms of narrative
literature, challenging the complacent fabric of an established
world, and inviting a fresh meeting with the life-giving mystery to
which mythology lays claim. If White's novel *Voss*, for instance,
has something of the character of an epic, its author lacks the confidence which would make his story a celebration of mythological
truth. The novel's open-ended denouement carries us towards the
parable form. The explorer, through his inconclusive journey, faces
the challenge of being human in a way which invites us to see him
as a symbol of our own existential plight.

[1]   *Habits of the Heart: Individualism and Commitment in American Life*,
Robert N. Bellah etc. (eds), New York (Harper and Row) 1986. See also *Individualism and Commitment in American Life: Readings on the Themes of 'Habits of the
Heart'*, Robert N. Bellah etc. (eds), New York, 1987; *Community in America: The
Challenge of 'Habits of the Heart'*, Charles H. Reynolds and Ralph V. Norman
(eds), Berkeley, Ca., 1988.
[2]   *Habits of the Heart*, p.vi. Cf. p.282 for a passing reference to the deeper
cultural community to which we are referring.
[3]   ibid., p.75.
[4]   ibid., pp.295–6.
[5]   Cf. 'Catholicism and American Culture: The Uneasy Dialogue', *America*, 27
Jan 1990, v. 162, pp.54–9.
[6]   ibid., p.55. Cf. Richard Campbell, 'The Character of Australian Religion',
Meanjin, 36 (1977) p.185.
[7]   loc. cit.
[8]   *Intruders in the Bush*, John Carroll (ed.), p.193, quoting Quentin
Anderson.

[9] *The Australian Aborigines: How to Understand Them*, Sydney (Angus and Robertson) 1968, p.220.

[10] *Traditional Aboriginal Society*, W. H. Edwards (ed.), Sth Melbourne, 1987, p.230.

[11] *Mimesis*, Princeton U.P., 1974, pp.19–20.

[12] The term 'numinous' (first used, it seems, by the German theologian Rudolf Otto, and derived from the Latin *numen*) has only recently been established in English usage; cf. *Concise Oxford Dictionary* (1954 ed.): ' "Numinous" n. ("The numinous"): the combined feeling of attraction and awe characteristic of man's communion with God and religion'.

[13] *Myth and Truth: An Essay on the Language of Faith*, Charlottesville (University of Virginia Press) 1964, p.35.

[14] *Preoccupations in Australian Poetry*, Melbourne, 1966, p.198.

[15] 'Political Ideology in Australia: The Distinctiveness of a Benthamite Society', p.159, in *Australia: The Daedalus Symposium*, S. Graubard (ed.).

[16] *A Discovery of Australia* (1976 Boyer Lectures), p.29.

[17] See the exchange between Erin White (grounding her approach in Ricoeur) and Neil Ormerod (acknowledging Lonergan as his 'major influence'), 'Is Ideology Always a Bad Idea?' (*National Outlook*, April 1990, pp.24–7).

[18] *Historical Disciplines and Culture in Australia: An Assessment*, J. A. Moses (ed.), St Lucia (Univ. of Q. Press) 1979, p.44.

[19] In *Australian Cultural History*, S. L. Goldberg and F. B. Smith (eds) Cambridge U.P. 1989, p.51.

[20] *Australia*, pp.43–4.

[21] Cf. E. Auerbach, *Mimesis: The Representation of Reality in Western Literature*, Princeton U.P., 1968; *Scenes from the Drama of European Literature*, Gloucester, Mass., 1973; T. R. Wright, *Theology and Literature*, Oxford (Blackwell) 1989; Northrop Frye, *The Great Code: The Bible and Literature*, San Diego, 1982; *The Educated Imagination*, Toronto, 1963.

[22] Cited, Wright, *Theology and Literature*, p.111.

[23] Cf. the remarks of Anthony J. Hassall, in 'Quests', p.395, in *The Penguin New Literary History of Australia*, L. Hergenhan (ed.), 1988.

3.

THE MYTHOLOGICAL FACTOR: NUMINOUS MEANINGS

Most white Australians would discount the idea that the mythological factor has played any part in the shaping of their culture.
What we have seen already, however, invites us to look again at
this assumption. This factor is fundamental to the shared ethos of
the United States. Moreover, two pioneers in Australian anthropology have assured us that the world-building processes of white
Australians are essentially the same as those which shaped the age-
old culture of Australian Aborigines.

Early this century, the culture of black Australians attracted a
special interest among those establishing the new discipline of
anthropology. It was coming to be recognised that this cultural
tradition possessed archaic mythological forms with few parallels
in the world, which provided precious insights into the world-
building processes of prehistoric human societies. It is only in
recent decades, however, that white Australians in general have
become aware of this remarkable cultural heritage, and of the
Dreaming, as the mythological lore of black Australians has come
to be called. While this awakening of interest is welcome, there is
something disturbing about the insensitivity with which white
Australians have begun to take over and even to commercialise the

folklore and art motifs of the Aboriginal people, with no thought of the reconciliation and healing which must take place if this is not to be seen by black Australians as yet another instance of white exploitation.

The right of the original inhabitants of this land to take part in the conversation which makes Australia is second to none. This right was recognised in the instructions both Captain Cook and Governor Phillip received from the British government[1]. The tragic failure of the whites who first made contact with the Aboriginal people to understand their culture and its relationship to the land led, however, to a disregard for the fundamental justice embodied in these instructions.

A strong case has been made, as we shall see in the next chapter, that the shameful history of our relationship with the Australian blacks has affected the moral fibre of our nation far more radically than we have recognised. The fact that, when the Australian Commonwealth came into existence through the federation of the colonies in 1901, citizenship was explicitly denied to the original inhabitants of this continent by the Australian Constitution, is an enormity which epitomises the injustices of our dealings with them. This sorry history gives a painful edge to a comment made by W. E. H. Stanner, the anthropologist already quoted. He suggested in 1968 that white Australia, then in the process of taking over Aboriginal motifs, had the appearance of 'an affluent society enjoying the afterglow of an imagined past...reaching out for symbols and values that are not authentically its own but will do because it has none of its own which are equivalent'[2].

These things having been said, the fact remains that an understanding of Aboriginal culture and its relationship to this ancient continent is of fundamental importance to all Australians.

1. The mythologies of Aboriginal Australia: the Dreaming

The Aborigines who first had contact with whites, we now know, had built for themselves a world in which the territory of each tribal group, and every feature of it, found its entire meaning through the mythological stories which were the expression of the life they shared. In other words, their human existence derived its meaning from the features of their physical environment. This meaning—expressed in the song cycles of their mythologies—gave each tribal group a totemic identification with their own land. So complete was this identification of each group with a particular section of the continent, seen as eternally determined by the totemic ancestors, that territorial disputes were practically unknown to them. 'For Aborigines', Judith Wright says, 'every part of the country they occupied, every mark and feature, was numinous with meaning. The spirit ancestors had made the country itself, in their travels, and fused each part of it into the "Dreamtime"—a continuum of past, present, and future—that was also the unchangeable Law by which the Aborigines lived. The spirits remained in the land, passing on their essence through the births and rebirths of Aborigines themselves, and still present in the telling of their stories'[3].

In other words, the Dreaming saw the human situation as determined entirely by the dispositions of the transcendent agency of the totemic ancestors. So radical was this process of interpretation, and so effectively did it speak to the existential needs of those who made it their world-building rationale, that mundane reality, including individual identity itself, almost disappeared in the identification it gave with the numinous world of the ancestors. Thus, for instance, the place of conception revealed one's identification with a particular ancestor and with the totemic economy whereby that ancestor still lived in particular features of the region: animals, rocks, mountains, or waterholes. This mutuality of life-experience and the order proclaimed in the mythology was so all-embracing that all nature was seen as 'coded and charged by the sacred' and the sacred was seen as present 'everywhere within the landscape'[4].

Because tribal life is a kind of sharing in the unchanging moment of the existence of the ancestors, time seems to stand still for the mythological awareness of the Dreaming[5]. Stanner, who compares the Dreaming to the *logos* of the Greek philosophical tradition, writes that he was never able to discover any Aboriginal word for *time* as an abstract concept, and that he came to conclude that the sense of existing in a historical continuum was wholly alien to the outlook essential to the dreaming[6]. As the anthropologist Aram Yengoyan whimsically puts it, 'Virtually all Aboriginals who possess the eternal through their totems would take delight in refuting Tillich's statement that "there are no societies which possess the eternal"'[7].

In the Dreaming, the Aborigine had a numinous identification with the land which it is important for white Australians to appreciate. In Stanner's words 'No English words are good enough to give a sense of the links between an Aboriginal group and its homeland. Our word "home", warm and suggestive though it be, does not match the Aboriginal word that may mean "camp", "hearth", "country", "everlasting home", "totem place", "life source", "spirit centre" and much more all in one... I have seen an Aboriginal embrace the earth he walked on'[8]. Stanner notes that the Aborigine used the same word for 'earth' and for parts of his own body. T. G. H. Strehlow, a scholar who grew up among the blacks of central Australia, tells how, in a typical ceremony expressive of the mythology of the Dreaming, a young initiate was presented with a totemic rock and told 'This is your body from which you have been reborn'[9].

Stanner describes the effect of white colonisation on the Aboriginal people. 'When we took what we call "land" we took what to them meant hearth, home, the source and locus of life, and everlastingness of spirit... the Aborigines faced a kind of vertigo in living. They had no stable base of life; every personal affiliation was lamed... no social network had a point of fixture left'[10]. The white person may get some inkling of what this cultural deprivation meant if he or she imagines suddenly being transferred to a situation in which *all* the institutions of civilised life are unaccountably extinguished: the processes of government are abolished; all law is abrogated; family and kinship are rendered meaningless; there is no longer any way of having access to the past; and there is no future to hope in. Something of this nature happened to the Aboriginal people. There can be little wonder that, generations later, they struggle to find themselves once more.

Describing the situation which many of them today experience Stanner writes: 'What we are looking at is one of the most familiar syndromes in the world. It is a product of four things —homelessness, powerlessness, poverty and confusion—all self-acknowledged and accumulated over several generations'[11]. It is true that most of them no longer live according to the mythology of the Dreaming. It is clear, however, that the subculture which has developed among them since they suffered the impact of white colonisation preserves many of the attitudes engendered by it. As the nature of their former culture is brought to light once more, it is for them to decide the degree to which they make use of their old ways within the context of a multicultural Australia.

2. The mythologies of white Australia

Some appreciation of the profound implications of the mythologies of the Dreaming is essential for white Australians. We cannot give the Aboriginal people their rightful place in our national conversation if we have no understanding of the remarkable culture which accounts for so many of their attitudes. Indeed, our own relationship to the Australian continent implies some sharing in their attitudes. But there is another reason why a fuller appreciation of Aboriginal mythology can assist us in the inquiry we are undertaking.

According to Stanner, as I noted in the last chapter, Aboriginal mythology is the product of something which belongs to the human condition itself: 'a "drive" to try to "make sense" out of human experience and to find some "principle" in the whole human situation'. To be human is to be unable to accept that our existence is ruled ultimately by chaos and meaninglessness. As often as not the unifying principles to which we have recourse, however, remain unacknowledged and are not reflected upon. A meeting with the mythological response of the Aboriginal culture invites us to reflect more deeply on the way in which the existential needs we share with them have been met in the Western culture which has provided the basis of our ongoing Australian conversation. If the conviction of the people of the United States, that they had had a 'manifest destiny' to take control of the North American continent, may be recognised as a modern equivalent of classical mythology, we Australians must ask ourselves what parallels to this conviction are to be found in our cultural development.

Although the Australian Aboriginals were a relatively small and dispersed population, their isolation for more than fifty thousand years—more than two thousand generations—led to the creation of a very distinctive mythological tradition. The mythologies of white Australians, by way of contrast, are not original but derive from the broader conversation of Western culture, and in particular from the British tradition of which it was for so long a provincial component.

The nationalism of the states of Europe in the nineteenth century was one of the most potent factors in the history of that century. Australia was not immune from this influence. The outlook that prevailed in our national conversation shared in the subtle mythological presuppositions of British imperialism and in the numinous overtones of Britain's self-understanding during this period. With the rest of the Empire, Australians hailed the 'Land of hope and glory' and joined in the prayer 'God who made thee mighty make thee mightier yet!' Sally Morgan's uncle, Arthur Corunna, tells how, about the turn of the century, the Drake-Brockman family who owned the Western Australian station where he grew up 'built a hump and stuck a flagpole in it', and 'raised the Union Jack' when visitors came[12].

Our main discussion of nationalism and imperialism belongs to the next chapter, where we shall be evaluating the ideological factors which have helped to shape our Australian culture. It is not difficult to recognise, however, that the relationship between ideology and mythology is a subtle and complex one. A nationalistic ideology such as that of imperial Britain had roots of a mythological kind, even if these were not clearly acknowledged. That remarkable Australian, Daisy Bates, who spent most of a lifetime among remote Aboriginal people, provides an illustration of this nationalism and its numinous overtones. Her efforts to celebrate Empire

Day each year with the blacks in the vicinity of her Oodea camp, and to give them an appreciation of its significance, seem somewhat ludicrous today[13]. Her attachment to the Empire and her understanding of its mission had all the marks of religious fervour: she pleaded that the neglected and demoralised Aboriginals needed, more than anything else, 'the administration of the British rule...what they most need is the governance and fatherhood of the Empire-makers, men of sterling British type that brought India and Africa into our commonwealth of nations'[14].

Daisy Bates's attitudes, of course, owed much to her Anglo-Irish origins, but she was giving expression to a tradition which went back a long way in the Australian conversation. Today most Australians would feel uneasy at the suggestion that patriotism should be linked with the sacred—an indication, no doubt, that we do not share fully in the mythological presuppositions of past generations—but we can be sure that Daisy Bates would have identified wholeheartedly with the sentiments expressed at the protest meeting of 1849 which blocked the unloading of the convict ship *Hashemy*. At that meeting, it will be recalled, the principal speaker appealed to 'the highest and holiest patriotism that could animate' the citizens of New South Wales.

The term 'destiny' has numinous overtones. We have seen it invoked as an expression of the mythology of the United States. Once again, today's secularised consciousness hesitates to use it as freely as it was used in the past. In the late nineteenth century, however, Vance Palmer tells us it was part of the vocabulary of Australian nationalism. There was at that time a 'desire of the ordinary citizen to keep the conflicts of old-world imperialism away from Australian shores so that the country would be free, as the phrase went, to work out her own destiny'[15].

Most Australians probably did not reflect upon the numinous implications of the themes we have just mentioned. In the minds of some, however, they became explicit enough. In the mid-nineteenth century, Dr J. D. Lang, the fiery Presbyterian who threw himself passionately into the building of an Australian nation which was a worthy antipodean replica of the tradition from which it originated, saw Australia's mission and destiny as including a rule over the islands of the Pacific, 'not only for the benefit of all these Australian colonies, but for the promotion of the interests of civilisation and Christianity throughout the vast Pacific Ocean'[16]. King O'Malley, the New South Wales politician who had come to this country from the United States, was almost certainly echoing the American mythology of 'manifest destiny' when he declared that 'the controlling destiny of the islands of the Southern Seas is sacredly vested in the Australian people'[17].

It was only to be expected that the moment of Federation should call forth expressions of confidence in Australia's national destiny. William Gay's poem 'Australian Federation', for example, is interesting in its movement towards an explicit mention of sacred implications. 'From all division let our land be free', he begins, 'For God has made her one'. The oneness of which these opening lines speak is that established by a 'single shore', etc. But as the poem progresses, this geographical oneness becomes a symbol of that unity which is the proper expression of 'sacred ties / Of one dear blood, one storied enterprise'. Australia is called to be 'one people — mighty, serving God'[18].

The words of J. D. Lang which I quoted were an expression of the 'myth' which Manning Clark sees as having a fundamental importance in the shaping of the Australian project from the beginning: 'The British in 1788 and in the early years of settlement', he writes, 'had their own myth — the myth of the benevolent influence of British civilisation. They believed that British political institutions and the Protestant religion were for men of heroic ingredients'[19]. What Clark is referring to is a complex amalgam of mythological, ideological and other cultural elements of the British tradition, which provided an essential and in many ways dominant component of the provincial conversation of early Australia.

Most Christians are understandably shy of the term 'myth'. According to the basic definition we have given, however, the message of Christian faith may be said to belong to the category of 'mythology'. The Judeo-Christian faith affirms that one great story, preserved in the record of the Scriptures, tells the universal truth about human existence, that the gospel story illuminates the homelessness of humanity on its journey through history[20]. One of the most puzzling aspects of our Australian experience is the fact that while the great majority of Australians have considered themselves Christians, the public conversation which has reflected the development of our Australian project has been reluctant to identify itself with the message of Christian faith.

The experience of Joseph Furphy clearly illustrates the paradox to which I refer. As he worked for a long time on his remarkable novel *Such Is Life*, this lonely idealist wrestled with the question of what Australia had become by the end of the nineteenth century and what it was capable of becoming in the future. In the end, he found no social program to compare with what the Christian story has to offer struggling humanity: 'the sunshiny Sermon on the Mount', he wrote, 'is no fanciful conception... but a practical, workable code of life, adapted to any stage of civilisation, and delivered to men and women like ourselves... by One who knew exactly the potentialities and aspirations of man'[21]. But the sectarianism and narrowmindedness of Australia's institutional Christianity in the late nineteenth century—something of which he would have been painfully aware, since his family came from Northern Ireland—left Furphy disillusioned: 'from generation to generation the multitudes stand waiting to welcome the Gospel of Humanity with psalms and hosannas as of old; while... phylacteried exclusiveness takes counsel against the revolution which is to make all things new'[22]. If his background would make us hesitate, perhaps, to see him as typical, Furphy was by no means alone in this sense of frustrated alienation. This question is one which will be considered in our final chapter.

In seeking to justify itself, racism has more often than not appealed to the mythological pretensions of nationalism. Australian racism, it is well to recall, was no exception. Hancock gives us an embarrassing account of arguments heard during the debates which shaped the White Australia Policy in the national parliament. 'During the debates of 1901, the rhetoricians declared that it would be unfair for "a nation of yesterday" (China) to interfere with the destiny of the "noblest race upon the sphere" (the Australians). They even doubted whether some European nations, such as the Italians, were "civilised in the ordinary Australian sense". However, their immediate concern was with black men and yellow men—"the servile nations of the world". In legislating against the entry of such people, they knew themselves obedient to the will of God, who had set aside Australia "exclusively for a Southern empire—for a Southern nation" '[23].

A number of assumptions which were in vogue in European culture during the nineteenth century and early twentieth centuries, and which were shared by many Australians, had something in common with mythology in the strict sense, in so far as they provided a pre-established framework within which human existence could be situated. The idea of 'progress'—which, as we shall see in the next chapter, provided the focus of one of the most influential ideologies of the nineteenth century—took on overtones which were almost religious. Carried along by the new energies of the industrial revolution, filled with wonder by the new horizons opened up by the advances of science, European society could see no limits to a progression that would carry them to ever greater achievements and well-being. When the bridge over the Firth of Forth—a pioneering feat of engineering—collapsed, plunging the passengers of a crowded train to their death, one British newspaper declared that it was 'a small price to pay for the benefits of Progress'. The terrible debacle of the war which overtook Europe in 1914 brought a bitter disillusionment, in which Australia shared.

The Darwinian notion of evolution as a law of being reinforced the rationale of 'progress'. Though Darwin himself hesitated to extend his theory to a natural selection among peoples and races, popularisers of his thought such as Herbert Spencer proceeded to do so. Social Darwinianism was taken up by white Australians as they sought to rationalise the tragedy which was overtaking Australia's Aboriginal people. One Australian Governor described the situation with unconscious irony, as one in which the advance of British civilisation made inevitable 'the natural progress of the aboriginal race towards extinction'[24].

For those whose beliefs made Darwinism unacceptable, another theory of nineteenth century rationalism was at hand to explain the superiority of the white race. 'The advocates of the theory of the Great Chain of Being', writes Richard Broome, 'ranked all living creatures from God down in a so-called order of merit. Since it was a European theory, the Europeans were ranked highest among the races of mankind, and the Aboriginals as one of the lowest, nearest the animals'[25].

[1]   Cf. Denis Edwards, 'Sin and Salvation in the South Land of the Holy Spirit', pp.92–3, in Peter Malone (Coordinator), *Discovering an Australian Theology*, Homebush (St Paul) N.S.W., 1988.

[2]   *After the Dreaming* (1968 Boyer Lectures), p.39.

[3]   'Landscape and Dreaming', p.31, in S. Graubard (ed.), *Australia: The Daedalus Symposium*, North Ryde (Angus and Robertson) 1985.

[4]   Aram A. Yengoyan, 'Economy, Society and Myth in Aboriginal Australia', p.215, in W. H. Edwards (ed.), *Traditional Aboriginal Society*, Sth Melbourne, 1987.

[5]   For this reason, Stanner's term 'the Dreaming' seems preferable to 'Dreamtime'. See Tony Swain, 'Dreaming, Whites and The Australian Landscape: Some Popular Misconceptions', *Jour. Rel. Hist.* 15 (1988) pp.345–50.

[6]   'The Dreaming', p.225, in W. H. Edwards (ed.), *Traditional Aboriginal Society*.

[7]   'Economy, Society and Myth in Aboriginal Australia', p.220, in W. H. Edwards (ed.), *Traditional Aboriginal Society*.

[8]   1968 Boyer Lectures, p.44.

[9]   *Aranda Traditions*, Melbourne U.P. 1947, p.116.

[10]   1968 Boyer Lectures, pp.44–5.

[11]   ibid., p.44.

[12]   *My Place*, Fremantle (Arts Centre Press) 1988, p.181.

[13]   Cf. *The Passing of the Aborigines*, London (John Murray) 1938, pp.222–3.

[14]   ibid., p.238.

[15]   'The Legend', p.12, in C. Wallace-Crabbe (ed.) *Australian Nationalists: Modern Critical Essays*, Melbourne, 1971.

[16]   Cited, Hancock, *Australia*, p.42.

[17]   Cited, White, *Inventing Australia*, pp.80–1.

[18]   L. Cantrell (ed.), *Writing of the 1890s*, St Lucia (Univ. of Q. Press) 1988, p.122.

[19]   'Heroes', p.58, in S. Graubard (ed.), *Australia: The Daedalus Symposium*.

[20]   Cf. T. R. Wright, *Theology and Literature*, p.84, citing Amos Wilder. Wright writes: 'the Christian claim is that one particular story, centred upon Christ, tells the universal truth about history'.

21   *Such Is Life* by Tom Collins (Furphy's pseudonym), London (Jonathan Cape) 1945, p.112.

22   loc. cit.

23   *Australia*, p.66.

24   Cited, Hancock, *Australia*, p.29.

25   *Aboriginal Australians*, Sydney, 1982, p.90.

4.

THE IDEOLOGICAL FACTOR: SHARED VISIONS

Marxist analysis has made us aware of the bias and self-interest which can characterise the ideological consensus through which groups find solidarity and a common purpose. It would be wrong, however, to see ideology in exclusively negative terms. The outcome of a sociological interaction and process which is essential to the life of any social group, ideological consensus shapes understanding and practical attitudes into that unity and equilibrium which gives the sense of solidarity essential to any group, be it political party or movement, national community or subculture.

Certainly the selective emphases of ideology formation easily lend themselves to distortion and self-serving. Examples are not difficult to find. Marx's social analysis makes us aware of the ideological bias which affects the outlook of social classes. Nations engaged in war show themselves capable of frightful distortions in the ideological consensus to which they have recourse. History is cluttered with examples which leave us in little doubt about the dangers inherent in the process, and the distortions of which it is capable. To remain healthy, any social group must be capable of critical reflection upon the ideological stance it has adopted.

This chapter begins by considering the development in our Australian culture of a tragically distorted ideological bias. This example should alert us to the importance of critical reflection upon the ideological developments which emerged in the course of the conversation which has made Australia as we know it.

1. Ideology and white Australia's struggle to be human

The art historian Bernard Smith is one of the most distinguished writers Australia has produced. In his Boyer Lectures, broadcast in 1980 and published under the title *The Spectre of Truganini*, he suggested that the relationship between our dominant white culture and Australia's Aboriginal people is 'of the greatest importance for the future of civilisation in our country', that it 'constitutes a central problem for the integrity and authenticity of Australian culture today'[1]. The present relationship, in his judgment, is the outcome of a development which is essentially ideological.

Ideology, as I have already noted, is one of the key concepts of Karl Marx's interpretation of history. Like many of his generation, Smith has been influenced by Marx's thought. As a child, his reading of the Bible gave him 'a feeling for the great drama of history'. After the Bible, he judges that Marx has been the greatest and most beneficial influence in his work as a historian, and upon his attitude to life; he assures us, however, that he has 'made a shrewd study of Marx himself, and has not been misled by the old guru'[2]. In the Boyer Lectures, Smith applies Marx's insight in a way which goes far beyond the narrowness of a doctrinaire Marxism.

Smith believes that historians can 'aim at a truth that is more than a relative truth, and sometimes hit it'. They can best do this through the ongoing conversation they have among themselves: 'historians not only aim at the truth, they also have a great habit of aiming at one another; indeed it could be argued that this is quite the best way of hitting the truth'. In the dialectic of this conversation, he notes, the ideological factor will always be at work, since the participants will speak 'from positions which are more or less determined by the social class into which they are born, the nature of their education and subsequent experiences of life'[3]. In his lectures, Smith extends this ideological analysis to the ongoing conversation of our Australian culture as a whole, and in particular to the attitude which white Australians have adopted towards the Aborigines.

From the Bible, Smith tells us, he has gained a 'vision of history as a moral drama'[4]. At the heart of this drama is the 'continuous struggle to be, and to remain human'[5]. In Smith's judgment, white Australians failed tragically to meet this challenge in their dealings with the Aboriginal people. Sally Morgan's *My Place*, which tells of her efforts to make contact with her Aboriginal origins, includes the story of Arthur Corunna, her grandmother's brother. His words illustrate the point Smith wants to make with an admirable directness and simplicity. 'Don't listen', he told Sally, 'to what others tell you about God. He's the best mate a man could have... You look away from God, you go to ruin. Take the white people in Australia, they brought the religion here with them and the Commandment, Thou Shalt No Steal, and yet they stole this country. They took it from the innocent. You see, they twisted the religion. That's not the way it's supposed to be'[6].

In the end, Smith writes, the essential worth and viability of a culture depends upon the measure of success it has had in this struggle 'to be human, and to remain human': 'its vitality and capacity for survival will depend largely upon the quality of the moral values it brings to human problems'. Moral values become real, Smith points out, not in abstract assertions and fervent denunciations, but in the flesh and blood options made 'at a particular place and particular time'[7]. The resources which white Australians brought to their 'struggle to be human, and to remain human' were derivative: 'we brought our moral values, such as they were, from Europe with us, in, so to speak, our travelling trunks'[8]. Here they had to undergo the test of a frontier experience. 'Frontiers are not places', Smith observes, citing Malinowski, 'where men meet nature but where they confront other cultures, and systems of law conflict'[9]. Undergoing this test, the moral principles we brought from the other side of the world were 'more often than not seriously affected'. In our relationship with the original inhabitants of this land, Smith concludes, ours is 'a history of damaged goods'[10]. White Australians turned their back on the remarkable respect for human rights and human dignity which was achieved by Western culture during the eighteenth century Enlightenment, and which found expression in the American Declaration of Independence and the French Declaration of the Rights of Man[11].

As our history progressed, this moral failure was compensated for and perpetuated at the heart of the emerging Australian culture in the ideological consensus through which white Australians attempted to come to terms with what had happened to the Aboriginal people as a result of European colonisation: 'confronted by the realities of the colonial frontier, the murder, the rape, abduction and servitude for victuals and clothing amounting to slavery, colonists turned away from the principles of universal justice enunciated by their European fathers and grandfathers, to take refuge in primitive tribal myths that lay at the heart of their own culture, in order to justify themselves'[12].

The colonial enterprise of the European powers during the nineteenth century produced many instances of this 'usurper mentality', as the sociologist Albert Memmi has named it[13]. Having failed in the 'struggle to be human, and to remain human' in their dealings with the blacks, the dominant white community moved further and further from the moral option which had been offered them in their frontier experience.

Bernard Smith and others[14] have traced the phases of this ideological development. Initially, the early settlers found a way of relating to the tragic condition to which the dispossessed Aborigines had been reduced by making them figures of fun. As the nineteenth century progressed, Herbert Spencer's application of Darwin's theory of natural selection to social development made it possible for the plight of the blacks to be seen as the working out of a natural process. One 1847 commentator quoted by Smith likened this process to such things as the 'drainage of marshes or the disappearance of wild animals'[15]. Sixty years later, this rationale had become capable of turning the whole situation upside down, and facetiously attributing the real blame for what had happened to the Aborigines themselves! James Collier, for a period Herbert Spencer's literary assistant, could write 'There can be no question of right and wrong in such a case. The only right is that of superiority of race, and the greater inherent capacity on the part of the whites; the only wrong on the part of the blacks is their all-round inferiority... All other wrongs were incidental and... trivial. This was the capital offence, and it was irredeemable'[16].

In an earlier series of Boyer Lectures[17], W. E. H. Stanner pointed to the remarkable fact that through the ideological mechanism with which it shielded itself, white consciousness moved towards the point of suppressing all reference to the very existence of the Aborigines. Having reviewed a series of substantial Australian works written this century, he was forced to conclude that a massive mechanism of repression had established itself in the Australian culture: 'inattention on such a scale cannot possibly be explained by absent-mindedness. It is a structural matter, a view from a window which had been carefully placed to exclude a whole quadrant of the landscape. What may well have begun as a simple forgetting of other possible views turned into a habit, and over time into something like a cult of forgetfulness practised on a national scale'[18].

This silence was the repression, not only of a past story, but also of an ongoing story of injustice, cruelty and exploitation. It was our novelists who first dared to speak openly of the sexual relations between blacks and whites which had taken place on the white man's terms since the beginning—Katherine S. Prichard in *Coonardoo*, published in 1929, and Xavier Herbert in *Capricornia*, published in 1938. As Smith writes, what these authors brought to light was the fact 'that at the heart of the Australian experience lay a sexual tragedy of enormous historical dimensions in which love, mockery and hatred battled for the mastery, and that tragedy was performed across the bodies of Aboriginal women'[19].

Together with others, such as the artist Margaret Preston and the writers of the Jindyworobak Movement, Prichard and Herbert signalled the beginnings of a new awareness of the Aborigines among white Australians. Randolf Stow's novel *To the Islands*, published in 1958 when Stow was twenty-three years of age, drew on first-hand experience of the meeting between black and white cultures in north-western Australia; it evidenced an emerging respect for the resources of Aboriginal culture. Given the ideological development we have briefly reviewed, it was only to be expected that the growth of this awareness would be slow and painful. Concluding the Boyer Lectures, Smith suggested the time was ripe for a new 'meeting of the two cultures'[20]. He hoped, with poet Les Murray, that this meeting could prove to be a real 'convergence' bringing *mutual* benefit. And not the least benefit it could bring to white Australia would be the possibility of redemption from the original sin that we have inherited with our culture, the possibility of taking up anew 'the struggle to be, and to remain human', in our dealings with black Australians.

We have dwelt at length on this ideological development because it has a fundamental importance in our Australian conversation, confronting us, as it does, with the deception and self-serving of which we white Australians have been capable. It prepares us to look with a more critical eye at some of the other ideological configurations which have been present in our ongoing conversation.

2. The original ideological baggage: the Enlightenment and Romanticism

As Bernard Smith has observed, cultural baggage brought by white Australians from the other side of the world was 'more often than not seriously affected', so that they had to make do with 'damaged goods'. It was the principles of the Enlightenment, as he points out, which were tested on the new frontier of Australia's penal colony. It was the spirit of the Enlightenment which animated Governor Phillip and his aides as they undertook their task.

This immensely successful movement which in the eighteenth century had united the creative energies of Europe, and given a

new and distinctive expression to the heritage of Western civilisation, had a strong ideological component. Behind its championing
of the autonomy of the secular order and the central place it gave
to human reason was a reaction against the highly sacralised
culture which had dominated medieval Christendom. It is this reaction which helps us explain the ambiguous relationship of Phillip
and his officers to the Christian tradition, as described by Manning
Clark: 'they mocked their religion in private as a false mythology,
while in public they supported it for its social utility'[21]. From the
first, the substance of the Christian message was being denied a
proper place in 'the struggle to be human, and to remain human'
which was at the heart of the project in which we were all to share.

It is not surprising that a cultural movement which had produced
the music of Bach and Mozart and the assured simplicity of the
Georgian architecture brought with it to the new colony enthusiasm and self-confidence. But the outlook of the Enlightenment was
a very limited resource with which to undertake the task of establishing our new society. By making human reason the measure of
all, the mind of the Enlightenment saw its world in very stark
terms. Captain Watkin Tench, an officer whose journals show him
a man of genuine sensibilities, illustrates this in the completely
negative evaluation he makes of the Australian Aborigine: 'a creature deformed by all the passions, which affect and degrade our
nature, unsoftened by the influence of religion, philosophy and
legal restriction'[22].

The outlook of the Enlightenment is very clearly expressed in a
pamphlet produced a year after the establishment of the colony to
publicise what Phillip had achieved. 'There are few things more
pleasing than the contemplation of order and useful arrangement,
arising gradually out of tumult and confusion, and perhaps this
satisfaction cannot anywhere be more fully enjoyed than where a
settlement of civilised people is fixing itself upon a newly discovered or savage coast'[23]. The civilised decorum of Georgian
London had its faint echoes in Sydney Town when Governor
Macquarie's 'birthday' was celebrated, and ceremonial odes—
written by a convict secretary of superior education named
Michael Robinson—were recited. One of these rejoiced that in
New South Wales 'Commerce and Arts enriched the social soil, /
Burst thro' the gloom—and bade all nature smile'. Barron Field,
the judge who was the author of the first book of verse to be
printed in the colony (1819), was impatient, however, with the
pace at which reason and civilisation were dispelling the savage
gloom; he saw the Australian countryside as an emptiness 'where
nature reflecting Art is not yet born'.

The spirit of the Enlightenment is still very much alive in our
Australian culture. In his *Ideas for a Nation*, Donald Horne sees it

as 'one of the best things Australia has going for it'[24]. For that reason it is well to ponder its limitations, limitations which are coming to be recognised by contemporary thought. While it was right that the sacralised culture of the medieval West should finally be challenged in the name of a rightful autonomy of the secular order—something I consider more fully in the final chapter—it was unfortunate that this challenge came in the concrete historical form it assumed in the Enlightenment movement.

As Johann Baptist Metz points out[25], by making a disembodied a-historical rationality the norm of cultural development, the Enlightenment spirit alienated that development from the manifold resources of tradition. Cultural traditions are a heterogeneous complexity. Because of the pre-reflexive nature of their development, they contain much that is vulnerable to critical analysis. At the same time, however, they give access to an accumulated wisdom that includes much more than can be articulated by reason: the truth we share as human beings is far more than can be spoken in words and recorded in the encyclopaedias of the Enlightenment. We disregard these additional resources at our peril.

Cultures which have been dominated by the Enlightenment spirit are impoverished by the fact that this spirit has alienated them from the traditional resources to which I refer: inarticulate wisdom concerning, for instance, human relationships, sexuality, material possessions, all of them problem areas in contemporary Western culture. The renowned Egyptian architect, Abdel Wahid El-Wakil, who recently visited Australia, sees the alienation to which we refer reflected in the physical environment which the spirit of the Enlightenment has tended to create: 'Modern architecture has proved a flirtatious mistress, a stranger to true emotion or love... Modern architecture cannot afford abiding commitment; its stillborn offspring litter our lifeless modern towns. Modern architecture lacks love'[26].

Of their nature, cultures of the new world imbued with the spirit of the Enlightenment are more likely to be affected by this alienation. Access to the resources of the cultural traditions in which they share is far more tenuous for them than it is in the lands in which they originated. I have already noted that this problem is an acute one for the culture which unites the people of the United States. The American authors of the remarkable work of self-criticism to which I have already referred, *Habits of the Heart*, seek to recover traditional resources which will help their people to take up moral issues arising from the spirit of individualism which characterises the American ethos. It is significant, as I have pointed out, that they look almost exclusively to the *articulate* wisdom which was an expression of the Enlightenment. They have little to say of the traditional wisdom communicated in many ways other than that of rational discourse—beyond a wistful, almost envious reference in their concluding paragraphs to the resources of other cultural traditions[27].

Even before the First Fleet set sail for Botany Bay the pendulum of Western culture was moving against the Enlightenment's unbounded confidence in the powers of reason. Deep instincts within European culture recognised the need to own the broader heritage to which I have referred, as the reaction of romanticism sought to give back its proper place to the emotional order, the instinctive, the symbolic, the dimensions of human existence which are beyond the measures of pure reason—what in fact had been too hastily discarded in the enlightenment's reaction against medievalism. Already in the eighteenth century a very different evaluation of civilisation from that of the Enlightenment had made its appearance. In this view, the ideal human existence was epitomised in the 'noble savage', in an existence removed from the pressures and denaturing influences of civilisation; genuine human impulses, it was suggested, would find their expression in an unspoilt natural world and human society.

Nineteenth century romanticism had many forms. It had a major influence upon our Australian culture through the nationalistic pretensions which it fostered among the peoples of Europe. For much of the nineteenth century this movement had a subtle but pervasive influence on the mood and perceptions of Australian culture.

As romanticism explored the darker, more enigmatic dimensions of human existence, the optimism so characteristic of the Enlightenment gave way at times to a more sombre view. Marcus Clarke (d.1881), the author of His Natural Life, one of our earliest novels[28], provides an excellent example of romanticism's influence in Australia during the last century. Clarke was given the honour of writing the Preface to an edition of the Poems of Adam Lindsay Gordon, published after Gordon's tragic death by suicide. This Preface contains a much quoted passage, descriptive of the Australian bush, showing clearly the way in which the perceptions of Clarke and many of his fellow Australians at the time were affected by European romanticism. Clarke writes 'What is the dominant note of Australian scenery?... The Australian mountain forests are funereal, secret, stern. Their solitude is desolation. They seem to stifle, in their black gorges, a story of sullen despair'[29].

The paintings of Clarke's contemporaries portray in visual form what he expressed in words. Conrad Martens (d.1878), for instance, the first artist to make his mark in this country, painted misty landscapes bathed in the soft light of early morning or late evening, seeking to capture a romantic perception far removed from the vivid sunshine and burnished Australian sky later Australians have taken for granted[30]. Nicholas Chevalier's (d.1902) *The Buffalo Ranges* reminds one far more of the European paintings of the period than it does of the familiar Australian landscape[31].

3. The aura of British imperialism

We see in Australia today the stirrings of a new nationalism. The flag is far more in evidence. Car stickers proclaim, in all serious-ness, 'I love Australia'. It is hard to imagine Ben Chifley, or even Robert Menzies, enthusiastic son of empire that he was, wearing the flag on their lapels and standing reverently, with hand on chest, while the anthem was played. The dry comments which would have come from rank and file Australians, come more easily to mind. Multicultural Australia, concerned to maintain identity and unity, is already moving, it seems, along the path taken by the United States from whom we have borrowed these new con-ventions. A review of the nationalism of our past may well help us to maintain the critical sense that is necessary if these devel-opments are not to foster the illusory slogans and myths which confuse nationalism and genuine patriotism[32].

The nationalism of our past was a sharing in the grand enterprise of British imperialism. British nationalism differed from that of the continental countries, many of whom were in the process of establishing new national identities for themselves as the map of Europe was transformed by nineteenth century developments. Her frontiers geographically determined, Britain was under no great pressures as far as domestic identity was concerned. She did not join the other European nations in establishing anniversary cele-brations of nationhood and making much of their past history and folklore. Britain's sense of identity and destiny in the era of nationalism was associated with the role she had assumed as the world's most successful imperial power. The ideology which main-tained British self-respect celebrated the greatness and benefits for humanity of her imperial exploits.

In the judgment of Judith Wright, European nationalism was related to the breakdown of traditional values in European culture. 'Europe was, for spiritual purposes, lost', she writes. 'As always, where a vacuum opens in the heart, action and violence rushed in to fill the space'. The vacuum was all the greater in a provincial culture like that of Australia, 'where not even the shell and struc-ture of European traditional values were available as a shelter for the naked'[33]. As the British project advanced, the legend of the imperial 'frontier' became a fundamental theme of its supportive ideology. What Rudyard Kipling did for the worldwide empire in celebrating this theme, writers like the Australian C. E. W. Bean did for the provincial corners of the British conversation.

Kipling is a far more interesting and engaging figure than the stereotype of our cultural memory would lead one to expect. His is a case of the legend displacing the reality. It was as if imperial Britain needed him to be the embodiment of its prevailing ideology. The brief autobiography Kipling wrote in the months before his death in 1936[34] helps us to distinguish the real man from the caricature. When he came to England at the age of twenty-four Kipling was hailed as a 'new Dickens'; his was 'the most notable case of literary fame achieved overnight since Lord Byron'[35]. During his time as a war correspondent covering the Boer War it probably suited Kipling to cultivate the caricature which portrayed him as a hardbitten champion of empire[36]. The fact that throughout his life, as Richard Holmes writes, 'he held to a Victorian code of decent silence on personal matters in public'[37] made it practically impossible to distinguish the real person from the public persona which had been created for him.

His autobiography makes it clear that Kipling's first love was writing itself, not the imperial frontier theme which served him so well as a writer[38]. *Something of Myself* certainly shows that Kipling had his limitations, and that he shared in the racist attitudes of his times. It also shows a man who was not insensitive to the lessons of history. He looked forward, for instance, to an autonomous India[39]. His surprising decision, in his autobiography, to make practically no reference to the world war in which he lost his only son, gives us to understand something of the disillusionment he felt[40]. He can speak with a certain detachment of the way in which journals like the *Manchester Guardian* had 'established' his '"Imperialistic" iniquities'[41]. The fact that he can formulate a perfect description of ideology and the distortions to which it gives rise, when commenting upon the outlook of the United States, gives the lie to the caricature which would make him a woodenheaded jingoist with a clever pen. 'Every nation', he wrote, 'like every individual, walks in a vain show—else it could not live with itself—but I never get over the wonder of a people who, having extirpated the aboriginals of their continent more completely than any race had ever done, honestly believed they were the godly little New England community setting examples to brutal mankind'[42].

It was the legendary Kipling, however, who was to capture the popular imagination. The name of the most popular writer of his day became synonymous with the saga of empire and the ethos which inspired it; his stories and verses gave Britishers everywhere a sense of identification with the romance and adventure of the imperial frontier.

What Kipling did for the empire as a whole, C. E. W. Bean did for Australia. Bean's writings contribute to our present discussion because they illustrate a less attractive side of the imperialist ideology which prevailed in Australia early this century. Before looking at this limited aspect of his writings, however, a word should be said about this author to whom I make frequent reference. As a person Charles Bean was a remarkable Australian, well deserving of a place in the telling of our story[43]. Bean was born at Bathurst, New South Wales in 1879. His father Edwin Bean was an English schoolmaster who had recently migrated to Australia; his mother was a third generation Australian whose family had been among the first free settlers in Tasmania. When he was nine years of age, his father took the family back to England where he became the headmaster of a grammar school. Bean's education was completed in England. After studies in Oxford he was admitted to the bar. In 1904, young Bean returned alone to Australia where it was not long before he decided to make writing his career.

Bean's relationship to his native land was complicated by the long period abroad during his formative years. In fact, before deciding to try his fortunes in Australia he had applied to join the British colonial service. The title of his first journalistic success 'The Impressions of a New Chum', a series of articles on Australia published in the *Sydney Morning Herald*, shows something of the ambivalence he felt at that time. It may well be however that his unusual situation heightened the awareness with which he observed his adopted land. His articles certainly provided clear evidence of an enthusiastic identification with things Australian. They indicated as well a promising journalistic talent, which combined a remarkable capacity for detailed observation and the ability to isolate the issues essential to a particular situation. It was this talent which eventually made him one of the greatest war historians the world has seen[44]. Henry Lawson, who read a book Bean published on naval matters in 1908, wrote to his sister, 'I am reading *With the Flagship in the South* over and over'; its style, he said, reminded him of Kipling at his best[45].

Bean's success as a journalist led to his being elected by the Australian Journalists' Association as the one Australian war correspondent allowed by British authorities to accompany the Australian Imperial Forces to the war zone. With an English accent and manner, wearing spectacles on a somewhat beaky nose, Bean was not the type to go down well with the Australian troops. He became, in fact, the object of some animosity when, at the request of the commanding officer, he wrote a somewhat righteous article on the lack of discipline displayed by some of the troops in training in Egypt—in order to prepare public opinion for the repatriation of offenders. At Gallipoli a short time afterwards, however, he soon won universal respect. Wherever the fighting was in progress, day or night, Bean was present, showing remarkable courage as he calmly gathered the data which he was to sift and record so meticulously. As a journalist he had developed a style which portrayed Australians from the point of view of the rank and file. This style served him well in his new task.

For his outstanding courage in assisting wounded troops under fire, Bean was recommended for the Military Cross. The fact that he had refused the military commission offered him, in order to maintain maximum independence for his work as a correspondent, meant that it could not be awarded. A man of remarkable personal integrity, he won the admiration of all who collaborated with him, both during and after the war[46].

Bean would have been horrified at the thought that his writings distorted the truth. Scrupulous about truthfulness in his personal life, he was outraged when General Hamilton's Chief of Intelligence questioned the wisdom of having correspondents at the front: 'In a properly organised nation', he said, 'the government... simply tells the people what it thinks will conduce to winning the war... if a lie is likely to win the war it tells them lies'. 'There are ways in plenty in which a war may be won', Bean replied, 'which conceivably do far more harm to a nation than defeat'[47]. The fact that a man of Bean's rectitude was betrayed into a racist interpretation of Britain's imperial project serves as a warning to all of us that, despite our best intentions, ideological consensus always runs the danger of distorting the truth in its efforts to promote the interests of the group.

In 1910 a series of articles Bean had written for the *Sydney Morning Herald* was published under the title *On the Wool Track*[48]. Bean's point of view was still, to a degree, that of an outsider. He was, as we have seen, a keen observer and a gifted writer capable of giving a sense of immediacy while at the same time putting his finger on the important issues involved in the situation he was describing. His book, provides a valuable record of outback Australia at the time he was writing, and we shall make further use of it. For the moment, however, we are concerned with the rationale which runs through the book as it endeavours to situate the Australian reality he is describing within the broader picture of the empire and its frontiers.

Bean interpreted the qualities which he admired in the Australian bushman as a manifestation of the greatness of the British race. It was an old theme. Hancock quotes the agreeable surprise of a visitor to Australia in 1827 that in the children of convicts 'the vigour of the stock reasserted itself'[49]. Henry Parkes, the champion of federation, hoped for the day when Australia would become 'the seat of a mighty empire under the banner of the Anglo-Saxon race'[50]. Bean took up this theme with a characteristic enthusiasm[51].

Bean saw the resourcefulness and independence which he admired in outback Australians as an achievement of the race. 'The roots of it seem to go back', he wrote, 'deep into the British stock'[52]. Indeed, 'the up-country Australian is possibly the most capable man among Anglo-Saxons'[53]. Comparing Australians with Britons in the home country, he was of the opinion that the 'genius of race' did not have the opportunity to express itself in the constrictions and regimentation of the British Isles; 'it does not come to the surface until the race gets to places like Australia, where the quality was to come out'[54]. He quoted Lord Kitchener's evaluation of Australian troops as 'the equal, if not the superior, of any people he knew'[55].

The Australian Bean was presenting as an ideal was one who was taking up the challenge of the imperial frontier: Australia's greatest need, if it was to realise its potential, was an influx of 'white British population'[56]. The question facing Australia was 'whether a territory of about the size of India can or cannot be used to advantage by a British people—will or will not be filled with the British race'[57]. Identifying with the view of the Anglo-Saxon establishment, Bean, like Henry Parkes in the passage just quoted, did not recognise the importance of the Celtic contribution to the ethos of the rank and file Australians he admired.

Bean contrasted the frontier type of the outback with the 'nervous, narrow, city-bred factory folk'[58] of Australia's cities. The qualities of the bushman 'are, of course, only drawn from the British race, because the people of Australia are as purely British as the people of Great Britain—perhaps more so than the population of London'. These qualities, however, could not develop in the soft life of the cities, they 'were never—and never will be—elicited from the race by such agencies as the sea-beaches and soft breezes, sweet fruits and easy hours of which the advertisements speak'[59].

Today the distorted assumptions of Bean's imperialist ideology make us smile. They were, however, what many Australians wanted to hear. The editorial staff of the *Sydney Morning Herald* saw nothing amusing about them. We have already cited Hancock's summing up of the situation: 'Among Australians pride of race counted for more than love of country'.

The issue was complicated for Australians by the need they felt to assert some kind of independence from Britain. Hancock explains this ambivalence by saying that Australians were 'pro-British' but 'anti-English'[60]. With characteristic dry humour—and a considerable unconscious irony!—the *Bulletin* made the point in its own way. Bean was probably echoing the *Bulletin* when he wrote that Australians may well be even more British than the population of London. The *Bulletin* boasted that the British race was better represented in Australia than in 'cosmopolitan and nigger-infested England'—especially among the people of London, who were often Poles and Jews![61].

Today, of course, the rationale with which C. E. W. Bean championed British imperialism would find no credible supporters. As three wars in the course of this century demonstrated, however, Australia's past investment in the imperialist ideology was immense. Disillusionment was inevitable. In a sense we are still recovering from it as we seek to find our place in the world.

4. Dreams of utopia

It is not surprising that Australia, as a new world country, should be taken up with the possibility of building a society freed from the injustices and shortcomings of the old world. As the nineteenth century progressed, a number of factors which contributed and gave expression to such aspirations helped to shape our ongoing conversation.

Many of those who immigrated to Australia brought with them a political idealism which had despaired of ever finding fulfilment in European society. The contribution to the emerging Australian ethos made by the Irish would be hard to exaggerate[62]. Among the convicts sent to New South Wales were about a thousand political prisoners. The six Tolpuddle Martyrs, for example, were transported in 1834 for attempting to organise a trade union. The Chartists constituted a noteworthy group. They derived their name from the 'People's Charter', in which they had advocated such reforms as universal franchise, voting by ballot, annual parliament and payment for parliamentarians. About sixty Chartists were transported to New South Wales between 1837 and 1848. Many of their sympathisers, disappointed at the rejection of their claims, came to the colonies as free settlers. Henry Parkes, for instance, was one. These immigrants found a colonial society, many of whom were emancipists or ex-convicts, jealous of their new-found freedom.

The gold rushes, coming immediately after 1848, the year of revolution and social upheaval in Europe, brought a flood of new citizens with heightened political awareness. The fight for justice on the goldfields, symbolised in the Eureka uprising at Ballarat, provided a common cause which sharpened political awareness during a period of rapid growth in population. In fact, by the late nineteenth century the objectives of the Chartists had been achieved in Australia, and Australian political institutions were attracting the attention and admiration of European observers.

The aspirations of the young Australian society were inevitably affected, of course, by the ideal of 'progress' which in the nineteenth century had almost assumed the place religion had had in the European tradition. Marcus Clarke concluded an essay entitled 'Civilisation without Delusion', which he contributed to the first number of the *Victorian Review*, with the hope that the new age which was dawning would prove to be one in which 'the interests now felt in churchmen's disputations will be transferred to the discoveries of science. The progress of the world will be the sole care of its inhabitants; and the elevation of the race, the only religion of mankind'[63]. It was an interesting marriage of the principles of the Enlightenment and the dreams of romanticism. Australians shared in the nineteenth century enthusiasm which made a series of international exhibitions 'national, and quasi-religious' festivals at the shrine of 'progress'[64].

As Australia's provincial culture shared in Europe's ideology of 'progress', 'the most convincing imported idea', as Donald Horne writes, 'was the English notion of Improvement'[65]. In Britain at this time John Ruskin's doctrine of the 'moral aesthetic' was winning widespread acceptance. Ruskin's view that exposure to artistic and intellectual culture would elevate the moral tone of civilised society seemed to explain the way in which 'progress' would unfold. The Schools of Arts and Mechanics Institutes which stand empty and forlorn in most Australian country towns are evidence of the fact that even rural Australia was touched by these hopes[66]. The aspiring novelist Joseph Furphy was one Australian who made use of the literature available in the Mechanics Institutes set up in country centres. The movement had much more substantial re-sults in Australian cities, of course, leading to the establishing of libraries and art galleries similar to those coming into existence in Britain's provincial towns. Our first universities had their begin-nings in this climate, and our public education systems received a new impetus.

If the Schools of Arts were more symbols of hope than places of real artistic endeavour, in the country as a whole much was achiev-ed. Considering the period which inaugurated the new century, Bernard Smith writes 'Between 1880 and 1914 the foundations of a new white Australian culture were laid down; and its achieve-ments were considerable'[67]. Notable among them were the paint-ings of the Heidelberg School which registered a perception of the Australian environment which, with the help of the French impres-sionists, had freed itself from the gloom of European romanticism.

Our dreams for Australia were more than an echo of European movements of thought and art. On a more popular level, the *Bull-etin* became the very embodiment of a lively Australian conver-sation. Founded in 1880, it was an immense success, achieving an astounding circulation of 80 000 by 1890. J. T. Archibald, who presided over its development, soon recognised that it could pro-vide an instrument for the expression of Australia's peculiar ethos, and most of its content came to be contributed by the readers themselves. The *Bulletin*'s style, irreverent and given to a dry, understated humour, at once echoed and promoted Australia's prevailing conversational tone. Many of its readers had a good basic education; many others were keen to educate themselves in the time they had for reading. The *Bulletin* became 'the bushman's bible'.

In 1923 the *Bulletin* captured the attention of D. H. Lawrence, who gave some pages of the novel *Kangaroo* to quoting excerpts which had amused him. Of Somers, his partly autobiographical character, he wrote 'The *Bulletin* was the only periodical in the world that really amused him... The horrible stuffiness of English newspapers he could not stand... But the "Bully", even if it was made up all of bits, and had neither head nor tail nor feet nor wings, was still a lively creature. He liked its straightforwardness and the kick in some of its tantrums. It beat no solemn drums. It had no deadly earnestness. It was just stoical, and spitefully humorous. Yes, at the moment he liked the *Bulletin* better than any paper he knew, though even the *Bulletin* tried a dowdy bit of swagger sometimes, especially on the pink page. But then the pink page was just "literary", and who cares?'[68].

The exchange of views recorded in the *Bulletin* was a varied mix. There was a strong republican contingent which found support in the journal's editorial policy. Ironically, that policy sometimes joined forces with the imperialistic ideology by espousing the ugly racism to which reference has already been made. Reformist social theories were discussed, such as those of Henry George who lectured in Australia on his proposed system of land tax; political radicalism, however, had few followers—a fact which I shall discuss in a later chapter. The political mood which prevailed has been summed up by Leon Cantrell as 'bourgeois reformist'[69].

The *Bulletin*'s outstanding service to the Australian conversation in this formative period of our history is made clear by the fact that many of its most memorable voices first found expression through its pages. A look at some of them tells us a great deal about Australia's aspirations during this period.

Henry Lawson writes, recalling the republican enthusiasm which fired him as a youth in 1887: 'I had to write then—or burst. The *Bulletin* saved me from bursting'. Four lines of his effort were published, with the characteristic comment, 'Youth: the first four lines are the best. Try again'. 'I haven't felt so excited over a thing since', he tells us[70]. If Henry Lawson does not rate serious consideration as a poet, Judith Wright tells us, he does 'as a symptom of the times, as the short story writer, and as a man'; there was a 'poetry', she adds, about the man himself. Like many of his contemporaries, Lawson was, in Judith Wright's words, 'passionately occupied with the notion of progress, of "civilisation", as a struggle towards some form of social justice'. What all this meant, she notes, was 'not clearly thought out', and often became mixed up with a nationalism which must stand up to the oppressor in an armed struggle: 'They needn't say the fault is ours', as one of his poems puts it, 'If blood should stain the wattle'. Lawson's real contribution to the Australian conversation was to come later.

Through the *Bulletin*, the youthful Miles Franklin (1879–1954) was able to make the acquaintance of Henry Lawson and ask him to write a Preface to her novel *My Brilliant Career*. It was published in 1901 while she was still in her teens, 'just a little bush girl' who 'has scarcely been out of the bush in her life' as Lawson put it in his Preface. Her precocious work portrayed the struggles and conditions of rural Australia with a realism and humour that were close to Lawson's own point of view. He said he was proud of the book because it came from lived experience of 'the country where I come from; where people toil and bake, and suffer and are kind; where every second sun-burnt bushman is a sympathetic humorist, with the sadness of the bush deep in his eyes and a brave grin for the worst of times'.

Franklin's views, expressed through her teenage heroine in the final paragraphs of her book, give us a glimpse of the idealism and hopes of adolescent Australia at the time. She is proud, she declares, to be 'an Australian'. She is thankful to be 'a peasant, part of the bone and muscle of my nation', glad she has not been born a 'parasite', one of those who live 'from the proceeds of human sweat and blood and souls'. She salutes the men of Australia, whom she has seen 'struggle uncomplainingly against flood, fire, disease in stock, pests, drought, trade depression and sickness', still able to reach out 'in true sympathy to a brother in misfortune' and 'to laugh and joke and be cheerful'. She salutes also the women, with 'a great love and pity'; through their toil they 'make the best of the few oases to be found along the narrow dusty track' of their existence. But she fears, in the end, that Australia's brave hopes will not be realised, because 'the rope of class distinction' seems to be 'drawing closer and closer, tighter and tighter'.

It was the encouragement and assistance of the *Bulletin*'s A. G. Stephens which made it possible for Joseph Furphy (1843–1912) to publish the novel *Such Is Life*. When submitting it for consideration, he described it: 'scene Riverina and northern Vic.; temper democratic; bias offensively Australian'. The work of a self-educated man, *Such Is Life* is not an easy book to read. Veronica Brady describes it as 'difficult, quirky, often garrulous'[71]. It has a place of great importance, however, in our Australian conversation, being described by Geoffrey Serle as 'the most freakish achievement of colonial Australia'[72].

Armed with the quiet humour of the bushman and his sense of irony, Furphy wrestles with the meaning of life and the realistic hopes it may offer in the Australia he observed at close quarters during the time he worked as a bullock driver. He employs a somewhat original device: a stream of characters from all backgrounds troop through his pages—bullock drivers and squatters, 'bosses' and 'men', stockmen, boundary riders, swagmen and prospectors, pious Catholics and cantankerous Orangemen, clergymen and government officials—all giving their views one way or another, and provoking reflection on the part of Tom Collins, the canny bush philosopher with a smattering of general reading who tells the tale. It is in effect a dramatisation of the Australian conversation as it was taking place in northern Victoria in Furphy's day.

In the judgment of Veronica Brady, Furphy succeeds in producing a novel that 'shows the spiritual possibilities of life in Australia' and which goes a long way towards 'describing what utopian dreams we are able to entertain'[73]. Furphy's hopes—we have already heard him on the 'sunshiny Sermon on the Mount'—are tempered by a realism akin to that of the later Lawson and that expressed by Franklin. 'The utopia he offers', Brady writes, 'involves learning to live comfortably, even joyfully, with the knowledge that an ideal society may not be possible in this world and yet we must go on hoping and working for it'[74].

These writers—Lawson, Franklin and Furphy—tempered their dreams for Australia with a realism they had learnt from the struggles which have marked Australian life. Bernard O'Dowd (1866–1953) was another writer whose first published works appeared in the *Bulletin*. The dreams he entertained for Australia were of a far more flamboyant kind. Australia's situation as the nineteenth century drew to a close gave rise to a predictable rhetoric of contrast with the old world. Furphy was well capable of it: 'this recordless land—the land of our lawful solicitude and imperative responsibility—is ... committed to no usages of petrified injustice; she is clogged by no fealty to shadowy idols, enshrined by Ignorance, and upheld by misplaced homage alone; she is cursed by no memories of fanaticism and persecution; she is innocent of hereditary national jealousies, and free from the envy of sister states'[75]. Associated with the prevailing ideology of 'progress', this rhetoric produced a heady mix. Such was the stuff of Bernard O'Dowd's dream for Australia.

As far as its intrinsic worth is concerned, O'Dowd's thought is not worth delaying over. As Judith Wright comments, the 'confusion of his rhetoric and the pedagogy of his half assimilated information' make it difficult to make a serious comparison with other writers. His verse, which she calls 'jerky doggerel', another critic, Brian Elliott, describes as 'poetic hemlock'! There is something moving, however, about O'Dowd's naive idealism. The enthusiastic response of his contemporaries shows that his efforts reflected something of the mood of the times—perhaps it is this which Hancock had in mind when he referred, as we have seen, to the 'exuberant, egotistical, idealistic nationalism' of the time. The novelist Katherine S. Prichard has described the reaction of those who heard O'Dowd's lecture 'Poetry Militant: An Australian Plea for a Poetry of Purpose': it 'made such an impression on those of us who were beginning to think seriously, that upon leaving the meeting we were almost too exalted and too exhilarated to speak'[76].

Summing up the mood of these audiences, Judith Wright writes: 'Australia, as the youngest of the continents and hence least trammelled by tradition, was to devote herself to the task of creating a new society on purely rational lines. Human thought had now been freed from all traditional claims; the Darwinian theory had done away with the notion of divine sanctions and the old political tyrannies had been broken. At last it was open to man to create a just society'[77]. The heritage of the Enlightenment, it is clear, had established healthy roots.

Judith Wright compares the approach adopted by O'Dowd with that of Lawson and the other writers mentioned, suggesting that they can be seen as representing different sides of the psyche of adolescent Australia. O'Dowd, expressing 'the self-confidence of adolescence', is 'reformist, scraping together for his utopia what he thought "the best of the old", but rejecting tradition and authority in favour of an ill-balanced political rhetoric'. Lawson, on the other hand, expressing the 'self-doubt' of adolescence, is 'bitter and moody', more obsessed 'by the world's sorrows and his own than by any brash intellectual plan to mend them'[78].

The program of O'Dowd's 'Poetry of Purpose', as Judith Wright comments, 'might well have daunted a committee composed of archangels'[79]. The coming of an awareness of 'evolution' called for a total reshaping of human society. 'All, all is being thrown, or has been thrown, into the crucible of re-evaluation, customs, morals, religions, laws, institutions, classes, castes, politics, philosophies: all, for at that apocalyptic word, "Evolution", a new Jerusalem descended upon the mental world...'[80].

During a 'transition period', when the power of theologians was waning and 'other dogmatists, possibly more dangerous because more superficially rational' were making their appearance, it was the poet who should give himself to answering the questions of the day. Poetry Militant, as distinct from Poetry Triumphant which belongs to eternity, must give itself to practical goals for 'the furtherance of the best interests of the human race'[81]. The task for this Poetry Militant was greater than ever before 'in the present reconstruction of all things beneath the wand of Evolution theories'; and in this work Australia should have a foremost place.

Nowhere was the need for Poetry Militant greater than 'in this virgin and unhandicapped land of social experiments, embryonic democracy, and the coming Race, Australia!'[82].

The task which lay ahead was no small one. 'The poet's function', O'Dowd explained, 'is to create gods, and in every age of human progress the poet has been the most authentic and effective creator of gods, and of the mythologies that give them bone and blood and power'. Poetry Militant 'may also have to destroy gods when their hour strikes'. This work of the poets is really 'the detection and unveiling of frauds...we disguise under the names of divinities...so subtle that we sometimes build codes of morality upon them, and buttress thrones, laws and religions by means of them; yea, nations have accepted them, have risen, flowered and fallen without knowing that they were frauds at all'[83]. The dismantling of whole civilisations for total reconstruction, it seems, does not daunt O'Dowd.

As we shall see presently, this program has much in common with Friedrich Nietzsch's Lebensphilosophie. But, as he leaves his work as a parliamentary librarian to deliver his lecture on Poetry Militant, O'Dowd knows nothing, apparently, of the existential terrors which overwhelmed Nietzsche. He does have doubts as to whether his hopes for an Australian utopia will be realised. They are expressed in his poem 'Australia'. This new nation can be either a place 'where the West / In halcyon calm rebuilds her fatal nest', or it can become the 'Delos of a coming Sun-God's race'; it could be a 'Light' for the new age, or 'a will o'wisp on marshy quest'; he asks whether beneath Australia's face 'lurks millennial Eden', or the country will become 'a new demesne for mammon to infest'. These doubts, however, are not the dismay of Nietzsche's recognition that to proclaim the death of God, as O'Dowd has done, is to assume a terrifying responsibility for all order and meaning in human existence, but a concern that the evangel of his Poetry of Purpose will not be taken up with sufficient enthusiasm.

Surely the most dramatic expression of utopianism in Australia, as the nineteenth century drew to a close, was the departure of several hundred Australians in 1893 to build a new society in Paraguay. Their leader was William Lane who, as a writer and union organiser, had been prominent in Australia's labour movement. Among them was the youthful Mary Gilmore. Though she was to return to Australia, her poetry kept alive her longings for a just Australian society where 'All men at God's round table sit, / And all men must be fed'. 'She expressed in her poetry', writes Vincent Buckley, 'the dream of a society which is as complete and simple as a lyric'[84]. 'Lane's departure in 1893', comments Leon Cantrell, 'marked the effective end of any dream of Utopia in the Australian colonies'[85].

5. Beyond disillusionment

If the Australian conversation at the turn of the century was in many ways adolescent, it also gave evidence of resources which were resilient and of great promise. The march of world events, however, was to work against their being given a fair test. We were soon to find ourselves caught up in a general disillusionment with the mythologies and ideologies which the nineteenth century had accepted so unquestioningly.

In 1893, the year in which William Lane led his ill-fated expedition to Paraguay, a slump on the world's wool market sent the vulnerable Australian economy into severe depression. Banks ceased to do business; one after another they collapsed and many Australians faced ruin. The trade union movement was demoralised, as force was used to break strikes. From 1894 until 1902 the country experienced severe droughts. Federation in 1901 saw the nation in a chastened mood. Within a few years it was to be caught up in the Great War. The conflict took a terrible toll in casualties and resources. Together with the rest of the Western world, Australia had to come to terms with a recognition that the magnitude and horror of the war had completely discredited European nationalism and the nineteenth century's assumption that humanity had embarked upon a path of ever ascending 'progress'. Recalling the 1914 night following the declaration of war, C. E. W. Bean tells us how he was overwhelmed by an awareness that much that he had taken for granted was collapsing: 'the clouds, dimly piled high in the four quarters of the dark sky above, seemed...like the pillared structure of the world's civilization of which some shock had broken the keystones... The stable world of the nineteenth century was coming down in chaos: security was gone'[86].

In his witty piece 'Mitchell on the "Sex" and Other Problems', Henry Lawson had picked up, perhaps, the beginnings of a mood of disillusionment, as he mocked some of the themes Australians seemed to spend so much time discussing. 'Socialism, or democracy, was all right in this country', Mitchell muses, 'till it got fashionable and was made a fad or a problem of' and started to breed 'a host of parasites or hangers on...they're generally the middle-class, shabby-genteel families that catch Spiritualism or Theosophy and those sort of complaints'. When he saw the 'problem spielers' beginning to hang around unionism 'he knew it was doomed'[87].

George Johnston's semi-autobiographical novel *My Brother Jack*—'a remarkable social document, a densely-textured recreation of life in Melbourne between the wars'[88]—reflects a far more serious note in its vivid portrayal of the spiritual emptiness and disillusionment which resulted from Australia's involvement in the two world wars.

The ideologies which had energised European culture in the nineteenth century had obscure mythological roots, not clearly recognised by those who took them up with an almost religious enthusiasm. Nationalism and imperialism found their justification in an appeal to the predetermined greatness of racial stock; the vision of 'progress' rested on presuppositions concerning the nature of evolution and historical development which had much in common with the mythologies of past cultures.

From where we now stand in history, it is clear that these presuppositions had little more to support them than the momentum of Europe's age-old heritage. By and large, they went hand in hand with the Deistic assumptions of the Enlightenment: human existence was situated within the framework of a world which had been divinely and wisely established. But what if these assumptions were called into question? The German philosopher Friedrich Nietzsche (1844–1900) recognised that once they were questioned, we were faced with the terrifying prospect of having to take an ultimate responsibility for all order and meaningfulness in our existence.

Nietzsche's parable of the madman who appeared with a lantern in the marketplace looking for God shows how profoundly he had grasped the shift taking place in Western culture[89]. The parable describes a dramatic confrontation between the madman and people in the marketplace. Because they no longer believe in God, they scoff at him and ask ironically where God could have gone to. 'Where has God gone?' shouts the madman, turning on them, 'I will tell you. We have slain him—you and I. We are his murderers'. And he confronts them with the stupendous thing they have done in excluding any notion of God from their understanding of their world. 'But how did we do it? How could we drink up the sea? Who gave us the sponge to wipe out the whole horizon? What did we do when we unchained this earth from its sun?... Do we not now wander through an endless nothingness? Does empty space not breathe upon us? Is it not colder now? Is night coming, and even more night? Must we not light lanterns at noon? God is dead. God stays dead. And we have slain him...' His hearers can only vaguely grasp the implications of his terrible proclamation, and they gaze at him in shocked silence. 'I came too early', the madman declares. 'It is not my time. The monstrous event is still on its way... This deed is still further from men than the remotest stars—and yet they have done it'.

The parable is made all the more poignant by the fact that its author, who clearly identified with the madman who came before his time, ended his days in an asylum for the insane. Nietzsche had diagnosed the essence of the problem emerging in Western civilisation: the God of the religious cultures of previous ages was 'dying', and this development called for a revolutionary transformation of our entire world-view. Perhaps God does not exist! If so we find ourselves in a featureless, transient cosmos, devoid of all norms. We are in the presence of an existential fear of living in meaningless chaos similar to that which the anthropologists Elkin and Stanner have recognised lies behind the world-building processes of the world cultures.

The tragic flaw in Nietzsche's position lies in the fact that as he seeks to define the existential option which must provide the basis of his *Lebensphilosophie*, he fails to consider the possibility that if *one* understanding of God—produced by the sacralised cultures which have tended to shape human awareness—could not survive in our culture, it does not follow that *other* understandings are not possible and necessary.

Situated within this broader cultural crisis, the superficiality of O'Dowd's utopian project—blithely calling for the 'creation' of gods to replace the divinity of his Christian past, and for their annihilation when their 'hour' had come—shows itself all too plainly. He knows nothing of the existential terror which cost Nietzsche his sanity.

As Judith Wright points out, the mood which preoccupied Nietzsche was not entirely unknown in nineteenth century Australia. The verses of Adam Lindsay Gordon, she writes, sometimes had the 'poison' of a 'swaggering emptiness', the kind that 'precedes insanity or suicide':

> I in vain
> Fall: I rise to fall again:
> Thou hast fallen to thy rest—
> And thy fall is best.

'The voice was the voice of Gordon', she writes, 'but the words were the words of Europe's own despair'[90].

This poison could prove lethal for those who admired Gordon and modelled themselves upon him. There is a chilling link, as Wright points out, between Nietzsche's 'God is dead', and the words of the despairing young poet Barcroft Boake who, before taking his own life, as Gordon had done, wrote to his father, 'civilisation is a dead failure'[91].

In a frequently cited article, 'Utopianism and Vitalism in Australian Literature'[92], Vincent Buckley took up the question of interpreting the directions taken by Australian literature. Those who try to force our literature into the shape of any one tradition are making a mistake, he judged, because it is too varied in its inspiration. He suggested, however, that taken as a whole Australian literature is shaped by 'two chief lines of influence': on the one hand, 'a kind of utopian humanism or insistence on the soul's radical innocence', and on the other, 'a kind of vitalism, or insistence on releasing the basic powers of life'[93]. Buckley's analysis sheds further light on the developments we are considering.

He saw the utopian inspiration as having lost its power in this century, turning away from a contemplation of the Australian project as a whole to a preoccupation with 'the lyricism of the isolated community or of the isolated, ecstatic sensibility'[94]. In Buckley's judgment, however, it is 'vitalism' which has been 'the chief formative influence in our literature' in the present century. Having roots in the Renaissance and nineteenth century romanticism, this movement he sees as having unmistakable Nietzschean affinities. 'I am tempted to say', he concludes, 'that if Australian literature has a beneficent grand uncle, it is not Karl Marx but Nietzsche... In the work of H. H. Richardson he beams grandly as the theorist of morals and art; in Brennan and Hope, he glowers as the heroic self-damning metaphysical poet going, as Swift did, half-mad at the top; and in Lindsay and all his school he is the faintly diabolical prophet of joy and physicality, a joy and physicality that are always being talked about but seldom realised in really compelling work'[95].

A closer look at creative Australians such as those Buckley has named can help us to understand more fully Australia's ongoing conversation during the present century. According to Geoffrey Serle, the work of Christopher Brennan (1870–1932) 'was the most weighty intellectual and artistic statement yet to have been made by an Australian'[96]. A study scholarship took Brennan to Germany immediately after he had graduated from the University of Sydney. From the first, therefore, he situated himself within the broader conversation of European culture. For this reason, it is not surprising that as he set out to salvage a meaning for human existence, by exploring the rich world to which he had been introduced by the French symbolist writers, his work has a close affinity with Nietzsche.

In his poem 'The Wanderer', published in *Poems 1913*, Brennan describes the journey he has undertaken. Setting out 'when window lamps had dwindled', and turning his back on a nostalgic inclination to rejoin the 'olden path, once dear' of the Catholicism of his youth, he finds himself 'alone with night'. Before him lies 'O what a horrible dawn... the homeless concave of the day' and 'the ever-restive, ever-complaining sea'. A 'wanderer for many years', he finds 'no ending of the way, no home, no goal'. Concluding a study of Brennan which expresses admiration for his poetic achievement, Judith Wright observes 'the poem, taken as a whole, represents a second loss of faith, this time in the possibility of man's attaining by his own powers, the realisation of self and the humanisation of the universe, to which Brennan had turned as a substitute for his early Catholicism'[97]. She judges that this second disillusionment was influenced in part by the barbarism of the First World War. If H. P. Heseltine is right in suggesting that the 'fundamental concern' of Australian literature in the twentieth century has been an acknowledgment of the 'terror at the basis of being', in order 'to explore its uses and to build defences against its dangers'[98], Brennan certainly stands at the centre of this concern.

Norman Lindsay (1879–1969) is also mentioned by Vincent Buckley. He and the group he inspired no doubt saw themselves as the followers of Nietzsche. Like Bernard O'Dowd, however, they failed to understand the radical nature of the German philosopher's insights. Lindsay's movement was, as Geoffrey Serle notes, 'escapist and reactionary'. If Lindsay shared Nietzsche's disillusionment with contemporary Western culture, what he proposed to replace it with was, in the words of the art critic Robert Hughes, 'to flee backwards into an illusory past whose true nature he could not and would not comprehend'[99]. Greek mythology, Lindsay suggested, was the best source from which to nourish the revitalised imagination of Australia's creative spirits.

His concern—a valid one—was to lead Australia beyond an art still too much entangled in outdated nationalism. But the model he proposed was 'the furniture of an escapist, a provincial rococo day-dream...a pantomime world of cavaliers, troubadours, Greek gods, courtiers, imps, panthers and magi; his art was a costume party'[100]. One could only applaud his determination to bring into the Australian culture a spirit of gaiety and a more positive attitude to sexuality. But his reaction to the narrow puritanism that had established itself in Australia was superficial, proposing as antidote an eroticism which Hughes describes as 'depersonalised and cow-like'.

Lindsay's magnetic personality won the support and admiration of talented poets such as Hugh McCrae and Kenneth Slessor. As it happened, the classical imagery he proposed provided an admirable foil for McCrae's lyrical talent. Slessor probably derived from Lindsay a confidence in pursuing the poetic quest which was to take him back into the mainstream of Nietzschean concern. 'It seems that in Slessor's poetry two conflicting forces meet—the Nietzschean cry that man must learn to suffice himself, must increase his capacities, must become physically and spiritually superior to himself; and the Nietzscean perception which underlay that demand, that when God is "dead" nothing can protect man from the malice of the universe'[101].

Whether or not Slessor had read Nietzsche's parable of the madman who announced the death of God, 'Stars', one of his early poems, contains a chilling echo of Nietzsche's parable and its

terror at the prospect of wandering through 'an endless nothingness': 'I was beating off the stars...I saw the bottomless black cups
of space—I could not escape those tunnels of nothingness'. Indeed,
'there are few of Slessor's later poems in which we cannot see the
gaps that lead out into the hollow universe'[102]. The theme appears
in Slessor's most celebrated poem 'Five Bells', in which he laments
the impossibility of communicating with his drowned friend. 'Yet
something forms its lips / And hits and cries against the ports of
space'. Even when they had been able to speak together it had been
in a mood of shared despair: 'We argued about blowing up the
world'.

Looking back at Slessor's poetic achievement, Judith Wright
judges that 'silence was always in the background of all he has said,
and has finally triumphed over his brilliant and feverish imagery'. It
was the silence of nihilism; his poems 'have about them something
rootless and desperate; even the increasing mastery of technique
does not quite disguise their lack of content'[103]. In Slessor's work,
she says, 'the emotional impasse of European civilisation appears as
affecting Australian writing directly...the despair and the lack of
direction beneath the poetry are authentically twentieth century,
and they stem, not from the Australian scene, but from European
civilisation and the rootlessness of the city'[104].

Slessor could speak brilliantly of the surface of life, but the nihilism of the times did not help him find the support or comfort of
a deeper meaning. It follows, as Judith Wright points out, 'that
despair, when he discovers it is part of himself and of the world, is
all the more irredeemable'[105]. As Richard Campbell writes, 'If it
cannot be shown that reality has some metaphysical and intelligible
structure which confers meaning on human life, the way is prepared for the existentialist picture of each individual as self-creator,
who through his decision projects himself out into nothingness'[106].

A. D. Hope, by way of contrast, *does* face the Nietzschean
concerns of our contemporary world by adopting an intellectual
perspective. At first his *riposte* to the world's apparent absurdity
is tense and strident. We have already heard Vincent Buckley
describing the Nietzschean spirit of Hope as 'the heroic self-
damning metaphysical poet going...half mad at the top'. Judith
Wright makes a similar comment: against the 'terrors of sexuality,
of impotence, of cruelty and of decay...and against the world's
ignorance and spite, he has armed himself with a kind of half-
hysterical cocktail party wit'[107].

This stridency is the expression of a deep conviction that a
meaning *can* be salvaged from a world in ruins, a conviction which
he expressed in the poem 'Australia', cited in an earlier chapter. At
first Hope's 'compelling and highly organised view of the world'
emerged as 'painfully dualistic...torn between a loathed reality

and a vision of eternal meaning'; his later poetry has 'been reached...through a cultivation and exacerbation of his perception of his own loneliness and despair, a meditation on moments that have seemed to offer a way out'[108]. His 'Ode on the Death of Pius XII', for example, explores one such moment—as standing among the glory of the Massachusetts Fall he hears of the pope's death and reflects upon his life, so that 'Emerging in its ecstasy of fire / The burning soul is seen'. Hope's mature poetry 'allows of the entrance of eternity into mortality, of essence into existence, of the world of legend into poetry'[109].

Writing in 1965, Judith Wright saw the image of the eternal, present in the changing temporality of human existence, in the 'standing wave' of a rushing stream, as a high point of Hope's thought:

> A standing wave through which the waters race
> Yet keeps its crystal shape and place,
> So shapes and creatures of eternity
> We form or bear. Though more than we,
> Their substance and their being we sustain
> Awhile, though they, not we, remain.
> And still, while we have part in them, we can
> Surpass the single reach of man,
> Put on strange visions and powers we know not of... [110].

The way from Nietzschean terrors to the image of the 'standing wave' has been arduous and lonely; beyond a disillusionment with the ideologies which sustained the world of the nineteenth century, Hope knows that he must find a faith such as 'the prophets' teach. In a passage from which I have already quoted, Judith Wright sums up the issue Hope has wrestled with as a problem facing Western culture as a whole: 'The intellect is only of real use in poetry when it begins from a starting point of faith—not necessarily religious faith, but simply faith in a meaning in the human world, a direction that governs the flow and eddy of event, an underlying and overriding destiny that is not confined to man's own conscious purpose and knowledge'[111].

The Nietzschean 'vitalism' to which Vincent Buckley refers is still an important component in Australian awareness. Donald Horne introduced his recent work *Ideas for a Nation* with the declaration 'A central concern of the book is that, objectively, existence is meaningless but that, as cultural animals, we provide meanings by creating "realities" and it is from these creations that we think and act'[112].

There were other responses to the disillusionment which tempered the Australian conversation as the twentieth century unfolded. Some of these were of a political nature. From the

1930s, Marxism had a considerable attraction for many young Australian intellectuals. While this may at first surprise us—and it often proved an embarrassment to them later on—it can be readily understood within the framework of cultural development we have been considering. Western culture in general was turning from romanticism to realism. If the world could not be made meaningful by the promise of a boundless 'progress', nor by the nationalism and imperialism which had shown their obscenity in the most appalling bloodbath humanity had ever seen, then a new basis must be found for the interpretation of the human project. Marxism, recently brought to the world's attention by the Russian Revolution, was ready to show the way.

Marx gained important new insights into the dynamisms at work in historical development. The realism of these insights had more substance than the ideologies of British imperialism and the nineteenth century idea of 'progress' had been able to provide. History was to show that these insights were open to reductionist and totalitarian abuse, but the fact that young Australian thinkers turned to Marx's social realism is very understandable. Marxism, they recognised, was able to bring to light the hidden agenda of economic self-interest which had been present in the ideological programs shaping the life of Western civilisation. We have already heard Bernard Smith acknowledge the influence Marx had on the development of his thought. A long list of prominent Australians would have been able to say the same. A social realism indebted to Marxism made an important contribution to Australian literature at this time, in the work of such writers as Katherine S. Prichard and Frank Hardy. In Marx's analysis of the dynamics shaping Western society, Prichard found something more substantial than the naive utopianism of Bernard O'Dowd. Hardy's *Power without Glory*, which had a considerable impact, had a similar inspiration.

If disillusionment brought an understandable reaction from the Marxist left, it was also to be expected that it should provoke a reaction from the other end of the political spectrum. There were many in Australia who still put their faith in the nationalistic and imperialistic values to which Australians as a whole had been so deeply committed. Russel Ward concluded his work *The Australian Legend* with the remark 'our profound suspicion of authority and pretentiousness provides some safeguard against the main danger of our times: dictatorship from either the right or the left...it is possibly harder to imagine a Hitler, a Stalin or even a Peron flourishing here than in any other country on earth, including England itself'[113]. Perhaps there is something in what Ward says; it is sobering, however, to find that the ideological vacuum created by Australia's disillusionment in the early part of this century gave rise to a number of fascist style movements.

Writing in 1930, W. K. Hancock reflected the mood which was behind these developments. He was himself critical of Australian democracy of the day for having settled for a 'middling standard', of being 'prepared to water good wine so that there may be enough for everybody'. 'The majority of men', in his judgment, however, 'want honest beer. A very small minority prefers rare vintages. When this minority wants them desperately enough it will get them ... If democracy is essentially mediocre it will become decrepit and be thrust aside. The warning comes from old countries'[114]. He refers of course to the way in which Fascism was filling the ideological vacuum of a Europe disillusioned by the world war and its aftermath.

Many Australians do not realise that our country saw the beginnings of such a movement. After the war, demobilised officers formed a number of shadowy organisations dedicated to the promotion of 'strong' government and opposing those whom they saw as out to ferment disorder and introduce a socialist society. In 1920 the King and Empire Alliance was founded in New South Wales. It was probably this group which provided D. H. Lawrence with a model for the secret right-wing organisation which features in his novel *Kangaroo*, written a few years later. Melbourne's White Guard was formed in the aftermath of a police strike in 1923. In 1930 the election of Jack Lang's government in New South Wales led to the formation of the All for Australia League and the New Guard.

This latter corps was dedicated to the 'suppression of any disloyal and immoral elements in Governmental, industrial and social circles', and to the prevention of socialisation, 'constitutional or unconstitutional'. It played with the idea of introducing uniforms and salutes imitating those of European Fascists, though not all went along with these ideas. The New Guard, which may have numbered as many as 50 000 members, petered out in 1935. Eric Campbell, its founder, said later that he 'became a Fascist without knowing what Fascism was'[115].

In the 1930s Robert Menzies and others found themselves impressed by the new style of leadership which had emerged in Europe: democracy must learn 'the technique of arousing the same kind of emotion' as was being seen in Europe[116]. Australia was adrift; the means were being sought of giving the country a new direction, and of safeguarding it against the evils of Marxist socialism.

Yet another outcome of ideological disillusionment in the twentieth century, it can be argued, was an accentuation of tendencies which have been present in the Australian ethos from our beginnings. In her work *A Crucible of Prophets* Veronica Brady discusses the existential concerns to be found in some of the classics of Australian literature. In the opening paragraphs of this work she quotes A. G. Stephens, writing in 1904: 'there is in the developing Australian character a sceptical and utilitarian spirit that values the present hour and refuses to sacrifice the present for any visionary future lacking a rational guarantee'. Perhaps the response of young Australians to the cause of imperialism ten years later showed that his judgment needed to be qualified; it remains true, however, that he was putting his finger on something in the Australian ethos which remains important for those who seek to understand the ongoing Australian conversation. There is something in our make-up which is not much discomforted by the spiritual vacuum of our century.

Brady goes on to comment that when she was writing in 1981, 'the public preoccupations of Australian society are with material prosperity in the present and economic expansion in the future'. She refers to the 'easy-going, unthinking hedonism' which has often been said to be typically Australian[117].

It is enlightening to note a parallel development in the culture of the United States, which I have already used as a term of comparison. Avery Dulles underlines the mythological factor at work in America's self-understanding. In the twentieth century, he notes, a new 'layer of culture' has emerged which, while it 'has not totally displaced' traditional cultural presuppositions, 'threatens to modify them profoundly'. Dulles describes something which we can recognise has a parallel in our own development:

> The whole syndrome of contemporary culture is well described by the term 'consumerism'. Each individual is seen primarily as a consumer, and heavy consumption is viewed as the key to social well-being. Wealth becomes a function of sales, which are increased to the extent that people can be induced to buy new goods. To provide such inducement business sponsors a gigantic advertising industry, which in turn supports and dominates journalism and mass communications. Advertising is funneled into programs that have the widest popular appeal. Nearly everything, from sports to education and religion, succeeds to the extent that it can arouse interest and provide entertainment. The desire for pleasure, comfort, humor and excitement is continually escalated. The traditional work ethic becomes tributary to, and is to some extent undermined by, the quest for affluence and sensory gratification. While the entertainment industries and business grow ever more fiercely competitive, alcoholism, drug abuse and obsessive sex proliferate in large sectors of the consumerist society[118].

The cultural syndrome which Dulles describes is symptomatic of the disillusionment of Western society with the ideals of the past. Its Australian form, of course, has its own peculiarities.

In his Introduction to *The State of the Art*[119], Frank Moorhouse writes: 'Australia appears to be still a robustly hedonistic society, but perhaps through art, and with heightened communication between men and women and within the sexes (about the meaning of gender), together with the cultural modification which comes subtly from travel, design, cuisine, we will add sensuality to the robust hedonism'[120]. The unrepentant hedonism of our Australian culture can only be understood when it is related to the puritanical tendencies against which it is in some measure a reaction.

John Rickard judges that these two tendencies have found an ambiguous coexistence in twentieth century Australia. Early in the present century, he writes, an accommodation had been reached 'between the hedonism of the "working man's paradise" and the morality of Protestant wowserism': showing itself in the approval, or at least acceptance, of strict laws relating to drinking and gambling, on the one hand, and a sardonic acknowledgment of such things as 'sly grog, off course S. P. betting and two-up as an authentically Australian sub-culture'[121]. Concluding his study of Australian culture and its development, Rickard comments 'The concern about a lack of spiritual core often sits uneasily with a bemused admiration for the simplicity, and even dignity, of Australian hedonism'[122].

This situation is the outcome of a long history. Russel Ward cites the astonishment of one visitor to Sydney in 1808 at seeing convicts literally gambling away the clothes they stood up in[123]. John Rickard suggests that the 'colonial passion for gambling' — something which has become part of the Australian way of life — may have its origin in the 'fatalism of the convict temperament'[124].

Judith Wright suggests that the puritanical strain in our culture may have been accentuated by the unusual conditions which prevailed in the early experience which was to shape our bush legend. The early bush ballads, as she points out, reflect a way of life which was 'often hard and cruel, almost always womanless, and because of this lack of normal balance, generally naive and sentimental under the tough hide induced by hardship and the remorseless conditions of the Australian outback'[125]. Australian attitudes to the pleasures of life, she suggests, owe a great deal to this originating experience.

To a certain extent, she wrote in 1965, the Australian male's attitude to women, 'both wary and sentimental', originated in this context; 'so does the unspoken assumption that the male-to-male relationship alone can be trustworthy and uncomplicated'[126]. Women have not fitted easily into the 'mateship' ideal upon which

Australians have prized themselves. In general, life in the outback established a pattern not calculated to promote a mature tradition of morality: 'occasional necessary outbreaks or "sprees"' constituted 'safety valves of which on the whole the perpetrators' were 'secretly ashamed'. Apart from these interludes, life was ruled by a fairly puritanical outlook which 'attached the notion of virtue to hard work, abstemiousness, monastic loneliness' in the 'strict solitudes of the bush'. Such a pattern of life gave rise to the 'peculiarly Australian dichotomy' which finds expression in 'the conflict expressed in the phrase "Sydney or the Bush"'. The City—where 'the temptations of civilisation robbed' the bush worker 'of his hard-won money and his hopes of a better life'—came to stand for Vice; the Bush—where he knew repentance and 'a reformation with which the hard bush life was associated'—came to stand for Virtue. If the Bush acted as a kind of conscience for Australians, however, 'it was a conscience that, for most, was too puritanical and demanding to be obeyed for long'[127]. As Judith Wright observes, 'No society can be as cruelly narrow and conventional as a small isolated community intent on respectability and the acquirement of wealth'[128].

The Christian churches, it is clear, played a part in this development. We are warned against an easy recourse to stereotypes in interpreting their involvement, however, by Patrick O'Farrell's judgment that Victorian standards of respectability and prudery in the late nineteenth century distorted a more balanced outlook which had prevailed among Catholics in Ireland and Australia[129]. Bruce Mansfield makes a similar point. 'We know now', he writes, 'that the temperance movement was a more complex phenomenon than a mere crusade of wowserism: David Bollen has demonstrated its politics, Anthea Hyslop its connection with the women's movement, and so on... It was widely believed that drink was the key to a number of social problems, including domestic violence'[130].

Australia's self-image in the early twentieth century, as Richard White points out, was associated with 'purity, innocence, wholesomeness, sanity, all of which were to be protected with an almost pathological obsession'[131]. The Lone Hand, a monthly from the Bulletin stable, set up in 1907, proclaimed that its policy would be 'an honest, clean, white Australia', taking 'a militant interest in the people's health'[132]. This approach would have appealed to C. E. W. Bean's imperialist outlook. Writing in 1907 in the Sydney Morning Herald, he spoke of 'the indescribable frankness' and 'cleanness' which made it possible to pick out an Anglo-Saxon face in a crowd of foreigners; he extolled the 'personal cleanliness' of the Australian type, whom he saw as 'pre-eminently a lover of the truth'[133]. Inspired by this prevailing outlook, Australian censorship provisions came to be among the most stringent in the world.

It was inevitable that the narrowness which had established itself in the Australian culture should eventually be challenged. Norman Lindsay took up a legitimate cause when he attacked the 'wowserism' which had become such a powerful force. It is only to be regretted that a crusader with more wisdom and with a greater grasp of the values upon which our Western civilisation had been established did not lead the attack. Contemporary Australia's hedonism is in some measure a reaction against an unreasonable puritanism; but it is a reaction which has left us with the unresolved ambiguities pointed out by Rickard.

It is not surprising that a utilitarian spirit should have shown itself in a young country where most were struggling to survive and talent soon became absorbed in the pursuit of the prosperity it seemed to offer. Geoffrey Serle notes that for the first century of our history, this atmosphere made the development of high culture very difficult. He cites Charles Harpur (1813–1868), one of our first native-born poets, bewailing the fact that he was condemned to the company of people 'who have faith for nothing in God's glorious universe that is not, in their own vile phrase, "money's worth"', and other visitors to the colony who remarked upon 'an enormous wealth in the hands of men utterly illiterate' and upon the 'crude provincial hedonism' of Australians[134]. In the disintegration of Mr Bonner, the patron who took possession of Voss the explorer, Patrick White holds up to ridicule this vulgar bourgeois spirit.

The selfish individualism which has drawn particular attention to itself in the prosperous Western world of recent decades was probably something to which we were already disposed. In the Preface to a special edition of *Daedalus*, Journal of the American Academy of Arts and Sciences, produced to mark our bicentenary, Stephen Graubard noted that there seemed to be 'a growing cupidity and materialism' in Australia[135]. In the same volume, Hugh Stretton expressed concern at the manner in which greed and selfishness are becoming entrenched in Australian society in a new way.

A suburban nation—history's first according to Donald Horne— we Australians certainly have a strong bourgeois component in our culture. As John Rickard observes, 'It became fashionable', in the mid-twentieth century, 'to regard suburbia as an Australian blight'. He cites D. H. Lawrence, describing 'the long street' of an Australian suburb as being 'like a child's drawing, the little square bungalows dot-dot-dot, close together yet far apart, like modern democracy'. For Norman Lindsay, the suburbs were a hateful evidence of American influence; for Vance Palmer, the 'picture theatres, gramophones, motor cars and villas' of suburbia were 'without pride of ancestry or hope of posterity'[136]. On the other hand, Donald Horne, as we have seen, came to the defence of suburban life. It is beyond question that today's consumerism has accentuated its peculiar features.

In a sense, the bourgeois spirit, with which we are so identified, symbolises the cultural revolution which has taken place in the Western world and its profound implications. The English historian Christopher Dawson describes the situation which now prevails in the West. 'Although the bourgeois now possessed the substance of power, he never really accepted responsibility as the old ruler had done... The bourgeoisie upset the throne and the altar, but they put in their place nothing but themselves. Hence their regime cannot appeal to any higher sanction than that of self-interest. It is in a continual state of disintegration and flux. It is not a permanent form of social organisation but a transitional phase between two orders'[137]. The link between bourgeois utilitarianism and the spirit of the Enlightenment already discussed is not difficult to recognise.

In the *Daedalus* volume to which I have referred, Hugh Collins, Research Fellow at the Australian National University, examines some of the implications of what Dawson has said, as far as contemporary Australia is concerned. He argues that it is an individualistic utilitarianism which gives essential shape to Australia's political life, 'that the mental universe of Australian politics is essentially Benthamite'. Collins's contribution, entitled 'Political Ideology in Australia', provides a valuable extension of what had been said already about the ideological and mythological factors at work in Australian culture.

The social philosophy of Jeremy Bentham, which Collins judges to have provided the basis of Australian political life, is essentially utilitarian, founding social order upon individual interests, as distinct from natural rights. This makes Bentham's understanding of social order essentially different from that of the American and French Revolutions, which took their stands upon an appeal to natural rights. His understanding is thoroughly secular. He has no place for the divinely established order of things presupposed by the eighteenth century enlightenment. In Collins's words, for Bentham 'political institutions are human contrivances, not divinely ordained' in any respect. Utility imposes a discipline on reality and sets its own limits. Collins cites Elie Halevy's summation of Bentham's basic position: 'Governments were instituted not because man had rights but because he had none...'[138]. The Benthamite position, in Collins's judgment, shapes public life in Australia as an ideology—in the sense in which I have defined the term—rather than as a doctrine critically upheld by philosophical reflection. In his judgment, critical assessment of Benthamite principles has been superficial to this point in our Australian conversation. As I have already pointed out, Robert Bellah and his associates have initiated a criticism of individualistic utilitarianism in the culture of the United States in their work *Habits of the Heart*.

Collins argues that the Benthamite doctrine has produced a social reality in Australia different from that of Britain for reasons which can readily be identified. The development of the Australian colonies, where in most instances a highly dispersed population was initially administered by a military autocracy, produced a state that was 'inevitably a stronger, more intrusive, legitimately interventionist instrument than Victoria's Britain'[139]. Moreover, the conditioning factors of a long established traditional culture—to which I referred in the second chapter when comparing Britain and the United States—were not present in Australia. 'Nineteenth century Australian democrats did not have to contend against the traditional restraints of established church, military service, and landed aristocracy'[140]. What, in Britain, has served as a convenient political instrumentality in the midst of a complex of potent vehicles of traditional values, becomes in Australia far more influential as a formative cultural principle.

The Benthamite ideology is seen by Collins as having been symbiotic with the ideology of British imperialism. First, Benthamite utilitarianism achieved 'domestic success' in Australia behind 'the shield of Britain's imperial protection...one of the "givens" in this settler society'; subsequently, utilitarianism provided the formula for operating within 'the larger world whose map was drawn by British imperialism'. Collins judges, however, that the essentially Benthamite character of our social self-understanding has hampered our development in various ways. It provided no satisfactory basis for a resolution of the Aboriginal question; it is inadequate as a rationale in the conducting of international diplomacy. He gives no concrete examples, but one could cite our reaction to the annexation of East Timor by Indonesia, which has left Australia as practically the only country supporting an intervention quite indefensible when considered in the order of natural rights. One recalls, also, the astounding occasion when a minister of the government described the right to privacy as a bourgeois indulgence.

Collins has strong criticism for the effects of this prevailing ideology on Australia's universities. They 'have been mostly post-Darwinian creations; the particular scientific paradigm they have enshrined has reinforced the tendencies of utilitarianism'[141]. In his judgment, this ideology has 'exhausted its capacity to cope with Australia's most serious political predicaments'[142].

As theologian Robert Gascoigne has pointed out, significant developments in contemporary Australian culture can be seen as responses to the ideological disillusionment we have been considering

and the void it has left in the Australian psyche. Christian fundamentalism is a naive attempt to fill the vacuum by once again
taking defiant possession of the substance of the Christian message.
The 'New Age' movement looks beyond the Christian tradition in
an effort to acknowledge the mystery in the depths of human and
cosmic existence[143].

Our Australian culture is still coming to terms with the profound
ideological disillusionment experienced by the western world this
century. While disenchantment with the ideological movements
which united Western culture in the nineteenth century was inevitable, it is possible to recognise that, beyond the distortions they
brought to the realities they interpreted, the ideologies of the nineteenth century also served as bearers of traditional values and
wisdom which deserve to be salvaged in more acceptable forms.

[1]   1980 Boyer Lecture, pp.7 and 10.
[2]   ibid., pp.11–12.
[3]   ibid., pp.12–13.
[4]   ibid., p.13.
[5]   ibid., p.11.
[6]   *My Place*, Fremantle, 1988, p.213.
[7]   Smith, op. cit., p.11.
[8]   ibid., p.14.
[9]   ibid., p.18.
[10]   ibid., p.14.
[11]   ibid., p.17.
[12]   ibid., p.19.
[13]   Cited, Richard Broome, *Aboriginal Australians*, Sydney (Geo. Allen and
Unwin) 1989, pp.91, 153.
[14]   Cf. Henry Reynolds, *Frontier: Aborigines, Settlers and Land*, Sydney (Allen
and Unwin) 1987; *The Law of the Land*, Penguin, 1987; Broome, op. cit., ch.6.
[15]   Smith, op. cit., p.17.
[16]   Cited by Smith, p.21.
[17]   *After the Dreaming*, broadcast in 1968.
[18]   ibid., pp.24–5.
[19]   Smith, op. cit., p.31.
[20]   ibid., p.50.
[21]   Manning Clark, *A Short History of Australia*, London, 1977, p.11.
[22]   Cited, White, *Inventing Australia*, p.14.
[23]   Cited, Rickard, *Australia*, p.43.
[24]   *Ideas for a Nation*, Sydney (Pan Books) 1989, p.72.
[25]   Cf. *Faith in History and Society*, New York (Seabury) 1980.
[26]   Cited from the prospectus of an *Exhibition of Arab Architecture*, at the Royal
Institute of British Architects, London, 1984 (ed., Anthony Hutt, University of
Durham). At the time of El-Wakil's visit, Australia was also being visited by
Grandmother Kitty (Deek Keel She Wa) of the Lakota Sioux Tribe, who was travelling to Aboriginal communities to acquaint them of her success in overcoming
alcohol dependency among her people by helping them to recover their indigenous culture and traditions (*Australian*, 11 April 1991). One is prompted to ask
whether the problem of drug and alcohol dependency in the contemporary

Western world is not associated with the vacuum created by the Enlightenment's disrupting of the continuity of our cultural traditions.
     27   They do refer to J. B. Metz's underlining, in his *Faith in History and Society*, of the importance of the 'memory of suffering', if a people is to become a conscious 'subject' of its traditional resources (*Habits of the Heart*, Robert Bellah etc. [eds], p.321, Note 17).
     28   Introducing her discussion of this novel, Veronica Brady observes that it 'marks a radical break with the Enlightenment's view of man' and notes that its 'corrosive melancholy tends to displace hope in this world', *A Crucible Of Prophets*, Sydney (Theological Explorations) 1981, p.4.
     29   Preface to *Poems* by Adam Lindsay Gordon, London, 1897, p.ix.
     30   Cf. Bernard Smith, *Australian Painting, 1788–1970*, Melbourne (Oxford U.P.) 1974, p.39.
     31   The link between Clarke's views in the Preface to the *Poems* of A. L. Gordon and the paintings of romanticist artists has been put beyond all doubt by the discovery of the fact that the celebrated passage I have quoted was originally written for an art exhibition prospectus: cf. Brian Elliott, *The Landscape of Australian Poetry*, Melbourne (Cheshire) 1967, p.24.
     32   Cf. George Orwell, 'Notes on Nationalism', in *Collected Essays*, London, 1961.
     33   *Preoccupations in Australian Poetry*, p.50.
     34   *Something of Myself*, Penguin, 1988. This edition is accompanied by an enlightening critical Introduction by Richard Holmes.
     35   Holmes's Introduction, p.19.
     36   op. cit., p.10.
     37   op. cit., p.16.
     38   Cf. *Something of Myself*, p.14, 65 etc.
     39   op. cit., p.65.
     40   Cf. Holmes's Introduction, p.15.
     41   *Something of Myself*, p.158.
     42   op. cit., p.106.
     43   Cf. Dudley McCarthy, *Gallipoli to the Somme: The Story of C. E. W. Bean*, Sydney (John Ferguson) 1983.
     44   Geoffrey Serle describes his later work as 'probably the finest war history ever', *The Creative Spirit in Australia*, Richmond, Vic. (Heinemann) 1987, p.151.
     45   McCarthy, *Gallipoli to the Somme*, p.63.
     46   Cf. McCarthy, *Gallipoli to the Somme*, pp.55, 175, 200, 214 etc.
     47   McCarthy, *Gallipoli to the Somme*, p.187.
     48   The edition to be quoted is a postwar revision, published in Sydney in 1925.
     49   *Australia*, p.35.
     50   Quoted, Hancock, *Australia*, p.56.
     51   Bean's biographer, an ardent admirer, writes of 'that naive simplicity... which he would never completely lose', McCarthy, *Gallipoli to the Somme*, p.63.
     52   Bean, op. cit., pp.103–4.
     53   ibid., p.37.
     54   ibid., p.122.
     55   ibid., p.115.
     56   ibid., p.129.
     57   ibid., p.97.
     58   ibid., p.x.
     59   ibid., pp.115–16.
     60   *Australia*, p.57.
     61   Cf. Hancock, *Australia*, p.57. Richard White quotes Joseph Chamberlain, Secretary of State for Colonies: 'I believe in this race, the greatest governing race

the world has ever seen; in this Anglo-Saxon race, so proud, so tenacious, self-confident and determined, this race which neither climate nor change can degenerate, which will infallibly be the predominant force of future history and universal civilisation'. We have smiled at Daisy Bates teaching the remote Aborigines about Empire Day. Sally Morgan quotes her mother's pride when, as an inmate of a childrens' home, she received a postcard from the place where the King and Queen lived (*My Place*, p.257). My first year of schooling was spent at a Brisbane State School in 1935; I have vivid memories, even today, of the awe with which we were made aware of British royalty, in the person of King George V.

62 One has only to consider convict statistics: 'By the time transportation to Australia's eastern colonies ended in 1853, just on 40 000 convicts (29 466 males and 9104 females) had been sent direct from Ireland. Of those convicts sent from England, estimates suggest that somewhere about 8000 were Irish-born and perhaps a similar number of Irish descent' (P. O'Farrell, *The Irish in Australia*, p. 23). A total of about 168 000 convicts were transported to Australia.

63 p.75.

64 Cf. Graeme Davison, 'Festivals of Nationhood', pp.158–77, in *Australian Cultural History*, S. L. Goldberg and F. B. Smith (eds).

65 Cf. *Ideas for a Nation*, p.73.

66 Cf. Gordon Dicker, 'The Search for Transcendence', pp.64–5, in Dorothy Harris etc. (eds), *The Shape of Belief*, Homebush West, N.S.W. (Lancer) 1982, citing Michael Roe's *The Quest for Authority in Eastern Australia, 1835–1851*, Melbourne, 1965.

67 1980 Boyer Lectures, p.22.

68 *Kangaroo*, p.274.

69 *Writing of the 1890s*, p.xviii.

70 ' "Pursuing Literature" in Australia', p.5, in L. Cantrell, *Writings in the 1890s*.

71 *A Crucible of Prophets*, p.45, Sydney (Theol. Explorations) 1981.

72 *The Creative Spirit in Australia*, p.66.

73 *A Crucible of Prophets*, p.45.

74 op. cit., p.46.

75 *Such Is Life*, p.81.

76 Wright, *Preoccupations in Australian Poetry*, pp.76–7, 78. 'We have the word of several contemporaries', she adds, 'that O'Dowd served as an inspiration to many of the young writers of the time'.

77 Cited, Serle, *The Creative Spirit in Australia*, p.69.

78 *Preoccupations in Australian Poetry*, p.73.

79 ibid., p.75.

80 'Poetry Militant', in *The Poems of Bernard O'Dowd*, Walter Murdoch (ed.), Melbourne (Lothian) 1944, p.9.

81 ibid., p.6.

82 ibid., p.8.

83 ibid., pp.20–1.

84 'Utopianism and Vitalism in Australian Literature', *Quadrant*, 3 (1959), p.43.

85 *Writing of the 1890s*, p.xix.

86 Cited, D. McCarthy, *Gallipoli to the Somme*, p.74.

87 *On the Track and Over the Sliprails*, Sydney (Angus and Robertson) 1945, pp.226–7.

88 *The Oxford Companion to Australian Literature*, W. H. Wilde etc. (eds), Melbourne, 1986, p.375.

89 *The Joyful Wisdom*, Section 125.

90 *Preoccupations in Australian Poetry*, p.65.

91 ibid., p.70.

92 *Quadrant* 3 (1959) pp.39–51.

93 ibid., p.40.
94 ibid., p.46.
95 ibid., p.51.
96 *The Creative Spirit in Australia*, p.97.
97 *Preoccupations in Australian Poetry*, p.100.
98 *Penguin New Literary History of Australia*, L. Hergenhan (ed.) 1988, p.88.
99 Cited, Serle, *The Creative Spirit in Australia*, p.92.
100 Robert Hughes, cited Serle, *The Creative Spirit in Australia*, p.92. Lindsay's disillusionment became, moreover, a reaction against contemporary European developments, many of which are acclaimed today as the masterpieces of the century. He scorned, for instance, T. S. Eliot, D. H. Lawrence, van Gogh, Picasso and Matisse.
101 Judith Wright, *Perceptions in Australian Poetry*, p.145.
102 Judith Wright, *Preoccupations in Australian Poetry*, p.147.
103 *Preoccupations in Australian Poetry*, p.135.
104 ibid., pp.156–7.
105 loc. cit.
106 'The Character of Australian Religion', *Meanjin*, 36 (1977) p.185.
107 *Preoccupations in Australian Poetry*, p.189.
108 ibid., pp.190, 193.
109 ibid., p.195.
110 ibid., pp.196–7.
111 *The Australian Legend*, p.198.
112 *Ideas for a Nation*, p.11; cf. pp.26, 42, 45, 257.
113 ibid., p.258.
114 *Australia*, p.238.
115 Cf. Rickard, *Australia*, pp.158–60.
116 Rickard, *Australia*, p.157.
117 *A Crucible of Prophets*, p.1.
118 'Catholicism and American Culture', *America*, 27 Jan 1990, p.55.
119 Penguin, 1983. This work is subtitled *The Mood of Contemporary Australia in Short Stories*.
120 ibid., p.3.
121 *Australia*, p.183.
122 *Australia*, p.269.
123 *The Australian Legend*, p.35.
124 *Australia*, p.99.
125 *Preoccupations in Australian Poetry*, p.53.
126 ibid., p.53.
127 Judith Wright, *Preoccupations in Australian Poetry*, pp.53–5.
128 *Preoccupations in Australian Poetry*, p.109.
129 Cf. *The Catholic Church and Community*, West Melbourne (Nelson) 1977, pp.375–6.
130 'Thinking about Australian Religious History', *Jour. Rel. Hist.*, 15 (1989) p.340.
131 *Inventing Australia*, p.115.
132 Cited, White, *Inventing Australia*, p.119.
133 ibid., p.117.
134 *The Creative Spirit in Australia*, pp.54–5.
135 *Australia: The Daedalus Symposium*, p.viii.
136 *Australia*, p.133. Cf. also Alan Gilbert, 'The Roots of Anti-Suburbanism in Australia', pp.33–49 in *Australian Cultural History*, S. L. Goldberg and F. B. Smith (eds), citing Hugh Stretton's 'brave words', pp.46, 44.
137 *The Dynamics of World History*, a collection of Dawson's writings edited by J. Mulloy, New York, 1957, pp.227–8.

[138] *Australia*, op. cit., pp.148–9.
[139] ibid., p.151.
[140] loc. cit.
[141] ibid., p.156.
[142] ibid., p.163.
[143] Cf. Gascoigne's article soon to be published in the *Australasian Catholic Record* under the title, 'Contemporary Culture and the Communication of the Gospel'.

5.

EVERYONE MUST HAVE A FAIR START

The mythologies and ideologies which white Australians brought with them from Europe played an essential part in the formation of our culture. It is above all, however, the experience we have shared in this strangest of continents which has given that culture a shape peculiarly our own. In the following chapters we will consider some of the experiential factors which have helped to shape Australian attitudes.

The title of this chapter is prompted by a paragraph in R. M. Crawford's *Australia*[1]. During the second half of the nineteenth century, Crawford writes, 'the accepted creed of Australian society' was summed up in the words of a Victorian conservative, 'every man should start fair in life, and have the same chance of making his way through the world'. It is significant, Crawford notes, that the words come from the conservative side of politics: indeed 'there were few in the colonies, even among those who were termed conservative...who would openly defend inherited inequalities'.

1. As others have seen us

From an early date, visitors who commented upon Australian society were struck by the egalitarian spirit which had established itself. In 1826, on the evening of the day of his arrival in Sydney, the English writer Alexander Harris visited a tavern in Market

Street. He was struck by the easy going manner of the Australians he met there—as he called it, a 'civility' which had 'no offensive obtrusiveness'—and by the way they treated each other as equals: 'every man seemed to consider himself just on a level with all the rest, and so quite content either to be sociable or not, as the circumstances of the moment indicated as most proper'[2].

The two great promoters of immigration in the mid-nineteenth century, Caroline Chisholm and John Dunmore Lang, both pointed to this egalitarianism as the basis upon which a sound social order should be built. Caroline Chisholm wrote 'We cannot be great as a nation, except every man be made to feel that his individual conduct is thrown into the national scale, unless he is made sensible that he forms one of the commonwealth'. J. D. Lang welcomed the injection of democratic spirit which came with the gold diggers to 'a land where already perhaps more than in any part of the world "a man's a man for a' that"'[3]. When he visited the Australian goldfields in 1871, Anthony Trollope was struck by the relaxed manner of the typical miner, which he found was not a 'submissive deportment, prone to the touching of hats and a silent reverence for his betters—but a manly bearing, which enables him to express himself freely'[4].

Francis W. L. Adams, a disciple of Matthew Arnold and a discerning writer, arrived in Australia for an extended visit in 1884. He was critical of what he found: a healthy, spirited people who spent their time chattering about trivialities such as dancing and the form of horses; a political life which was, in his words, 'positively so base that there is danger of it becoming the monopoly of those whose verbose incompetence is only equalled by their jovial corruption'. But he was much impressed by the self-respect and egalitarianism he found. 'The people in Australia breathes free... Workmen do not go slouching down the street as they do in England, crushed under their sense of inferiority. This is a true republic; the truest, I take it, in the world. In England, the average man feels he is an inferior; in America he feels he is a superior; in Australia he feels he is an equal. This is indeed delightful. It is the first thing that strikes a new arrival in the country, and though Australia's sins—sins against true civilization I mean—are as many as they are heinous, still a multitude of them is covered by this; namely that here is a people that is neither servile nor insolent, but only shows its respect for itself by its respect for others'[5].

Among the qualities of the frontier life which C. E. W. Bean came to admire in his travels in the outback in 1910, he singles out this same independent, egalitarian spirit. The boss of the sheep station, Bean observes, has 'unquestioned authority among men who do not readily recognize authority at all'[6]. These men 'do not pull their forelocks, or touch their hats, or even, it may be, remove their pipes' when dealing with the station boss. 'If they call him "Sir" once in each separate conversation it is enough for them', he writes. 'But they will do what he tells them, and often a good deal more, with the quiet resource few Europeans could compass'[7].

A spirit of equality is taken for granted in the outback: 'it cuts utterly against the whole grain of the people there to recognize any social distinction at all, except, perhaps, that between a good man and a useless one'. The thought 'that he is the social inferior of the man he serves and obeys' would not enter the head of a bush stockman[8]. He can be relied upon, but he is not a 'feudal retainer', and loyalty in the sense the retainers of the old world take for granted 'is not a feeling to which he generally owns'[9]. A readiness 'to stand by one's mate, and to see that he gets a fair deal whatever the cost to oneself... means more to Australia', Bean concludes, 'than can yet be reckoned'[10].

The free and easy discipline of Australian troops during the 1914–1918 war caused some consternation among the imperial authorities, and stories arising from their reluctance to salute officers are legend. One senses Bean's British loyalties were being put under a certain strain when he refers to this question in his official history. 'The fact that a man had received a good education, dressed well, spoke English faultlessly and belonged to the "officer" class', he wrote, 'would merely incline them, at first sight, to laugh at him... But they... were readily controlled by anyone really competent to teach them... At first there undoubtedly existed among them a sort of repressed resentfulness, never very serious, but yet noticeable, of the whole system of "officers"'[11].

In the early pages of his novel *Kangaroo*, D. H. Lawrence was drawn to reflect upon the egalitarian spirit he had encountered in Australia. It left him puzzled, perhaps a little disturbed. The life of Sydney seemed to run well, with little fuss: 'there seemed to be no policemen and no authority, the whole thing went by itself, loose and easy... no authority—no superior classes—hardly even a boss... everything rolling along as easily as a full river'. J. D. Pringle thinks that Lawrence is mistaken here: that Australia, despite appearances was 'a much, if rather badly, governed nation'; that the easy going approach of the Australian 'has merely allowed bureaucracy to impose on him more easily'[12].

In themselves Lawrence's reflections are interesting[13]. He puts his finger on what makes Australia different from his native England, reiterating the common theme of the comments already quoted: 'There is really no class distinction'. He recognised that differences existed, such as those 'of wealth and of "smartness"'. 'But nobody felt *better* than anybody else, or higher; only better-off. And there is all the difference in the world between feeling *better* than your fellow man, and merely feeling *better-off*'.

Somers, Lawrence's principal character, 'for the first time felt himself immersed in real democracy'. Here 'Demos was...his own master, undisputed, and therefore quite calm about it'.

Perhaps it was Lawrence's Nietzschean strain which left him uneasy: surely one 'cannot fail to admit the necessity of *rule*'. Among citizens there must be those who are responsible for where society is going. 'The only alternative is anarchy'. Perhaps, too, his sense of a 'vacancy' in the Australian culture, already referred to, added to his uneasiness. He reflected that with the undoubted 'good temper' and 'genuine tolerant nature' of Australians, this democratic system may be able to 'just go by itself' and that 'for quite a long time'. But that would seem to leave it like 'a machine which is running on but gradually running down'. Lawrence's hesitations invite us to recognise the ambiguities which have been present in Australia's egalitarianism.

2. The legend of mateship

It is easy enough to recognise what must have been the origins of the ethos which has been identified and described in such remarkably similar terms. A colonial society in which for many decades the bulk of the population were emancipated convicts or their descendants could not be expected to uphold the things that the authorities of the colony stood for, especially inherited status and privilege.

Robert Hughes's work *The Fatal Shore*[14] provides a vivid picture of the oppression and brutality which prevailed in Australia's penal colonies. Forty per cent of Australian convicts, we are told, were subjected at some time to flogging—an ordeal so terrible that it is impossible to expect that it did not leave a permanent resentment against the authoritarian system which it symbolised.

Constant reference has been made here to the refusal of Australians to touch their hats to their superiors. In his novel *Geoffrey Hamlyn*, an adventure story for English readers published in 1859, Charles Kingsley refers to the origins of this reluctance. 'The touching of the hat is a very rare piece of courtesy from working men in Australia', he comments. 'The convicts were forced to do it, and so the free men made it a point of honour not to do so'[15].

Another writer, Price Warung (William Astley), who came to Australia in 1859 and became well informed on the convict system by interrogating old-timers who had experienced it, tells, in his story 'The Liberation of the First Three', of a terrible oath of solidarity taken by convicts and sealed with blood. Independent evidence, Russel Ward suggests, indicates that the author is basing his narrative upon fact[16]. Judith Wright considers that this oath and the solidarity it established was 'for Australia the germ of something new that we now feel to be in some sense our own'[17].

The temper of the convict community is clearly enough expressed in a startling incident which occurred in the early days of Hobart when the Lieutenant-Governor and the chaplain assembled the female convicts to address them. The women convicts 'all with one impulse turned round, raised their clothes, and smacked their posteriors with loud report'[18]. While still serving their time, Australian convicts, most of whom were assigned to work for free settlers or emancipists, objected to being called 'convicts'; the euphemism 'government men' became current. From fellowship found in the common ordeal of life in the penal colony a convict subculture originated which was fundamental to later Australian development[19].

Having obtained their freedom, the emancipists resented any claim to a higher station of life on the part of other Australians. As Russel Ward writes, the fact that initially 'practically all the "lower class" Australians were also convicted criminals strongly underlined the dividing line between them and their masters and intensified mutual hostility'[20]. It is not surprising that the 'currency lads and lasses', the vast majority of whom had convict parents, showed a similar resentment to those who considered themselves their superiors, being described as 'more intolerant and intolerable than the bowery boys of America', and 'systematically insolent' to English visitors[21].

Rivalry between Hume and Hovell for the principal honours deriving from the first expedition from Sydney to Port Phillip, and the 'unseemly bickering' to which it gave rise, were symptomatic of the uneasy relationship which existed between native-born Australians and Englishmen coming to the colony. Hume was a 'currency lad'; Hovell was an Englishmen and a gentleman. Manning Clark comments that this dispute marked the beginning of 'the long and anguished struggle of the native-born for recognition', a struggle often carried on 'with the truculence of men with a chip on their shoulder'[22]. No doubt the Irish tradition's rejection of 'undue solemnity, pomposity, repression' and 'sourpussery' made an important contribution to this emerging ethos[23].

Statistics, Russel Ward argues, leave little doubt that the outlook which had developed among convicts and emancipists prevailed in New South Wales before the discovery of gold. In 1828 this group outnumbered free settlers by seven to one; in 1851 they were still three to two[24]. Those who came in search of gold in the years which followed were socialised, by and large, into the existing ethos. Rather than obliterate the convict legacy, John Rickard observes, these 'new migrants had, in social terms, to negotiate with the old. The values of convict society may have been diluted, but elements were necessarily incorporated in the new culture'[25]. If the native-born Australians greeted the new-comers with their customary air of superiority, the immigrants upheld the existing culture by paying it, in Russel Ward's terms, 'the supreme compliment of imitation'[26].

The harsh attitude initially adopted by the colonial authorities over the question of mining licences only strengthened this new-found solidarity. Once again the contribution of the Irish tradition is worth noting. The number of Irish on the goldfields was remarked upon. Of the diggers of the Eureka stockade, a witness to the Gold Fields Commission declared 'Quite half of them were Irishmen'[27].

Observing the gold diggers of Victoria, one visitor spoke of the 'marked contrast' between their attitudes and those prevailing in England and in Europe generally. 'As a rule, every man there is, may be, or expects to be, his own master...this causes a spirit of independence... Here are no conventionalities; no touching of hats. Men meet on apparently equal terms; and he who enjoyed the standing of a gentleman in England becomes aware, on the diggings, that his wonted position in society is no longer recognized; and the man, who in former days might have...served you respectfully...shakes hands with you, and very likely hails you by a nickname, or by no name at all'[28].

In the last decades of the nineteenth century, as the country settled down after the gold rushes, this Australian ethos 'emerged stronger than ever', in the judgment of Russel Ward, 'when it tended to coalesce with, and colour deeply, middle class political and literary nationalism'[29]. The quotation from a Victorian conservative which suggested the title of this chapter comes from the circles Ward is referring to.

Ward's much discussed thesis is that the ethos of egalitarianism we have considered was now becoming the basis of a legend of central importance in the self-awareness of Australians. This legend sees the bushman, the itinerant worker of the outback, and the tradition he lived by as the embodiment of qualities which are most typical of Australians as they would like to think of themselves. According to Ward, the Australian of the legend is

> a practical man, rough and ready in his manners and quick to decry any appearance of affectation in others. He is a great improviser, ever willing 'to have a go' at anything, but willing too to be content with a task done in a way that is 'near enough'. Though capable of great exertion in an emergency, he normally feels no impulse to work hard without good cause. He swears hard and consistently, gambles heavily and often, and drinks deeply

on occasion. Though he is 'the world's best confidence man', he is usually taciturn rather than talkative, one who endures stoically rather than one who acts busily. He is a 'hard case', sceptical about the value of religion and of intellectual and cultural pursuits generally. He believes that Jack is not only as good as his master but, at least in principle, probably a good deal better, and so he is a great 'knocker' of eminent people unless, as in the case of his sporting heroes, they are distinguished by physical prowess. He is a fiercely independent person who hates officiousness and authority, especially when these qualities are embodied in military officers and policemen. Yet he is very hospitable and, above all, will stick to his mates through thick and thin, even if he thinks they may be in the wrong[30].

Ward's *The Australian Legend* has provoked much discussion. He left himself open to challenge because he did not make clear his theoretical presuppositions. While sound enough as far as it goes, his discussion of what he means by 'legend'—he seems to make no distinction between 'legend', 'mystique' and 'myth'—is brief and undeveloped. One of his main contributions is the wealth of historical material he has gathered concerning the developing Australian ethos. Other authors have given a more adequate analysis, however, of what was involved in the formation of this legend of the typical Australian at the turn of the century.

As we have seen, some years before Ward's book appeared the historian R. M. Crawford gave an account of the formation of the Australian legend which clarifies some of the questions Ward left unresolved[31]. More recently Bill Gammage—profiting from the discussion which was aroused by Ward's book, which he describes as 'one of the most important books ever written about Australia'— has given an enlightening analysis of the principles at work in the formation of a legend such as this[32]. His analysis has much in common with the analysis of ideological development made in an earlier chapter.

National traditions, Gammage points out, are 'new and illuminating ways' of looking at the *past*, which are dictated by the needs of society in the *present*. These traditions, rather than being a simple recreation of the past are the creation of society in which writers play an important part. The present needs of the social group lead to a selective presentation of facts of the past which serves the prevailing national consensus[33]. As a consequence, he notes, these traditions may lose their effectiveness as the present reality of the society and its needs for consensus change.

By the mid-nineteenth century, Australia had become one of the most urbanised societies in the world. Before the end of the century, Melbourne and Sydney ranked thirteenth among the world's cities in terms of population. As the century drew to a close, the bohemian and nationalistic circles living in the cities identified the 'real' Australia of their utopian aspirations with the outback. They were attracted, in Richard White's words, 'to the cluster of symbols and principles which they associated with Australia: sunlight, wattle, the bush, the future, freedom, mateship and egalitarianism'[34]. How is this move towards the creation of what was to prove a very powerful national legend to be explained?

R. M. Crawford, in the article to which we have referred, gives a very straightforward and persuasive explanation: 'the radical bush tradition with its edge of social revolt' came 'to be accepted as representative of Australian national character and aspirations', so that the 'bush legend had become the Australian legend'. A legend, as Gammage has noted, meets the needs of the present. The need which Crawford points to in Australia of the late nineteenth century was that discussed in an earlier chapter, the need for the Australian provincial conversation to find itself within the broader conversation of British culture. The 'ruling assumptions' of the metropolitan culture, still firmly in control in Australia, were, Crawford points out, 'not Australian, but English', and it was taken for granted that colonial life was 'too crude to serve for artistic inspiration'. Reacting against this establishment, Australian writers and thinkers sought to 'break the tyranny of old-world motifs' by turning to 'distinctively Australian sources of inspiration'. They found these in the bush, he concludes: 'Here was to be found the Australia that was most distinctive, most unlike the old world'.

As Crawford points out, Australian townspeople, by and large, for all their high level of urbanisation can hardly be considered 'town-lovers'. On the other hand, they have kept 'a romantic if unsentimental feeling for the bush'. This may well be linked with something Ward has touched upon: the potency of the frontier symbol in new world cultures, the assumption that the real action was taking place in the outback—after all, the cities were only servicing and transport centres for an essentially agricultural economy. Perhaps D. H. Lawrence was intuiting this when he described the bungalows of Sydney as 'still hinting at the temporary shacks run up in the wilderness'; he was offended by the 'ragged bush loused over with thousands of small promiscuous bungalows'.

We may well add—recalling with Gammage that legends are based upon facts, even if these facts are used selectively—that the bush attitudes of mateship, solidarity and egalitarianism were, at an earlier date, the outcome of an essentially similar reaction to the structures and expectations of the British establishment.

Manning Clark adopts a similar point of view, pointing to another essential element of Gammage's analysis of the process of legend formation. He writes 'The question was, if the Australians were not British, what were they? Perhaps the most memorable attempts to answer this question were in the short stories of Henry Lawson'[35].

It is through its articulation in literature that a legend is fed into the conversation of a historical community. It was the Bulletin, of course, which provided the forum of a literary articulation in which city dwellers like Henry Lawson and Banjo Paterson were in regular communication with the journal's immense readership and their expectations. As Patrick Morgan writes, the Bulletin 'achieved its balance and its greatness by being generously eclectic: it included all groups—city, country towns and the bush, the wealthier and poorer classes—and many modes of expression', developing 'a unique rapport with the clientele, who were encouraged to be contributors as well as readers'[36].

By portraying the factual reality which lay behind the legend, Henry Lawson and Joseph Furphy made an important contribution to the emerging Australian awareness. Lawson, as Manning Clark writes, had a 'vision of mateship' which touched his own existence very deeply. He wrote 'with simplicity and fire on mateship and the dignity of man'; he wrote 'with compassion' about the lives of simple men and women who battled on in the bush 'against the soil, the weather, the market, and the evils of the capitalist system'; he captured in words typical characters of the bush such as 'his Mitchell, the cheeky irreverent, roguish man, a cheat and a liar in his dealing with his opponents but the soul of honour and the repository of all the virtues in his dealing with his mates'[37]. 'Mateship' was essential to the Australia of Lawson's dreams:

They tramp in mateship side by side—
The Protestant and Roman—
They call no biped lord or sir,
And touch their hat to no-man!

As Australia's most popular writer of verse, A. B. (Banjo) Paterson (1864–1941) had an immense influence on the articulation of the bush legend. For Paterson, the bush and the bushman stood for the real Australia. As Geoffrey Serle writes, 'he translated the experience of a huge "uncultured" audience into art'; his strength was his 'easy *rapport* with the bush audience of all classes'. Like Lawson, he reacted against what he saw happening in the pastoral industry, 'the takeovers by banks, companies, urban capital', a concern immortalised in his 'Waltzing Matilda' ballad. But his remedy was a romantic one, a 'nostalgic harking back to the pure old days'[38]. In the small world of Paterson's Australia, he was on good terms with Charles Bean. He had been a boy at Sydney Grammar when Bean's father was teaching there. As the editor of the *Evening News*, he helped Bean when he was beginning his career as a journalist[39].

Paterson identified with Rudyard Kipling's imperial frontier ideal. In the judgment of Judith Wright, however, he really began to exploit the bush ideal. Establishing a 'cult of the independent sun-tanned bushman, of mateship and self-reliance, of egalitarianism and the outback and the "droving days" ', Paterson made the legend 'become less real and more formalized'[40]. As we have become aware, there is an inherent temptation for any national ideology to become self-serving, in Judith Wright's words 'pandering to the natural desire for some simplification, something recognizable and familiar, a predictable hero typifying a predictable country'. She describes the effect of the development of such a legend as 'paralysing': 'we have our stereotype of Australia... this is what we want to believe of ourselves; and while this is so, and while we dismiss all other notions as somehow a betrayal of the "Australian legend", it will be of no use examining further into the various and treacherous reality'[41]. Judith Wright would, no doubt, express herself somewhat differently today; the Australian conversation has changed considerably in the twenty-five years since she wrote *Preoccupations in Australian Poetry*.

Initially, C. E. W. Bean, like his friend Paterson, identified with the ideology of the imperial frontier and took up the Australian legend with enthusiasm. The way in which he fell under the spell of the outback, discussed in an earlier chapter, brings home to us the fact that even if Bean was selective in his view of what he found the legend was not lacking a factual foundation. His *On the Wool Track*, written a few years before the 1914–1918 war, is legend-making stuff.

But it was in his *Official History of Australia in the War of 1914–1918* that he made his remarkable contribution to the elaboration and carrying forward of the Australian legend. What Bean did was to draw upon the bush legend to provide Australians, shocked and bewildered by the horror of the war, with an interpretation that helped them to come to terms with Australia's entry to the international scene on the field of battle. Donald Horne, echoing Bill Gammage, describes the Australian self-awareness Bean sets out to interpret:

after Anzac, in the concept of 'the Digger', the soldiers made their own creation of who they were and why they mattered. Self-perceived gatekeepers of the public culture had wanted only brave boys, preferably from the bush, who could enoble the world through their shedding of blood: but the Diggers added to the concept of bushman-hero the Irish concept of larrikin and the fraternal concepts of mateship. That made the Diggers feel more democratic, and more Australian[42].

There exists today a tendency to debunk the Anzac legend. It is important to weigh up the factual basis upon which it rested in order that we may judge what abiding significance it should have in our national story. This issue could easily be confused by the fact that Bean's biographer acknowledges in our key witness 'a capacity for hero-worship which he never lost'[43]. Many factors, McCarthy points out, contributed to this. Bean's family history had engendered memories of Waterloo and the Indian Mutiny; his home environment and schooling fostered 'the British virtues of courage and hardihood and decency'. 'It was little wonder, then', writes McCarthy, 'that because of his being a constant witness to the heroic achievements and endurance of his countrymen at Gallipoli, a great part of his capacity for hero-worship should come to be directed at the A.I.F. This was not to say that he was uncritical and could not be objective...but these men became to him objects of such love and admiration that they would remain so until the end of his long life. To write of their doings was his job; but it rapidly became more than that—the driving purpose of his whole being'[44].

McCarthy continues, 'It seems as though he was never able to elude the whole revelation of those Gallipoli days...for a revelation to him indeed they were. All the heroism and devotion he had dreamed about was first given daily visible form to him there, the ideals of duty, courage and sacrifice that he had grown up to cherish'. He would immortalise the story so that future generations 'could see for themselves and feel with wonder just why, and how, it came about that those men "once rang out like a bell"'[45]. The remarkable qualities shown by the Australian troops at Gallipoli are beyond question. Bill Gammage has argued that the legend of the Anzacs was denatured by those who contaminated it with the old imperialist ideology before the facts were able to speak for themselves[46].

Bean's testimony is all the more significant in that he was undergoing a profound disillusionment with the British as he came to know them during the months of the campaign. McCarthy gives many instances of his indignation with British officials during the campaign. Of the British troops he commented 'Poor little chaps—they struck me as wretched specimens of men—dirty, skinny, rather spiritless'[47]. As a prisoner of war in the Second

World War, Sgt Stan Arneil made a similar comparison between the spirit which prevailed among Australian troops and the demoralisation of British troops undergoing the same ideal[48].

As Robin Gerster writes, Bean told the story of the war as an 'Australian *Iliad*'. He did not betray his duty as a historian to disclose the past accurately. But in doing so he made use of the bush legend as an interpretative device, 'with the missionary fervour of an epic poet'. He made use of Homer's technique 'of concentrating on small-scale (often man-to-man) infantry skirmishes'; his portrayal drew on the attributes of the bushman he had come to admire before the war 'to evoke a warrior whose virtues and foibles (virtues mostly) are further illustrated in an enormous catalogue of anecdotes contributed by the soldiers themselves'[49].

Another lesser variant of the Australian legend—that of 'the Australian larrikin' which had been articulated for an appreciative readership by C. J. Dennis, in his portrayal of Ginger Mick, *The Sentimental Bloke*—found expression in *The Anzac Book* of 1916. In this volume Bean put together contributions written by the troops themselves. There the 'digger is portrayed as an ideal type on the one hand and, with self-mocking humour, as an unkempt larrikin on the other'[50]. In the *Official History*, however, it is the idealised type, the transmogrified bushman, which carries forward the legend[51].

Donald Horne points to the influence of sport in the development of Australia's egalitarian ethos: participation, it was proudly pointed out, was open to all classes, in contrast to the situation prevailing in England; and Australia led the way in 'the standardisation of spectator sport as a principal form of leisure'[52]. The 'invention' of Ned Kelly as a 'mythical outlaw' by Australians, Horne suggests, is an example of an often-found mechanism of commoners' solidarity[53].

H. M. Green's *Outline of Australian Literature*, published in 1930, continued the articulation of the Australian legend. Once again the small world of Australia's creative writing is apparent in the fact that Green was a friend of Charles Bean, having commenced work at the *Sydney Morning Herald* on the same day as Bean. Bean discussed with Green the approach he should adopt in his *On the Wool Track* series[54]. Peter Pierce judges that Green's identification of Australian characteristics—'an independence of spirit, a kind of humorous disillusion, a careless willingness to take risks, a slightly sardonic good nature and a certain underlying hardness of texture'—made the stuff of the legend an important part of literary discussion as the twentieth century progressed[55].

The writing of Les Murray grounds itself on the premise that the bush is still an important and viable element of Australia's self-awareness. He is not concerned to revive the 'paralysing' legend of

Paterson and Bean, but to share a vision of the bush according to a 'Boethian' model, which promotes 'transaction between town and country' which 'do not relegate one to the other'—as does the 'Athenian' model of civilization 'which is hierarchical and centred on the city'[56].

3. The reality behind the legend

Our discussion of the formation of the Australian legend at the turn of the century has already begun to make us aware of its dangers and shortcomings. Its selectivity in its portrayal of the past can leave important issues—in 'the struggle to be human, and to remain human'—not confronted. John Hirst points to the paradox of nineteenth century Australian society: it accepted the egalitarian principle as axiomatic; at the same time, however, it included many who were desperate to climb the social ladder and achieve 'gentleman' status with the recognition it brought[57].

Judith Wright, who in 1965 drew attention to the 'paralysing' form the legend can take, also warned that 'in our present reaction against the "Australian legend", we may forget the truth that lies behind it and thereby lose the strength it gave us'[58]. Those who have observed our life together have been struck by something remarkable in the Australian ethos. It may have had ambiguities in its convict origins. Its spirit of egalitarianism may have owed a lot to the need to stick together in the struggle for survival. It may have been inconsistent and cruel in that it did not admit all to its 'mateship'. It contains, however, the germ of something which could become a great strength and a remarkable resource.

If Bean seems to see only the noble side of the nomad tribe of bush workers, they certainly had their limitations. Behind the icon of the legend was a reality of mateship which was in many ways flawed. In the opening pages of Furphy's *Such Is Life*, a group of bushmen who have been thrown together for the evening have no hesitation in pulling one of their number to pieces as soon as he is out of earshot. Veronica Brady describes the characteristics of mateship, as it is painstakingly portrayed by Furphy, in the following terms: 'mutually suspicious'; sharing their goods, yes, but as 'a kind of insurance against the time they themselves will be in need'; yarning around the campfire, 'not as a means of self-revelation but of defending oneself against the claims of personal intimacy'. Mateship was indeed 'a temporal expedient, the means used by lonely, vulnerable people to grapple together for some protection against the twin enemies of their own thoughts and the world outside them'[59].

One of the first and most obvious criticisms which we should make is that the legend, and the ethos it celebrated, had no place for women. Women were not 'mates'. One of the most mordant pieces of Australian literature is Barbara Baynton's short story 'Squeaker's Mate'[60]. The title refers to Squeaker's woman, but the use of the term is ironical in the extreme. Squeaker—a study in spineless selfishness—confronted with the problem of coping with his woman when she has had her back broken chopping down a tree for him, tells her 'double up yer ole back and bite yerself'. Though Squeaker is hardly typical of the outback, the extremity of Baynton's story, told with a breathtaking irony, may be seen as expressing something of the resentment women felt at the strange place left for them by the mateship ethos. However, Baynton's sarcastic portrayal of the women neighbours who found a ready excuse for not making a second visit to Squeaker's injured 'mate' seems to indicate that this was not her main concern.

The disproportion of males to females in the Australian population was extreme in the early nineteenth century. In 1831 there were three males to each female. The situation improved gradually, and by the end of the century there were eleven males to ten females. Of course, this disparity was much greater in the bush, where many survived as nomad workers. Such a situation, as Geoffrey Blainey notes, 'must have flavoured society in countless ways'[61]. He points to some obvious ones: 'the material standard of living was unusually high' since most workers had no dependents to support; the high incidence of drunkenness until late in the nineteenth century would have been linked with this situation. Blainey thinks that a comparison with the United States leads to the conclusion that the male predominance contributed to our becoming 'one of the most sports-crazy nations in the world'. He thinks that this passion for sport led to 'a higher priority being given to shorter working hours and longer leisure rather than to higher wages' in the fight for better working conditions.

The situation which fostered mateship among a predominantly male population had effects of a more subtle kind. We have already mentioned the link between the bush ethos and the puritan strain in Australian culture suggested by Judith Wright. The enforced quasi-monastic pattern of life in the bush came to represent virtue, whereas the city with its pleasures and temptations stood for vice. The widespread lack of normal male–female and family relationships constituted a serious deprivation for the developing Australian culture. As Manning Clark writes, a 'hugh excess of men over women in the bush ... probably explains why in Australia there was an extreme form of male dominance'. It also accounts, he argues, for 'the brutalization of the relationship between men and women'. He notes the remarkable fact of 'the complete absence of any reference to romantic love in the folk literature' of early Australia[62].

Deprived of the possibility of wholesome intimacy with the opposite sex, Australian males reacted in two apparently opposed ways. In practical terms, they were insensitive to the situation and needs of women. Veronica Brady points to this insensitivity in Furphy's picture of outback mateship in the late nineteenth century. On the one hand, he is able to look very critically at the ambiguities of the mateship ethos as it existed among males. We have already contrasted his approach with the mateship legend proposed by Bean and Paterson. He is a realist and portrays, in Brady's words, 'a world in which self-interest not only prevails but has to be taken for granted, so that suspicion rather than love is the norm'[63].

But when he comes to portray the relationship of Tom Collins, his storyteller in *Such Is Life*, with a woman, her attempts to establish a romantic relationship with Tom give rise to a recurring theme of male humour at her expense. To quote Brady, this 'shows remarkable insensitivity to her situation and indeed to the plight of women in general in the society in which they must depend on a man not only for social position but even for the sheer necessities of existence'[64]. Furphy's talent as a novelist does lead him to open slightly the door which leads to the world of Baynton's 'Squeaker's Mate': telling of how he deserted his wife Molly when she was disfigured by an accident, Warrigal Alf adds 'there are queer things done when every man is a law to himself'[65].

But alongside this insensitivity, and in a way that is related to the puritanism we have mentioned, the Australian male put women in a zone of idealism and unreality which excluded them in a more subtle way from the world of mateship. Manning Clark expresses it well: 'A male dominated society elevated woman into the Madonna of the Australian bush—the pure one whose ears must not be defiled by coarse language, and whose body must not be debauched by men'; she 'belonged in the home', she 'had the children, and the comforts of religion: men had that wonderful moment when their eyes met over the tops of two glasses of beer'[66]. The tendency of mixed gatherings of Australians to disintegrate very soon into two groups, the men at one end of the room, the women at the other, has often been remarked upon. In her hard-hitting *Damned Whores and God's Police*[67], Anne Summers took up discussion of the prejudices and stereotypes which have captured Australian awareness as far as women are concerned.

It is not surprising that D. H. Lawrence, fascinated as he was with the whole question of human relationships, should have observed the peculiarities of the Australian situation. Somers, the character in *Kangaroo* who is Lawrence's mouthpiece, observes of Victoria, his Australian next-door neighbour, 'sometimes she seemed a little afraid of' Jack her husband, 'physically afraid—

though he was always perfectly good-humoured with her'. Jack's emotional make-up puzzles Somers. He seems to have a strange 'animal' quality: 'a certain slow, dark, lingering look of the eyes, which reminded one of some animal or other, some patient, enduring animal with an indomitable but naturally passive courage'[68]. The 'only consecutive thing' to be observed in his make-up was his 'facetious attitude ... of taking things as they came', a 'sort of ironical stoicism'; he certainly 'had a sort of passion', but it was 'not what Somers called human'[69]. He was hearty, greeting everyone with the 'same breezy intimacy', yet 'the moment they had passed by, they didn't exist for him ... His friends, even his loves, were just a series of disconnected, isolated moments in his life'[70].

If women did not have any place in the mateship fellowship, neither did those who did not share in the patterns of kinship Australians had brought from the British Isles. As Judith Wright observed in 1965, in her criticism of the 'paralysing' legend of mateship, 'at the back of most of our observations of the foreigner, the misfit, the coloured man or the person who refuses to submit to our categories, there is a more-or-less hidden sneer. That sneer was built-in in the early days of the century'. It was not unrelated to the form of the legend promoted by Paterson and Bean, which had been 'slyly built into our character' as Australians[71].

The sneer was sometimes very obvious. As Russel Ward comments, most Australians would probably agree that the most discreditable component of the mateship legend was its racism. 'The sentiments of mateship', Manning Clark concludes, 'tended to be reserved for the native-born, and the ideals that were the offspring of their loneliness and isolation became in turn forces to strengthen ... provincialism and ... xenophobia'[72]. One of the most disgraceful episodes in Australian history was the astonishing violence which broke out in Victoria and New South Wales against Chinese prospectors. Clark describes an incident at Lambing Flat, near Young in New South Wales, in which more than a thousand white diggers ran amok with bludgeons and whips in a rampage which lasted a whole day. All those who were later charged and tried in Goulburn were shamefully acquitted[73]. The same pattern showed itself, later in the century, on the Queensland canefields where 'cruel fancies about the behaviour of other human beings poisoned ... minds as they fumbled and groped towards ways and means of defending their way of life and their civilization'[74].

It goes without saying that the mateship and egalitarianism of the white Australian way of life had no relevance to the Aboriginal people. They could never be thought of as mates. Ward can only point to 'hints' that the men of the bush felt 'some indebtedness to the Aborigines'. Many a lost white person owed his or her life to the skills and caring of the blacks. Ward has to admit, however, to 'overwhelming evidence that the usual overt attitude to the Aborigines continued to be almost as brutal and contemptuous at the end of the nineteenth century as it had been earlier'[75].

Furphy reflects this attitude accurately enough. Chinese boundary riders are objects of scorn and of a mean vindictiveness which he seems to take for granted. The blacks are a shadowy presence in the background, only referred to as objects of fun or as a term of comparison in obloquy. When Rory O'Halloran's child is lost in the bush, Thompson, the bushman recounting the incident to Tom Collins, asks derisively 'Did anybody know where to find a blackfellow, now that he was wanted?'[76]. This is a question which deserves a fuller discussion later in this chapter.

Commenting on the way the 'idea of mateship flavoured Australian Democracy', Geoffrey Blainey writes 'Ambition and desire to raise oneself beyond one's station were considered to be vices by a majority or an influential minority of Australian men'[77]. The editor of *Australia: The Daedalus Symposium*, Stephen Graubard, indicates that this attitude is still perceived as a dominant characteristic of Australians. He speaks of constraints within the Australian culture 'that derive in part from the values of people who . . . are constantly charged with not encouraging the growth of the "high timber" in their midst that so impresses others'[78].

Back in 1930 W. K. Hancock made a searching comment on this Australian attitude. 'Intolerance of oppression and sympathy with the underdog', he writes, situating himself within the mainstream of the Australian legend, 'are among the most attractive features of the Australian character'. These virtues, however, have their darker side. 'The passion for equal justice can easily sour into a grudge against those who enjoy extraordinary gifts, and the aspiration for fraternity can so easily express itself by pulling down those lonely persons who are unable to fraternise with the crowd'. The ideal of mateship can be more concerned, he says, 'to put down the mighty from their seat', than with 'eagerness to exalt the humble and meek'. This spirit made him hesitate as he considered Australia's future. 'If ever the ship of Australian democracy enters the calm waters of its millennium it will carry a fraternal but rather drab company of one-class passengers'. He went on to cite one of Henry Lawson's early ballads which predicted that 'the curse of class distinctions from our shoulders shall be hurled', when there is 'higher education for the toilin' starvin' clown' and 'the rich an' educated shall be educated down'[79].

Hancock returns to this theme later in his text. Australian democracy is different from its American counterpart, the equality it promotes is of a different kind. It is 'not content merely to attack privilege nor to remove the handicaps which birth imposes'; it tends to 'ignore capacities in its preoccupation with needs'.

Equality of opportunity will of necessity create 'new inequalities', but Australian democracy resists this, preferring 'equality of enjoyment'. It seeks 'a fair race', but resists 'a fast race': in fact, 'it dislikes altogether the idea of a race, for in a race victory is to the strong'. In its solicitude for the weak, Australian democracy's instinct 'is to make merit take a place in the queue'[80]. He feared that these attitudes condemned Australia to a 'middling standard' even more bleak than what Tocqueville feared for America[81]. Echoing Hancock, Donald Horne suggests the principle that everyone deserves a fair start seems to have degenerated into an assumption that 'everyone has right to a good time'[82].

It is not difficult to see evidence of an enduring problem for the Australian culture: in Lawrence's 'vacancy', Hancock's 'drab company of one-class passengers', Patrick White's 'Great Australian Emptiness' and Manning Clark's 'Kingdom of Nothingness'. The changes which have taken place in Australia since Hancock wrote have brought greater inequalities than existed in his day, but has this happened because we have looked critically at the legend's distortions and corrected them? In fact, at another level we are probably still 'paralysed' by the legend in a passive acceptance of much of what Hancock and Lawrence were criticising.

Like all legends, the bush legend which won widespread acceptance early this century was partisan in its tone. It favoured a particular group at the expense of others. We may well ask ourselves why our national story did not give rise to a 'pioneer' legend. The reason why no legend developed around the heroic struggles of the pioneers who opened up the outback, however, is easy enough to recognise: the egalitarian temper and resentment of privilege which was deeply ingrained in the legend taken up so enthusiastically at the turn of the century was antagonistic to any celebration of the achievements of the squatters. The later struggles of the selectors on their small holdings were so often marked with desperation and failure that they were unlikely to become the stuff of legend.

There is something tragic about the relationship between the three groups of white Australians engaged in developing Australia's agricultural industry in the outback. It should be pondered as we reflect critically upon the legend which has influenced our self-awareness for most of the present century. The squatters, the nomad workers and the selectors were really fellows in what was—for all the undercurrent of sardonic humour so often present in their dealings with one another—a tragedy of gigantic proportions.

The nature of the continent was unable to make the only kind of agricultural methods they knew enormously successful. The extremes of climate, veering from drought which may last for years to floods of a magnitude unknown in Europe, meant that the squatters were constantly struggling to keep ahead of their creditors, more often than not without success. Those who had not been able to take part in the scramble for land holdings were calling for the release of smaller parcels of land. The legislation which attempted to achieve this placed the small farmers on holdings where their position was even more precarious than that of the large holders. They were resented by the squatters, whose land they had encroached upon; they often resorted to stealing their big neighbours' stock in order to survive. The itinerant workers' demands for better working conditions and for forage for their animals were a further pressure on the embattled squatters who, though they may have seemed wealthy, were really living on the advances of their creditors. As Geoffrey Blainey observes 'One reason why' Australia's 'city streets were dominated by ornate banking chambers and why upcountry villages in Australia had three competing banks when similar-sized villages in England or the U.S.A. had none was the need of rural industries to borrow heavily to buy or retain their land'[83].

Furphy's *Such Is Life* gives a good cross-section of the interaction among these three groups from the point of view of the itinerant worker. The bullock drivers and drovers were engaged in a battle of wits with the squatters, upon whose depleted fodder they often depended. The selectors, whose poverty made it impossible for them to show hospitality, were despised and taken advantage of by the bush workers. The setbacks of the 1890s only made the situation of all three groups more difficult.

Like the other actors in this three cornered struggle, the squatters had their two sides. Greed was a real temptation for many of those taking up new holdings. Both Hancock and Blainey compare Australia's pastoral development to the gold rushes. 'This was not an orderly neat invasion of new country', writes Blainey. 'It was more like a gold rush'[84]. 'Not all the armies of England, not 100 000 soldiers scattered throughout the bush' could contain them within the bounds of official policy, one of the early Governors of New South Wales complained in his report to London. Their sometimes arrogant pretensions alienated them from the emerging ethos. John Macarthur could write scornfully to the colonial office 'that the opinions of emancipated convicts' about access to the land 'were not the opinions of the moral and respectable part of the community, who were in fact anxious to disclaim the violent and absurd demands of publicans, bakers, Jews and other common people'[85]. They believed that their influential position gave them a right to a special say in the government of the colonies, something which quickly led to their being dubbed a 'bunyip aristocracy'. They could be devious and even ruthless in dealing with the problem of encroaching selectors.

On the other hand, though we must add a grain of salt to the frontier romanticism of C. E. W. Bean when he declares that the station boss is 'the finest of all Australians'[86], there were certainly many pioneers whose courage and leadership deserve to be part of our national memory. No one could fail to be moved by the story which Judith Wright tells so well of her family's struggles and endurance, as their changing fortunes led them to move from district to district in New South Wales and Queensland, wealthy one month, travelling to negotiate relief with creditors the next[87]. Mary Durack tells a similar story on behalf of her family[88].

As we have said, only a small proportion of pastoral families survived for more than a couple of generations. The good use these people made of their material success is evidenced in their distinguished descendants, who include such people as Judith Wright herself, Anne Fairbairn, the Duracks, Patrick White, Russell Drysdale, John Manifold and Geoffrey Dutton. It is an accident of history that our dominant legend has tended to inhibit the development of the pioneer legend normally found in the tradition of a frontier society[89]. Paterson's verse pre-empted the sympathies of generations of Australians: 'Up rode the squatter mounted on his thoroughbred'!

The legend's egalitarianism also leaves a legacy of ambiguity in our attitudes to the organs of government, and to those charged with the maintaining of public order, which has often been remarked upon. As we shall see, we probably demand more of government than we have a right to expect; on the other hand we give those responsible for the nation's public life scant respect. Indeed, we are predisposed to giving support to someone who is 'taking on the authorities'. The legend of Ned Kelly amply illustrates this. Member of a selector family reduced to desperate straights, he resorted to violence and bravado when he judged, probably rightly, that he and his family had been victimised. He murdered several policemen who were carrying out their duty. What other country would have made such a man a national hero and thought it a supreme compliment to be called 'as game as Ned Kelly'?[90].

4. 'A fair start' for black Australians

History, they say, is written by the winners. In the case of the Aborigines it was not written, it was suppressed. As Sally Morgan put it, when she was persuading her uncle Arthur Corunna to tell his story: 'All our history is about the white man. No one knows what it was like for us. A lot of our history has been lost, people have been too frightened to say anything. There's a lot of our history we can't even get at... There are all sorts of files about

Aboriginals that go way back, and the government won't release them. You take the old police files, they're not even controlled by Battye Library, they're controlled by the police. And they don't like letting them out, because there are so many instances of police abusing their power when they were supposed to be Protectors of Aborigines that it's not funny! I mean, our own government had terrible policies for Aboriginal People. Thousands of families in Australia were destroyed by the government policy of taking children away. None of that happened to white people'[91].

The 'cult of forgetfulness' to which W. E. H. Stanner has drawn our attention makes it doubly difficult for white Australians to come to grips with the reality of the situation of the Aboriginal people. Yet if we do not do so, does not our mateship tradition become something of a sham? Sally Morgan's work is one of a number of publications now appearing from which we white Australians, if we are honest enough and courageous enough, can come to understand the magnitude of the tragedy for which our forebears have been responsible. If we cannot be held responsible for past events, we must take up our responsibilities as far as the present situation of the black people is concerned.

It is an incontestable fact that the rights of the Aborigines, which were acknowledged by the instructions received by Captain Cook and Governor Phillip, came to be disregarded. Few Australians realise the extent of the determined resistance put up by the blacks in many parts of the country. Richard Broome judges that 'the Aborigines were eventually written out of frontier history, and the misdeeds of Europeans whitewashed'. In the struggle to which he refers, he judges that there were between a thousand and fifteen hundred white, and about twenty thousand, or even more, black deaths[92].

For twenty years I lived at Toongabbie near Parramatta, where I took an interest in local history. It was only in reading for this work, however, that I have become aware of Pemulwuy, an Aboriginal warrior who belonged to that district and for twelve years carried on an effective guerilla campaign against the white invaders—so effective has been the suppression of his memory. When he was killed in 1802, his head was sent to England. 'Altho' a terrible pest to the colony, he was a brave and independent character' wrote Governor King to Sir Joseph Banks[93]. Eric Willmot, a distinguished Aboriginal academic, concludes his introduction to a novel in which he recreates the story of Pemulwuy with a reference to the 'conspiracy of silence' that concealed the story of his brave resistance. 'It was apparently not in the interests of a crookedly intent or racist establishment to promote such parts of the Australian story. If this is true, then these people have stolen from generations of Aboriginal and non-Aboriginal Australians a heritage as important, as tragic and as heroic as that of any other nation on earth'[94].

It is clear that fear and misunderstanding prevented Europeans from taking up the opportunities which were present in their first encounters with the Aboriginal people. *Tom Petrie's Reminiscences of Early Queensland (Dating from 1837)*, a reprint of articles published by Tom Petrie's daughter in the *Queenslander* at the turn of the century, gives a picture full of life and immediacy of this encounter seen through the eyes of someone who first came to know the Aborigines as a child, who was familiar with their languages, and who remained on friendly terms with them throughout his life[95].

An incident which took place in the area near Brisbane's Fortitude Valley, recounted by Petrie, gives an idea of the kind of misunderstanding which must often have arisen through the ineptitude and fear of the whites. A young black came to the Petries' house with a story of other blacks stealing one of Petrie's bullocks. Tom's father did not believe him: in fact, it soon turned out that the story was fabricated for purposes of revenge. The young Aborigine then went to the police. A detachment of troops was hastily dispatched. Several innocent blacks were wounded and many more would probably have been killed if one of the Petrie boys had not intervened and explained that the story was false[96].

Tom Petrie never feared the blacks. As a youth he travelled hundreds of miles inland with them to the bunya festivals, where a great concourse of blacks from many tribes spent weeks together. In the early days of the colony, he told his daughter, he 'would sooner trust them than most of the whites'[97]. His experience in setting up his farm north of Brisbane gives us a glimpse of what might have been possible if more of the settlers had had similar attitudes:

> the Blacks were very good and helpful, lending a hand to split and fence, and put up stockyards... For the young fellow was all alone, no white man would come near him, being in dread of the blacks... On his return (from an expedition to Brisbane) all was as it should be, not even a bit of tobacco missing!... Father says he could always trust them; and his experience has been that if you treated them kindly they would do anything for you... Many a time when the blacks wished to gather their tribes together for a corroboree (dance and song), or fight, they would send on two men to inquire of father which way to come so as not to disturb his cattle. This was more than many a white man would do, he says. To him they were always kind and thoughtful, and he wishes this to be

clearly understood, for sometimes the blacks are very much blamed for deeds they were really driven to; and of course they resented unkindness'[98].

Petrie gives first-hand evidence of shooting and poisoning of the blacks which was soon to provoke very different attitudes. He quoted one leading Aboriginal who, when questioned years later about the killing of whites, said: 'Before the white fellow came we wore no dress, but knew no shame, and were all free and happy; there was plenty to eat, and it was a pleasure to hunt for food. Then when the white man came among us, we were hunted from our ground, shot, poisoned, and had our daughters, sisters, and wives taken from us. Could you blame us if we killed the white man? If we had done likewise to them, would they not have murdered us?' Asked why innocent whites were sometimes killed, he appealed to the tribal sanctions practised by the Aborigines[99].

Tom Petrie saw what had happened to the Aboriginal people as a tragedy: 'They used to be fine, athletic men, remarkably free from disease, tall, well-made and graceful, with wonderful powers of enjoyment; now they are often miserable, diseased, degraded creatures. The whites have contaminated them'[100]. In the pioneering days of central Queensland, fear and distrust on the part of many whites led to a policy forcing settlers who had established friendly relationships with the local blacks to drive them away from their homesteads[101]. No doubt the same thing happened in many parts of Australia.

Arthur Corunna, Sally Morgan's uncle, in telling his story makes it clear, though quite unconsciously, that the whites whom he dealt with had no sense of the opportunities they were missing in their treatment of Aborigines of his calibre. His story shows him to be a man of nobility and character whom anyone should be proud to have as a friend. He became what he was, in spite of the whites he had dealings with! His white father, with whom he often had contact, never acknowledged him; in the mission school—to which he was taken against the protests of his mother—he was treated with a cruelty that was shameful and almost certainly perverted, being stripped naked with other Aboriginal lads and beaten until his flesh was lacerated; after running away from the school, he was several times deprived of his rightful earnings by white employers; he was blatantly victimised by jealous white neighbours when he made a success of his small farm. The remarkable thing about Arthur Corunna as he tells his story is the lack of self-pity and bitterness with which he looked back on what he had been through.

We have another insight into the way in which our white 'respectability' set up barriers to what might have been when we hear of Henry Lawson's meeting with Aboriginal people. Manning Clark writes 'the only times he (Lawson) ever looked as though he were enjoying life were when he met Aborigines in the streets of Sydney. There seemed to be an instant secret bond between them and him. As they chatted away to him, their faces temporarily losing that sullen look with which they confronted most white men, Lawson, who probably did not hear a word of what they were saying, rubbed his hands gleefully...'[102]

Katherine S. Prichard's tragic novel *Coonardoo*, based on first-hand experience in north-western Australia, shows us the admirable qualities of the Aborigines engaged in working on the cattle stations, the people Arthur Corunna came from. The woman whose name gives the novel its title is by far the greatest character in the story and gives a wonderful insight into the qualities of the Aboriginal people living in circumstances such as hers. She is destroyed, however, by white Australians, one who lusts after her for years and finally rapes her, and another, her childhood friend, whose son she bears and who is upright in a pathetic, puritanical way, but quite incapable of finding a genuine relationship with 'a gin'. Xavier Herbert's novel *Poor Fellow My Country* is the fruit of many years' observation of life in the Northern Territory. It portrays with a relentless realism in the period between the wars, the commerce between the whites and blacks which ruins the life of a half-caste lad. All conducted on the white man's terms, it brings only pain, bewilderment and humiliation to the blacks, taking from them whatever dignity and tradition they had managed to retain.

There is ample evidence that given a 'fair go' the Aboriginal people would have managed much better then they did. Two examples point to a story that could be told over and over again. In 1863 Aborigines who were frustrated by their treatment as far as land was concerned, squatted on a traditional camping site named Coranderrk on the Yarra flats near Healesville. Photos of those who made this settlement an outstanding success after the government made the land an Aboriginal reserve show well dressed, self-respecting young men and women. The government refused to give title, however, and white property owners became covetous when they saw the success with which the blacks had developed the land.

The subsequent history was a struggle for survival. While the land remained a reservation, the Aboriginal people's security was constantly threatened by changing government policies. Those who saw what they had done, however, could only be impressed. A Melbourne paper wrote, revealingly if somewhat patronisingly, of a deputation which came to Melbourne from the reservation in 1882. 'From each face there comes a calm, steadfast, civilised look; each of these manly figures is costumed in civilised and decent fashion; the attitude of each individual is not slouching but erect, as that of a self-respecting man, conscious of his manhood'[103]. Eventually, a new government policy of removing young people of mixed descent proved fatal for the struggling community. What could have been a model for Aboriginal people in many parts of the country disappeared.

Patsy Cohen is a remarkable woman. With the help of Margaret Somerville of Armidale University, she reconstructed the story of her Aboriginal family and the community to which they belonged in Ingelba, near Tamworth[104]. Her mother was Aboriginal and her father was white. When her father joined the army during the Second World War she was taken from her mother and made a state ward. At the age of ten she was sent back to stay with her grandparents who lived on the small Aboriginal reservation at Ingelba. There a small colony of black people lived dignified, if frugal, lives. They provided for their own needs by farming the small area of land available to them, taking in the washing of white families, and so forth. By bringing old-timers to the site and re-cording the memories these visits stimulated, Patsy and Margaret have pieced together the picture of a people in cultural transition who were coping remarkably well.

With the passing of time, and no government interest in their struggle, they found themselves having to move to a life of shame-ful conditions in shacks on the Armidale rubbish tip. After whites took up their cause, they were eventually provided with better accommodation. The story that emerges leaves the reader in admir-ation of the patient dignity and courage this strongly bonded community has shown. Understandably, in the white man's world it was the Aboriginal women who coped best and provided the leadership which helped the group stand together in an ordeal few white people would have been aware of. Ella Simon, the first Abor-iginal woman to become a Justice of the Peace, tells a similar story of black people in the Taree district of New South Wales[105].

I have already described what the loss of tribal land meant to the Aboriginal people: the virtual annihilation of all the landmarks of their culture. Mistreatment by white Australians did not end there. From the first they were denied the most basic respect. Pemulwuy's body, like those of many others, was dismembered so that his head could be examined by English phrenologists. Petrie tells of an Aborigine being shot and skinned at Kangaroo Point in Brisbane, and put up like a scarecrow among the corn to deter blacks tempted to steal it[106].

Aborigines were exploited. The family which owned Corunna station where Arthur Corunna was born paid no real wages to the blacks who worked for them on the station, and virtually none to those taken to Perth to provide domestic help. Sally Morgan's narrative makes it clear, time and again, that the blacks were virtually slaves. Her mother sums up her situation: 'I was owned' by that family 'and the government and anyone who wanted to pay five shillings a year to Mr Neville (a government official) to have me'[107]. Sally's grandmother's story would have been even more shameful for her white masters and mistresses if she had been persuaded to tell it.

As we have seen, Aborigines were excluded from citizenship by the Australian constitution. In some states they required a permit to travel freely outside reservations. This provision proved a very effective means of intimidation and control. Perhaps the greatest injustice of all was that which has already been referred to by Sally Morgan. Families were broken up against the will of parents. Well into the present century, legislation in various Australian states gave officials power to round up Aboriginal youths of mixed descent, take them forcibly from their parents and place them in apprenticeships and training homes. Sir Doug Nicholls, who was to become the Governor of South Australia, describes how he saw his sixteen-year-old sister Hilda taken in this way: 'The police came without warning except for the precaution of ensuring that the men had been sent over the sandhills to cut timber. Some of the girls eluded the police by swimming the Murray. Others were forced into the cars, with mothers wailing and threatening the officers with any weapons at hand'[108]. Charles Perkins was forcibly separated from his tribal relatives, so that the only communication he had with his grandmother was through the wire of the reservation fence.

The family whose story Sally Morgan has shared with us was reduced to a fear of revealing their Aboriginal descent to their children—terrified that the break-up of families they had experienced before would be repeated. When Sally's mother finally told her story, she said 'Mum said she didn't want the children growing up with people looking down on them. I understood what she meant. Aboriginals were treated the lowest of the low. It was like they were the one race on earth that had nothing to offer'[109].

The reading I have done during the past months has made me aware how ignorant I was of the real story of the Aborigines. In his 1968 Boyer Lectures, W. E. H. Stanner expressed the opinion that white Australians should be given the true facts about the Aboriginal people, beginning with 'the first primary classes'[110]. How much has been done? Many white Australians who have smouldered with indignation at the thought of the apartheid regime in South Africa have little knowledge of the reality we have been describing which without a doubt involved greater injustices.

Aborigines were not given a 'fair start'. With the passing of the decades things become progressively worse. However, many very positive developments which have taken place among the Aboriginal people in the last decade or so have received little attention from the media.

Generosity and patience are the least we can give them in their present struggles to find their rightful place in a genuine Australian society. Just provisions, especially in the form of a treaty, seem demanded by the facts of our history[111]. In a sense the contemporary situation offers us an opportunity to take up the struggle 'to be and to remain human' at the point where we failed before. White Australians must not fail a second time.

As Caroline Jones points out, we have much to gain from this renewed relationship. She speaks of the reverence she has come to have for Aboriginal religion. 'The Aboriginal people', she writes, 'give meaning to my life by showing through their suffering, their courage, their unselfishness, their sense of family, their forgiveness, their survival, and their sense of the sacred, what it is truly to be human. For me, they are the steady beating heart at the centre of our Australian spiritual identity'[112].

5. The politics of 'a fair start'

Critical reflection upon the mateship legend which has upheld Australian egalitarianism must consider its relationship to the nation's political life. There is a basic human truth, which should be one of the first concerns of government, in the axiom that every Australian has a right to a fair start in life. The owning of that truth can bring the resilience and strength we need as we enter the multicultural phase of our national history.

As Hancock pointed out sixty years ago, 'In Australia the assertion of rights has been less a matter of theory than of instinct'[113]. It has been argued in an earlier chapter that the barely recognised Benthamite assumptions which have provided a kind of rationale for our instinctive gropings have outlived their usefulness. It is time for renewed reflection.

One of the most remarkable facts of Australian political life, especially when it is considered together with the egalitarianism upheld by our national legend, is its constant refusal to follow the path of radicalism. This has been a disappointment to doctrinaire socialist planners, from the socialists of the nineteenth century to the Marxists of the mid-twentieth century. The Fabian Socialists Sidney and Beatrice Webb visited Australia in 1899, attracted by the description of Australia as a 'social laboratory' fashionable at the time. They were profoundly disappointed. Beatrice wrote in her diary 'The working men seem largely non-political'. Michael Davie finds in their reactions a constant 'note of resentment that these descendants of British and Irish working-class migrants should be prospering so unabashedly and enjoying themselves so greatly'[114]. A couple of years later a French observer, in a much quoted phrase, summed up Australia's political program as 'socialism without doctrines'[115].

The fact was that already ten years after the discovery of gold in Australia all the Chartists' objectives of political reform had been realised. European socialism in all its confused and bickering forms was, in large part, a reaction against the age-old structures of privilege and inequality embedded in European culture. The egalitarian ethos of Australia's developing political community had never accepted these structures and Australians were well on the way to exercising their own choice about the shape the Australian political community should take. The 'instinct' of which Hancock speaks was based on the unreflective recognition of this fact and, perhaps, on something of a recognition of the limited expectations one should have of government initiatives in the life of a healthy human community. The majority of Australians have refused to be persuaded by the champions of radical political revolution that their proposals would bring real benefit to the Australian people. Even William Lane, the social idealist who led his band of disciples to Paraguay in 1893, taught that 'socialism is just being mates'[116].

Australians saw their country as already 'free from the clogs and accumulated hindrances which act as drags upon the progress of other countries... having nothing to undo'. Crawford, who cites this statement as typical[117], points out that class conflict played no important part in the political issues of the nineteenth century—the opening up of the land and trade protection between the colonies. That a fair and reasonable standard of living should be available to all was accepted as axiomatic by all public figures. The fact that there were no major conflicts of principle concerning the nature of the political order meant that use of the old world labels 'conservative' and 'liberal' was gratuitous and misleading[118]. The problems of Australian politics in the nineteenth century were factionalism and corruption.

If revolutionary socialism was to emerge in Australian politics, it was clearly the Labor Party which was destined to be its standard bearer. Historians are agreed, however, that it never really took that path. There were certainly radical socialists within the party, of course; and a danger existed that members of the party would confuse working for social justice with the more radical aspirations of this wing of the party. There is general agreement, however, that the party as such was never identified with a doctrinaire socialism.

In Hancock's judgment, 'the old Australian experimentalism which some people called socialism was not really socialism at all' but 'practical utilitarianism'[119]. John Rickard finds that in its essential thrust the Labor Party 'adhered loosely to its populist tradition, whilst focusing its energies on campaigns for specific reforms'[120]. Manning Clark traces the various stages of the party's development. At its inception, he writes 'Labour's aim was to capture rather than destroy the institutions of the bourgeois state...to make the bourgeois ideals of liberty and equality a reality for all members of society, not just for the privileged few'[121].

In 1921, when the Labor Party, at its conference, voted for 'The socialisation of Industry, Production, Distribution and Exchange', the policy 'meant different things to different members of the party'[122]. In practice the party retained its original direction: reformist and evolutionary rather than revolutionary. In 1963 the A.L.P. leader Arthur Calwell campaigned on the promise that, if elected, the party would not implement any socialist policies[123]. In 1973, the French journal Le Monde marked the election of the Whitlam government by publishing a series of articles on Australia. In one of these Robert Hawke, President of the A.C.T.U., summed up the Australian situation: 'For a large part of the A.L.P. and the unions, the walls are sound; a coat of paint is all that is needed'[124].

The 'instinct' that Hancock refers to owes something also to the Anglo-Saxon tradition of legislation and common law, which has been remarkable for the way it has seen human rights as being best upheld in practice rather than through legal definition. At the time of the gold rushes, the contrast between the maintenance of public order on the Australian diggings and the breakdown of law and order on the Californian fields was remarked upon. Ward cites one observer at the time as attributing this to the cultural homogeneity of the Australian diggers, together with the English tradition of justice. Manning Clark notes that the Anglo-Saxon instincts of those in authority headed off radical tendencies by quickly acceding to the reasonable demands of the moderates after the Eureka Stockade debacle[125].

The fact that Australian politics have not become radicalised has meant that both wings of politics have found it difficult to achieve a focus of concern which clearly distinguished them from their opponents in the perceptions of the electorate. As social objectives have been achieved by the A.L.P., it has come to look more and more like its opponents. The conservative wing of Australian politics has found itself acting more as a moderating influence than as an initiator of social policies. As the parties become more and more indistinguishable in their essential policies, attempts to project themselves as rivals in the struggle for power easily descend to issues of personality or distorted detail, to the neglect of a creative debate of the essential questions facing the country.

The Australian Democrats have helped to improve the quality of that debate. The confrontative type of debate in which Australian

politicians often indulge undermines the confidence of the electorate in the parliamentary process. Perhaps in order to deal with the
important questions Australia is facing in the contemporary world,
sound government should adopt far more often a bi-partisan
approach, so that issues may be debated on their intrinsic merits
rather than become elements in a theatrical struggle for power
which consumes the energies of the nation's elected representatives.

Hancock pointed to another aspect of Australian democracy
which he judged to be linked with the 'middling standard' deriving
from the egalitarian ethos. 'Australian democracy', he writes, 'has
come to look upon the state as a vast public utility, whose duty it is
to provide the greatest happiness for the greatest number'[126]. I
have already noted Hugh Collins's observation that 'the state that
was delivered to Australia's colonial democrats was inevitably a
stronger, more intrusive, legitimately interventionist instrument
than Victoria's Britain'[127]. The vastness of the land, the impossibility of a dispersed population's providing structures of local
government, made a greater centralising of the governing authority
unavoidable. To an extent this situation still prevails. Moreover,
Australia's economy is locked into a volatile world system so that it
requires careful management in a way that affects all aspects of our
common project.

This situation, however, must not be allowed to call up the caricature of a 'fair go' which feeds on the illusion that government
must provide for us in all things. The function of government,
upholding a framework of justice within which we may live
together and the weak and needy may find protection, is fundamental to the nation's survival and welfare, but our future will be
determined even more by the initiatives undertaken by individuals
and free associations quite independently of any government
initiative.

1   London, 1974, p.112.
2   Cited, Ward, *The Australian Legend*, p.67.
3   Cited, Hancock, *Australia*, pp.39, 42.
4   Cited, Manning Clark, *In Search of Henry Lawson*, Sth Melbourne
(Macmillan) 1978, p.18.
5   Cited, V. Palmer, 'The Legend', in C. Wallace-Crabbe, *The Australian
Nationalists: Modern Critical Essays*, Melbourne, 1971, pp.1–21.
6   *On the Wool Track*, p.31, Sydney (Cornstalk) 1925 ed.
7   ibid., p.32.
8   ibid., p.183.
9   ibid., p.125.
10   ibid., p.218.
11   Cited, Ward, *The Australian Legend*, p.231.
12   *Australian Accent*, p.33.
13   *Kangaroo*, pp.16–17.

[14]   London (Pan Books) 1987.

[15]   Cited, Ward, *The Australian Legend*, p.232.

[16]   *The Australian Legend*, p.31.

[17]   *Preoccupations in Australian Poetry*, p.xx.

[18]   Cited, Robert Dixon, 'Public and Private Voices', p.130, in *Penguin New Literary History of Australia*, L. Hergenhan (ed.).

[19]   Cf. J. B. Hirst, *Convict Society and Its Enemies*, Sydney, 1983.

[20]   *The Australian Legend*, pp.38–9.

[21]   Cf. Ward, *The Australian Legend*, p.65.

[22]   *A Short History of Australia*, London (Heinemann) 1977, pp.51–2.

[23]   Cf. P. O'Farrell, *The Irish in Australia*, p.19. John Hirst notes the link between 'the disrespect of the Irish for English pretension' and our egalitarian ethos ('Egalitarianism', p.69, in *Australian Cultural History*, S. L. Goldberg and F. B. Smith [eds]).

[24]   *The Australian Legend*, p.16.

[25]   *Australia*, p.83.

[26]   *The Australian Legend*, p.115.

[27]   Cf. P. O'Farrell, *The Irish in Australia*, pp.90–1.

[28]   Cited, Ward, *The Australian Legend*, pp.120–1.

[29]   *The Australian Legend*, p.114.

[30]   ibid., pp.1–2.

[31]   'The Australian National Character: Myth and Reality', *Jour. of World Hist.*, 2 (1955) pp.704–18.

[32]   'Truth and Tradition in Australia, New Zealand and Papua New Guinea', in J. A. Moses (ed.), *Historical Disciplines and Culture*, St Lucia (Univ. of Q. Press), 1979; see especially pp.41–4. More recently, Gammage has carried forward his analysis of the Australian legend in 'Anzac', John Carroll (ed.), *Intruders in the Bush*, pp.54–66.

[33]   Cf. Auerbach's definition of legend, *Mimesis*, pp.19–20, cited in an earlier chapter.

[34]   *Inventing Australia*, p.97.

[35]   *A Short History of Australia*, p.185.

[36]   'Realism and Documentary', pp.247–8, in *Penguin New Literary History of Australia*, L. Herganhan (ed.).

[37]   *A Short History of Australia*, p.185. The writer is aware that his exploration of the complexities of Henry Lawson has only begun, and that Manning Clark's biography is open to criticism; it has been pointed out to him that Lawson's 'fictive strategies', such as 'his manipulation of tone, his understated symbolism and his often-guilty narrators' may be seen as contesting the themes of mateship and endurance. Perhaps it could be suggested that in these aspects of his writing Lawson is acknowledging and exploring the ambiguities which have been present in the Australian character.

[38]   *The Creative Spirit in Australia*, p.62.

[39]   Cf. McCarthy, *Gallipoli to the Somme*, p.51.

[40]   *Preoccupations in Australian Poetry*, p.81.

[41]   ibid., pp.81–2.

[42]   *Ideas for a Nation*, p.163.

[43]   McCarthy, *Gallipoli to the Somme*, p.154.

[44]   *Gallipoli to the Somme*, p.154.

[45]   ibid., p.212.

[46]   'Anzac', pp.63–65, in J. Carroll (ed.), *Intruders in the Bush*.

[47]   *Gallipoli to the Somme*, p.183.

[48]   Arneil wrote in his diary 'I worry about the Englishmen under my care. They practically walk to the cremation pyre. They stop eating, lie down and refuse to live. It is incredible, instead of hanging grimly on to life with both hands

they start to criticize their meals and that is the finish' (*One Man's War*, p.124; cf. pp.28–9). See also Patricia Shaw, *Brother Digger: The Sullivans 2nd AIF*, Richmond, Vic., 1984, for first-hand evidence of the qualities of representative Australians involved in the Second World War.

[49]   'War Literature', p.342, in *Penguin New Literary History of Australia*, L. Herganhan (ed.).

[50]   White, *Inventing Australia*, p.136.

[51]   In the judgment of John Rickard, Bean's portrayal is still, to a degree, 'flavoured by nationalistic romanticism' (*Australia*, p.125).

[52]   *Ideas for a Nation*, p.77.

[53]   loc. cit.

[54]   McCarthy, *Gallipoli to the Somme*, p.65.

[55]   'Forms of Literary History', p.82, in *Penguin New Literary History of Australia*, L. Hergenhan (ed.).

[56]   Bruce Clunies Ross, 'Literature and Culture', p.15, in *Penguin New Literary History of Australia*, L. Hergenhan (ed.). Cf. also pp.444, 478.

[57]   Cf. 'Egalitarianism', pp.58–77 in *Australian Cultural History*, S. L. Goldberg and F. B. Smith (eds).

[58]   *Preoccupations in Australian Poetry*, p.xx.

[59]   *A Crucible of Prophets*, p.60.

[60]   in Cantrell, *Writing of the 1890s*, pp.216–30.

[61]   *The Tyranny of Distance*, Sun Books, 1966, p.171.

[62]   1976 Boyer Lectures, p.28.

[63]   *A Crucible of Prophets*, p.60.

[64]   ibid., p.60.

[65]   *Such Is Life*, p.183.

[66]   1976 Boyer Lectures, p.28. Clark derived this magnificent image from Henry Lawson: cf. *On the Track and over the Sliprails*, Sydney, 1945, p.85. On the place given to women in the Australian ethos, see Barbara Baynton's 'The Chosen Vessel'.

[67]   Melbourne (Penguin) 1975. Cf. Donald Horne's comments, *Ideas for a Nation*, p.259.

[68]   *Kangaroo*, p.54.

[69]   ibid., p.55.

[70]   ibid., pp.54–5.

[71]   *Preoccupations in Australian Poetry*, p.82.

[72]   *A Short History of Australia*, p.110.

[73]   ibid., 125.

[74]   Clark, *A Short History of Australia*, p.163.

[75]   *The Australian Legend*, p.201.

[76]   *Such is Life*, p.234.

[77]   *The Tyranny of Distance*, p.171.

[78]   Graubard, op. cit., p.x.

[79]   *Australia*, p.63

[80]   ibid., p.153.

[81]   ibid., p.226.

[82]   Cited, Rickard, *Australia*, p.268.

[83]   *The Tyranny of Distance*, p.166.

[84]   ibid., p.131.

[85]   Cited, Clark, *A Short History of Australia*, p.60.

[86]   *On the Wool Track*, p.40.

[87]   Cf. *The Generations of Men*, Melbourne, 1970, which is based upon family diaries, and *The Cry for the Dead*, Melbourne (Oxford U.P.) 1981, which is the result of a study of the historical circumstances surrounding the story recorded in the diaries, particularly as they touched the Aboriginal people.

88   *Kings in Grass Castles*, London, 1957.

89   Cf. J. B. Hirst, 'The Pioneer Legend', *Hist. Studies* 18 (1978) pp.316–37.

90   Cf. Angus McIntyre, 'Ned Kelly: A Folk Hero', pp.38–53, in J. Carroll (ed.), *Intruders in the Bush*.

91   *My Place*, pp.163–4. Cf. Henry Reynolds *Frontier*, Sydney, 1987, *The Law of the Land*, Penguin 1987, for painstaking studies of the shameful realities of White Australia's dealings with our Aboriginal people.

92   *Aboriginal Australians*, Sydney, citing the studies of H. Reynolds and N. Loos.

93   Eric Willmot, *Pemulwuy: The Rainbow Warrior*, Sydney, 1987, p.14.

94   ibid., p.19.

95   First edition, 1904; quotations from edition published in Brisbane in 1932 (Angus and Roberason).

96   *Tom Petrie's Reminiscences*, pp.143–5.

97   ibid., p.187.

98   ibid., pp.5–6.

99   ibid., pp.182–3.

100   ibid., pp.14–15.

101   Cf. Judith Wright, *The Cry for the Dead*, Melbourne (Oxford U.P.) 1981, ch.5. This work provides ample evidence of the disastrous history of relationship between the races.

102   *In Search of Henry Lawson*, p.125.

103   Cited, Broome, *Aboriginal Australians*, p.81.

104   *Ingelba and the Five Black Matriarchs*, North Sydney (Allen and Unwin) 1990.

105   *Through My Eyes*, Blackburn, Vic. (Collins Dove) 1987 (Foreword by Les Murray).

106   *Tom Petrie's Reminiscences*, p.234.

107   *My Place*, p.350.

108   R. Broome, *Aboriginal Australians*, p.83.

109   *My Place*, p.305.

110   1968 Boyer Lectures, p.41.

111   See the text of the treaty proposed by prominent Australians, R. Broome, *Aboriginal Australians*, pp.202–3. Cf. also, Reynolds, *The Law of the Land*, p.175.

112   *The Search for Meaning*, Crows Nest (Collins Dove) 1989.

113   *Australia*, p.62.

114   'The Fraying of the Rope', p.379, in *Australia: The Daedalus Symposium*, S. Graubard (ed.).

115   Cited, Rickard, *Australia*, p.147.

116   Cited, Crawford, *Australia*, p.124.

117   *Australia*, p.112.

118   Crawford, *Australia*, p.120.

119   *Australia*, p.179.

120   ibid., p.147.

121   *A Short History of Australia*, p.169.

122   Clark, *A Short History of Australia*, p.212.

123   Cf. Michael Davie, 'The Fraying of the Rope', in *Australia: The Daedalus Symposium*, S. Graubard (ed.).

124   7 May 1973.

125   *A Short History of Australia*, p.122.

126   *Australia*, p.61.

127   'Political Ideology in Australia', p.151, in *Australia: The Daedalus Symposium*, S. Graubard (ed.). Cf. also G. Blainey, p.21, and Henry S. Albinski, p.399, in this same volume.

6.

A WISDOM FOUND IN ADVERSITY AND FAILURE

It is at the limits of human existence that many have found wisdom. Because our Australian experience has often taken us to these limits, it has also offered us a way to wisdom. From the beginning, the very nature of this strange, weathered continent made it inevitable that our history would be marked with hardship and failed hopes. Those who initiated the history of white settlement were not heroic pioneers but Britain's convicted criminals, taken to the ends of the earth against their will. The explorers who set out to discover rich resources in the continental interior found a barrenness such as they had never imagined to exist. Many of them did not survive to tell what they had found. The military campaign with which we bravely entered the arena of world affairs, and which we have given a place of honour in our national celebrations, was a disastrous failure. In a sense our national history has turned everything upside down. And yet, for that very reason, the experience we have shared has taught us lessons with few parallels among the world's peoples, something which could be our peculiar contribution to the great conversation of humanity.

1. A history that does not foster self-aggrandisement

A comparison with the United States immediately suggests itself, as we seek to understand what our experience has made us. We occupy territories of comparable size; we both had our origins as British colonies, bearing the distinctive mark of the Georgian era of the late eighteenth century; the formative periods of our histories belong to the same two centuries. But what begins as a comparison soon becomes a distinct contrast. The regions we occupy gave rise to very different kinds of experience. As Les Murray puts it, North America promised its colonists that it could be 'a vaster repeat performance of primeval Europe, a new Northern Hemisphere with familiar soils and seasons into which a liberal variation on inherited European consciousness might be transplanted with prospects of vast success'[1]. Australia's colonists saw immediately that the seasons were out of joint. It was only with much heart-break that we have come to recognise that the soils of our island-continent are old and thin, and that its climate is capable of destructive variations which often bring to nought the toil of years.

Les Murray quotes novelist George Johnston's remark that the land has humbled us, that nothing human is able to stand out above the strange, massive reality of the continent itself. We are coming slowly to recognise, Murray says, 'that the land does not finally permit of imported attitudes that would make it simply a resource, a thing; it has broken too many of us who tried to make such an attitude fit it'[2].

At the level of those events which provide the symbols of national identity, the contrast between our two countries is a strik-ing one. 'The Yanks', George Johnston writes, 'proved themselves long ago'. Their history is filled with the stuff that legends and symbols are made of: 'Revolution, civil war, frontiers to subjugate, mountains to climb, rivers to ford, plains to cross, the Redman as the perfect adversary, the right sort of issues like slavery and liberty'[3]. Our history, on the other hand, is peopled with 'ghosts', to call upon a metaphor which both D. H. Lawrence and Manning Clark have used. 'Our country is full of...ghosts', writes Manning Clark, 'the ghosts of what our ancestors did to the Aborigines, of what they did to the land, the ghost of convictism, and the ghosts of foreign wars'. 'We must live with our ghosts', he concludes, 'as best we can'[4].

Henry Albinski, an American who knows Australia well, points to the way in which national experiences have produced very different political tempers in our two countries. The United States has its origin 'in overtly political acts—a declaration of independ-ence, war, the crafting of a novel constitutional document'. As a result, Albinski writes, the 'American national mythology became heavily infused with constitutional reverence'[5]. Manning Clark fills out the details of this contrast. 'With Australia there was no declaration of independence, no statement of what Australia stood for, let alone what it was'. The Americans had established their nation with 'the profession of a credo': 'We hold these truths to be self-evident...' The cornerstones of their republic were proudly declared: that all are 'created equal'; that the republic was founded upon the recognition of 'certain inalienable rights'; and that amongst these are 'life, liberty and the pursuit of happiness'. By way of contrast, Australia's instrument of federation 'seemed dull and dreary as some of our critics and detractors find our life to be': 'Whereas the people of (naming the States in turn) humbly relying on the blessing of Almighty God, have agreed to unite in an indissoluble Federal Commonwealth'[6].

As Albinski puts it, 'Australian federation...was a leisurely process, inspired mostly by considerations of efficiency...Australia slipped into formal nationhood, almost unobtrusively; it had no specific legacy of emotive political symbols; it lacked heroic figures, and has not developed them since'. The American legend invests the state itself with an almost sacred aura, with the result that in the United States 'wars have generally been fought and recalled more as national events, glorifying such principles as national destiny or the bringing of democracy to other people'. Australians, in Albinski's judgment, have viewed their military involvements as testifying 'more to the nobility of individual character than to the power of national causes', and looked upon their remembrance as commemorating 'Australians more than Australia'. If Americans see the state as the embodiment of the nation itself, Australians see it as the nation's tool[7].

Albinski cites Jeanne MacKenzie's observation that the seemingly limitless possibilities for expansion that marked America's experience encouraged 'a boundless optimism, vitality and drive and joy for living'; on the other hand, Australians, whatever their achievements, found the 'going was always too tough to leave any energy for the sheer joy of the struggle'. She judged that an American optimism and a cynical pessimism on the part of Australians are derived from this pattern[8].

In a similar vein, Veronica Brady cites R. W. B. Lewis's description of 'the American Adam' evoked by the United States experience: 'an individual, standing alone, self-reliant and self propelling, ready to confront whatever awaits him with the aid of his own unique and inherent resources'. Australia's counterpart, she judges, is 'more paradoxical, even ironic', because he has had to come to terms with weakness and defeat[9]. Unlike the North American continent, our land could not be made immediately into something heroic. 'The land could not be metamorphosed', Manning Clark writes, 'into a hero of the people. It seemed designed by nature or possibly by an otherwise inscrutable providence, as a testing place for heroes'[10].

A nation's heroes give an insight into the ideals it has espoused and the stance it has adopted. As both Clark and Albinski observe, Australia has been slow to venerate heroic figures. Our national struggle was not one that ended in triumph; the prize more often than not was mere survival. And so ours is a strange catalogue of heroes—heroes who have won our admiration for the way in which they have conducted themselves when they were up against it: the early bushrangers, the gold diggers of the Eureka Stockade, the explorers who did not survive, Burke and Wills, the troops of the abortive Anzac expedition, Phar Lap the race horse, Les Darcy the boxer, and Ned Kelly, the strangest national hero of all! It is interesting to reflect upon the absence of women in this catalogue. Perhaps Dame Mary Gilmore could be included: she was certainly identified with the qualities to which I have referred. This exclusion of women must surely be related to the fact that they had no place in the legend of mateship.

We were not to be given the easy way of making a national legend. 'Australia presented a blank and negative front to our efforts at self-aggrandisement, either through easy wealth or heroic conquest'[11]. Perhaps an experience in which the seductive symbols of self-aggrandisement have little place can prove for us, in the end, a source of wisdom. That depends on whether we are ready to learn from what that experience has to teach. As John Rickard writes 'It might seem appropriate, even admirable, that Australia should escape the lurid excesses of patriotism, but it raises questions about the kind of society the colonists had created and the loyalties it fostered'[12].

Anthony J. Hassell sees Patrick White's novel Voss as having a place in Australian literary history which it would be difficult to exaggerate, because the novel wrestles with this issue, so important in our national culture. He compares Voss with Anzac. Both, he writes, 'are stories of failure, of idealism and courage recklessly spent on quests that were in objective terms of little value, though of profound subjective value to those involved'[13]. The explorers, the Anzacs, Phar Lap and Les Darcy are admired by Australians, Hassall writes, 'for taking on overwhelming odds, battling courageously, and, if they failed, showing courage and determination to the end'. He sees White as interpreting these legends for twentieth century Australians still troubled by them and who, in remembering the explorers, still 'sense the interior of the continent as a reservoir of meaning about the essential Australian experience'. 'Voss is defeated', he writes, 'and his will eventually fails;

but in the process he learns something of the country and its people, something of love and humility, and his spirit haunts the land as his story will haunt his countrymen'[14]. Pringle's reply to Topp in the last paragraphs of the novel captures something of this peculiarly Australian lesson: 'the mediocrity of which he speaks is not a final and irrevocable state; rather it is a creative source of endless variety and subtlety'[15].

2. The challenge of realism or the paralysis of legend

Henry Lawson has great importance in Australia's developing conversation. In Lawson, a considerable literary gift—making him comparable, in Geoffrey Serle's judgment, with Maupassant and Chekov[16]—was hampered by a lack of educational background which ran the danger of isolating him in a provincial point of view.

His tragic life took him to the limits of human existence. 'For Lawson there were, in the end, nothing but human relationships', writes Judith Wright, 'and these were doomed to failure as the body was doomed to death'[17]. What he went through as a person made it possible for him to be aware of the limits of human existence as they presented themselves in Australian experience at the turn of the century. Geoffrey Serle quotes H. M. Green's judgment of Lawson's genius: 'it would be hard to find any writer of his calibre, in whom so deep and romantic a love of his fellows is accompanied by so keen and humorous a perception of their inconsistencies and pettinesses, and, on the whole, by so conscientious a determination to show them just as they are'[18].

At first sight, Lawson and Banjo Paterson have much in common. Both of them, through their writings, play a key part in the elaboration of the Australian legend. But their points of view were very divergent. This difference was brought to light in an exchange which they carried on in the *Bulletin* in 1892. 'For weeks', Serle writes, 'they "slambanged" away at each other, on the whole good-humouredly, to the great delight of the mass audience, several of whom made entertaining contributions'[19].

Lawson, in 'Up the Country', wrote of 'shattering many idols out along the dusty track', and of how he 'Burnt a lot of fancy verses'. He concluded 'I intend to stay at present, as I said before, in town / Drinking beer and lemon-squashes, taking baths and cooling down'. Paterson replied, in 'In Defence of the Bush', that 'the men who know the bush-land—they are loyal through it all'. 'You had better stick to Sydney', he admonished Lawson, 'and make merry with the "push", / For the bush will never suit you, and you'll never suit the bush'.

Beneath the banter an issue of great importance for the Australian conversation had been raised, though neither of the protagonists could have been expected to appreciate it with full clarity. B. Nesbitt[20] concludes his discussion of this debate, in which literary issues and cultural issues became hopelessly entangled, by quoting an observation of the Canadian scholar Northrop Frye. Frye identified in the writing of a new world society two distinct currents, 'one, romantic, traditional, and idealistic, the other shrewd, observant and humorous'. Lawson represented the latter point of view. Paterson's approach was romantic and selective, idealistic in its perception of reality, giving rise, as we have seen, to what Judith Wright has called a 'paralysing' form of national legend.

Paterson, Manning Clark reminds us, 'went to a school which had prefects and a cadet corps, and attended those chapels where the emblems and trophies of war were displayed in a building dedicated to the teachings of the Galilean fisherman'. He was a fine example, Clark says, 'of what might be called the Australian brand of British Philistinism'[21]. We have seen already what Clark is driving at: Paterson took up the Kipling style legend of the frontier of empire. If Lawson 'was putting a serious case for realism against romanticism', Serle writes, 'Lawson's argument was one to which Paterson would not or could not reply'[22].

Lawson *did* love this 'worst dried-up God forsaken country' and its people. But he argued that the realities of life which he had seen in the bush, and portrayed so honestly, carried with them immense challenges that Australians must face—'Till the plains are irrigated and the land is humanised', as he writes in 'Up the Country'—if they were to find their true selves and build their nation on the qualities he admired in the midst of the 'inconsistencies and pettinesses' which he fully acknowledged. At his best in his short stories, Serle writes, 'he is a highly finished artist and craftsman... a writer of high originality—precise, restrained, constantly understated—and almost the only Australian protest-writer whose art successfully carries his message...a radical who sensed the futility of radicalism and of Australian utopianism'[23]. The contrast with Bernard O'Dowd's inflated idealism could hardly be more extreme. The exquisite humour and irony which salts Lawson's understatement saves him from the pitfalls of a writer with a message, in a way we now recognise to be authentically Australian.

Patrick Morgan compares Lawson's portrayal of the setbacks that marked so much of Australian life with Steele Rudd's *On Our Selection* (1899) and Barbara Baynton's *Bush Studies* (1902), situating Lawson between the extremes they represent[24]. For Rudd's characters 'Everything goes so wrong...that they just sit down and laugh at it all...incidents become memorable tales to be recalled and laughed at in the future'. For Baynton 'All civilised restraints have gone, hell is let loose, and women, potential carriers of human decency bear the brunt of it all'. Lawson's stories, he says, 'avoid the extremes of blandness and despair'. 'They brilliantly combine', Morgan writes, 'horror and humour, each keeping the other in check'.

The issue was, and remains, one of great importance for Australians. The legend championed by Paterson invited Australians to forget their troubles and to dream of the pure bush, to find inspiration in that romanticised outback which he describes in the much quoted line 'the vision splendid of the sun-lit plains extended'. As Judith Wright has pointed out, this legend brings a 'paralysis'. An appeal to some imagined innocence of Australia's past becomes an avoiding of the real challenges 'to be, and to remain human' which face us in the continent which gives us our existence. Lawson, on the other hand, knows that we shall only be true to ourselves by facing the reality of the Australia we share.

Lawson is not alone in exploring the limits of human existence as they presented themselves in Australian experience at the turn of the century. The picture of bush life painted by Joseph Furphy and Miles Franklin is very close to Lawson's. 'Such is life', the phrase which suggested the title of Furphy's novel—said to have been the last words of Ned Kelly—recurs like a refrain in the reflections of Furphy's main character, Tom Collins. 'Self-communion in the back country will never leave a man as it found him', Furphy writes, 'he becomes a fool or a philosopher'[25]. John Barnes observes that this 'is only a hint, but it implies disturbing depths of bush experience which are not confronted directly in *Such is Life*, although Furphy had experienced them'[26].

If, in his first enthusiasm for what he found in Australia, C. E. W. Bean identified with Paterson's version of the Australian legend, in his later and best work he made an important contribution to the tradition of realism championed by Lawson. Even though this displeased the editors of Australian newspapers, in his work as a correspondent Bean refused to resort to sensationalism. His rationale was clearly expressed and it was a point of view with which Lawson would have identified: 'I can't write that it occurred if I know that it did not, even if by painting it that way I can rouse the blood and make the pulse beat faster—and undoubtedly these men here deserve that people's pulses shall beat for them. But War Correspondents have so habitually exaggerated the heroism of battles that people don't realise that real actions are heroic'[27]. The powers of observation which made him a remarkable journalist also made it inevitable that he would follow the path of realism. Ashmead Bartlett, the leading British correspondent whose praise of the first assault of the Anzacs contributed greatly to the worldwide attention they received, is reported as having said 'Bean! O, I think Bean actually counts the bullets'[28].

If Lawson is not a great poet, Judith Wright observes, he stands in our history as 'a poetic legend, a figure who remains real to us, when more rational and persuasive writers are forgotten'. As the tragedy of his life unfolded, 'his polemics vanish behind a far more human figure, a man who identifies himself with human woe, a man of compassion and sensitivity, the eternal scapegoat who suffers for and with others'[29]. These qualities are well portrayed in Manning Clark's moving biographical sketch, *In Search of Henry Lawson*[30]. The Australian public somehow recognised the significance Henry Lawson has in our national tradition. His immense popularity, despite the humiliating tragedy of a life plagued by alcoholism, was evidenced in the fact that he was the first Australian writer to be given a state funeral. If Paterson's 'vision splendid' entertained, deeper instincts responded to the stronger medicine of Lawson's realism.

This seems to be the case still. As an American who knows Australia well remarked to me, it would be difficult to imagine Albert Facey's *A Fortunate Life* attracting much attention in the United States. No doubt there have been many Americans who could tell an equally moving story of triumph over adversity, and tell it with a similar naive dignity. The fact that Facey's story won an immediate response from Australians of every background tells us something important about ourselves. As Chris Wallace-Crabbe comments, it was 'full of common topics to which every bosom returns an Aussie echo'. He quotes Freud's observation, 'Childhood memories come in general to acquire the significance of screen memories, and in doing so offer a remarkable analogy with childhood memories that a modern nation preserves in its store of legends and myths'[31]. Wallace-Crabbe compares Facey's text with Alan Marshall's I *Can Jump Puddles*. Both authors, he writes, provide readers 'with the deepest of mimetic consolations, the assurance that they have come fully into contact with the real Australia'[32].

In her own way, Judith Wright has contributed to the strain of realism so important in our Australian tradition, seeking in her various writings to express its truth and its strength. Her poem 'Bullocky', for example, invites us to share in the genuine Australian legend in all its tragic realism. The old man is, in Brian Elliott's words, 'a tutelary shade, and his madness—poignant evidence of the power of the bush to "chasten and subdue"— becomes a kind of divine frenzy which possesses, and also blesses, the land'[33]. Somehow it is the humble bullock driver rather than the brave squatter or the heroic explorer who most fittingly embodies our Australian experience.

3. Australian humour: wisdom in a lower key

A study such as this runs the risk of giving all its attention to the confident voices of the intelligentsia, and to the 'intimidatory' voices, as Donald Horne describes them[34], of the media, as if what they have to say constitutes the Australian conversation. These confident and assertive speakers easily drown out the quieter, more diffident voices of ordinary Australians. Their specialised conversation often leaves their inarticulate friends somewhat uneasy and bewildered, uncertain whether what they hear squares with what their instincts tell them to be the real nature of things.

Henry Lawson had to battle with something of this sense of inadequacy, in handling such things as the niceties of grammar and punctuation, as he tells us in 'The Uncultured Rhymer to His Cultured Critics'. The fact is, as Judith Wright has reminded us, his message 'remains real to us when more rational and persuasive writers are forgotten'. It was humour which provided the vehicle for most of Lawson's message, so much so that it is hard to imagine him without it.

It is especially in humour that ordinary people become articulate. For that reason, it has the greatest importance to us as we assess the drift of the Australian conversation. Like all peoples, Australians have a distinctive kind of humour. There are few people, probably, to whom it has been as important a way of communing as it has been to Australians. Through our humour we have made existence bearable and not devoid of meaning. In our formative period, it was through humour, as Geoffrey Serle observes, that we Australians 'were achieving self-expression and enjoying the shock of self-recognition'[35]. 'Comedians, rather than historians', writes Manning Clark, 'taught Australians who they were'[36].

Australian humour has some characteristics which come to mind immediately. It can be exuberant and boisterous, but more usually dry and understated. It delights in an irreverence which cautions us not to take ourselves, or the things we most revere, too seriously. Irony is one of its favourite devices—'sardonic' is the adjective constantly used by those who have attempted to categorise its distinctive flavour.

Dorothy Jones and Barry Andrews, who write on 'Australian Humour' in the *Penguin New Literary History of Australia*, point to an overriding rationale which helps to explain the part played by these various elements. What is characteristic of Australian humour, they suggest, is not a specific content but 'a specific configuration of attitudes'. 'Irony predominates', they write, 'and individuals manipulated by circumstances, or a destiny they are unable to control, wryly resign themselves to their own powerlessness'[37]. If the Irish made a contribution to the Australian ethos—through 'a creative exchange which compelled Australia's inhabitants, of all kinds and persuasions, to take stock of the nature of their society'[38] —there can be little doubt that this contribution is recognisably present in Australian humour as it has just been described.

It is not difficult to recognise a link with the realism championed by Lawson. The significance of his writing and the lasting affection in which he is held by Australians are no doubt related to the success with which he captured the tone and accents of popular humour. He evidences the 'configuration of attitudes' to which Jones and Andrews refer when, for example, he suggests to the young Australian writer that, given the frustrations which lie ahead, it would be advisable 'to study elementary anatomy, especially as applies to the cranium, and then shoot himself carefully with the aid of a looking-glass'[39].

Typically, Australian humour registers reactions to an intractable situation. Reactions are of different kinds. At one extreme we find what Manning Clark calls 'a ghastly savage humour', a response to a 'ghastly country'—the chilling irony, for example, which spoke of a back lacerated by flogging as 'a red shirt', or of freed convicts as 'Botany Bay swells'. Since the convict era, Clark writes, 'Australian humour always had the sardonic savage flavour of a disenchanted, embittered people, a people who knew one certain thing in life was defeat and failure'[40].

This strain can become, as Clark also observes, a humour whereby 'life is made bearable by being treated as a joke'[41]. In Steele Rudd's Dad and Dave, for example, the tragedy of the small selector farmer is portrayed by being 'cut back to size as subjects for bar-room humour'[42]. But it can also take the form of mildly self-mocking parody, such as one finds in John O'Brien's ' "We'll All Be Rooned", Said Hanrahan'; or in the deadpan advice of the wharfie who met a *Bulletin* writer in a pub at Wyndham, Western Australia: 'So you are up here to write about us... Put this in mate. Cambridge Gulf is the arsehole of the world, and Wyndham is sixty-five miles up it'. Jones and Andrews, who retail this joke, comment that it gathers together much that is basic to the tenor of Australian humour: 'protest at the harsh environment and its alienating effect on the individual, resignation to the impossibility of change, and pride at being able to endure it all'[43].

Henry Lawson sums it up in a gentler form in the Preface he wrote for Miles Franklin's novel *My Brilliant Career*, describing Australia as a land 'where every second sun-burnt bushman is a sympathetic humorist, with the sadness of the bush deep in his eyes and a brave grin for the worst of times'. This 'you can't win' theme has been developed in a more flippant style in C. J. Dennis's larrikin character 'Ginger Mick', and in J. C. Banks's comic cartoon character 'Ginger Meggs'.

Australia's egalitarian ethos expresses itself in a humour which deflates the pretensions of those who take themselves or their causes too seriously. D. H. Lawrence's English character Somers encountered humour of this kind when he innocently asked the sanitary man who was collecting the can from the outdoor privy whether he took ashes and rubbish as well. 'Neow, we take no garbage', was the reply. To his further question 'Then what do I do with them?', he was told 'Do what you like with them'. Somers reflected, somewhat bemused, as the sanitary man marched off with the can, 'It was not rudeness. It was a kind of colonial humour'[44].

C. E. W. Bean recorded humour of this same kind at Gallipoli. 'The General (Birdwood) and General Bridges used to have a guard, by name Bill, when they went round the trenches. Bill was from Sydney and in one trench he met a Sydney friend. "Ullo, Bill", said the friend, "who's yer prisoners?"'. On another occasion a batch of men saw three generals (Walker, Bridges, Birdwood) coming along. '"Say Jim", one was heard to say ... "better put a guard over the biscuits—here's three bloody generals"'[45].

Those dealing constantly with the public have often excelled in this levelling kind of humour. Father Phil Reeves took himself very seriously by all accounts. The conductress on a Ryde tram, clearing a passage near the crowded entrance, looked at him and directed in typical jaunty fashion, 'Move down. Move down, please!'. 'Do you know who I am?', said Father Reeves, 'I'm Father Reeves from Ryde'. 'I don't care if you're Father Christmas from Grace Brothers', was the reply, 'move down!'

Australia's remarkable tradition of black and white cartoonists belongs to this same genre. Leaders in public life have to take it for granted that they will see themselves portrayed in a way which brings a smile to fellow Australians as they open their daily papers. This levelling humour can take less defensible forms, as when 'pommies' and other immigrants are victimised merely for being different, or achievers are cut down to size. 'Our past has made us cruel mockers', Manning Clark observes. 'All vulnerable men need to wear a mask when talking to Australians'[46]. At its best, however, it is dismissive in a good-natured, dry way, as in the swaggy whose reply to the squatter who offered him a lift was 'No flamin' fear. You can open your own gates'. Paul Hogan's *Crocodile Dundee* belongs to a tradition of humour enjoyed by Australian city-dwellers as they find themselves put down by the man from the bush. Banjo Paterson's 'The Man from Ironbark', about the barber's joke that backfired, belongs to this same tradition.

Jones and Andrews identify another typical mood of Australian humour. Reaction to the impossibility of the situation can sometimes take the form of 'outbursts of anarchical disorder'. This breakdown of normality into anarchy—whether physical or verbal—they suggest 'provides a saturnalian release, charging ordinary life with renewed energy'[47]. This is clearly a function of the slapdash humour found in most cultural traditions; but in Australia, the peculiar difficulties of our situation have given it a special flavour. The authors cite Henry Lawson's hilarious tale 'The Loaded Dog' as an example of this. The chaos provoked by the playful retriever with an ignited blasting charge in his mouth is set against a background of the desolate landscape of the diggings, the lack of success which prompted the diggers to give up for the moment and prepare a blasting charge to catch fish in the waterhole, and the desultory mood of the country pub at midday. 'Although the dog's mad spurt of energy is potentially lethal, it nevertheless challenges the unyielding pattern of the men's daily lives'[48].

No Australian cartoon is more famous, probably, than that depicting two construction workers dangling from a girder, one of whom has grabbed his mate around the legs, pulling down his trousers. Despite his predicament, he is overcome with the giggles. 'For gorsake stop laughing', mutters his mate, 'this is serious'. This cartoon, it should be pointed out, appeared at the height of the depression. As Jones and Andrews observe, these anarchic outbursts in Australian humour are 'not celebratory'; they are 'not so much a reaffirmation of order as reminders of how precariously it is maintained'[49].

If such humour reacts to the harshness of life, the Australian tall story, the authors suggest, may register a reaction to the strangeness of the Australian environment: 'tall tales with their deadpan accounts of grotesque impossibilities were one means of coming to terms with the land's strangeness'[50]. They instance such stories as that of the bushman who 'shot so far he needed salt bullets so the game would keep until he got up to it'[51].

The best Australian humour has a severe economy—of language, in its laconic wording, and of emotional expression in its deadpan style. This reflects a situation in which, though wits must be kept alert, energies must be saved for the continuation of the struggle to remain on top of things. A true story I heard recently illustrates this economy. Fifty years or so ago, a Brisbane kid decided with his mate to hold up the train which rattled past his backyard each afternoon. Faces masked, they stood on the line with their guns, and the train had to stop. 'This is a stick-up', said the kid. 'This is a kick up the arse when I speak to your father', replied the engine driver.

Summary descriptions of the configurations of Australian humour given by Jones and Andrews are worth quoting. They describe one as 'the ironic acceptance of a losing situation' which 'balances on the edge of a barely evident self-parody'[52]. They note that 'while bleak irony and anarchic exuberance are played off one against the other, in the end irony prevails...so that no matter how vigorous or absurd the eruption of comic disorder, everything remains as it was before'. 'For all its deflationary irreverent quality', they point out, 'Australian humour is usually an acknowlegement of the status quo'[53]. A relationship to the intractability of the physical environment of the continent and the conditions of life it has imposed is hard to deny.

Les Murray's comments on Australian humour lead us back to the recognition of its importance as a vehicle of the folk-wisdom of our culture. He notes the importance of what he calls 'clown-icons', the derisive symbols that have emerged in our culture— instancing such things as tomato sauce and gladioli. Although these clown-icons are not unique to Australia, he judges that they are 'more highly developed in Australia than anywhere else'. He contrasts the 'complexity and restraint' of the derisive humour they exemplify with the 'fatigue and angry despair' one finds in European parallels[54].

The 'ability to laugh at venerated things' in a way which is not essentially destructive 'may, in time', Murray writes, 'prove to be one of Australia's great gifts to mankind'. At bottom it can bespeak a profound wisdom, 'a spiritual laughter, a mirth that puts tragedy, futility and vanity alike in their place'[55]. This resource belongs to our 'vernacular culture', which has developed a 'wise and subtly ramified levity' with its origins in the 'underground traditions of working people's irony and fantastical peasant wit'. In most cultures, he points out, this wit has been submerged by a dominant upper class culture; but in our culture 'these things emerge into the daylight and grow, and the clown-icon is one of their first fruits'[56]. And so 'it may be, in the end, that humour is the touchstone for the viability of any import here...for Australia really seems to be where God put a sardonyx to the lips of Western man and teaches him to laugh wisely'[57]. Australian humour, it is clear, has roots in the egalitarian ethos.

4. Finding wisdom

What we have to say of the wisdom offered us in our Australian experience gathers together much of our discussion to this point. Our national story has taken European experience onto a new testing ground: in coming to terms with the barren reality of our island-continent, we have been invited to make a new evaluation of the pretensions which so often shape human existence. It is here, nonetheless, that we have found our true home. This continent has become our beloved and only land, the place where we must take up the struggle 'to be, and to remain human'.

Judith Wright points to the fact that two of our foremost novelists, H. H. Richardson and Patrick White, have dramatised in their works the situation just described. Both *The Fortunes of Richard Mahony* and *Voss* take up the theme of a meeting between 'the European mind' and Australia's 'raw, bleak and alien life and landscape'. In each case, Wright notes, the meeting has been a 'struggling...a suffering whose only consummation and reconciliation is found in death'[58]. The story of each of these seekers invites us, however, to recognise the possibility of understanding, loving and interpreting this strange land, even though it is a costly reconciliation. 'Knowledge', Voss's friend Laura Trevelyan tells us, 'was never a matter of geography. Quite the reverse, it overflows all maps that exist. Perhaps true knowledge only comes of death by torture in the country of the mind'[59].

'The South Land, with its "futile heart within a fair periphery", as James McAuley described it', writes Anthony Hassall, discussing the quests reflected in our Australian literature, 'was to elude many of its early seekers; and to disappoint many of its would-be exploiters'[60]. The result was that 'the expectation of disappointment entered into the national mythology; to be laughed at by Joseph Furphy, made tragic by Henry Handel Richardson, and mournfully celebrated by Henry Lawson'. This acceptance of a future which is going to bring disappointment to European expectations is at the heart of the dying which Richardson and White see as inevitable for those who are to share fully in the Australian project. But dying can also be the beginning of a new life, as White's novel invites us to recognise.

The European expectations to which we Australians must die were to be dramatically fulfilled in the North American continent. We must discover our own 'equilibrium', Judith Wright suggests, an equilibrium which allows us to find that this shy, sometimes cruel and capricious country 'is truly ours by right of understanding and acceptance', so that our existence may take to itself the new qualities it has to give as we begin to grow again[61].

Judith Wright's observations in the essay just cited serve as a good summary of what has emerged in the course of this discussion. Our success here was not to be a flattering triumph, but a survival through which we learnt 'endurance, persistence, a home-made ingenuity and a sardonic attitude to the failures and reverses' that were inevitable[62]. In this survival, the egalitarian spirit of mateship was 'the germ of "something new" that we now feel to be in some sense our own'[63]. If it developed as a necessity for survival, that germ nevertheless makes it possible for us to develop something of incomparable value in the tradition we share. As Judith Wright says, 'Furphy and Lawson were supremely right in seizing on it as their deepest theme': an Australian understanding of mateship which affirms 'that mutual trust implies for us equality... of the kind that transcends the necessary differences of circumstances and work and intelligence and income... this sense in the best of us that we are equal'[64].

In this Australian way, Wright suggests, we find 'the chief difference between, say, the Australian and the American dreams'[65]. The American ideal stresses the competitive individualistic element in life, the Australian ideal, on the other hand, 'emphasises man's duty to his brother, and man's basic equality, the mutual trust which is the force that makes society cohere'[66]. If they are rescued from the 'paralysis' of a self-serving legend, these values can provide 'the key to our proper nationhood' and make possible the 'separate contribution' we have to make to the world at large[67].

Other commentators extend the lesson. Manning Clark, speaking of the 'wisdom' that is to be found in the experience of failure, writes 'with such a wisdom a man can feel tenderness and compassion, indeed, can look with the eye of pity on all who are being tried in the fiery furnace of life in the Australian bush or the Australian suburbs'[68]. Clark acknowledges that Australians of Irish background found strength in 'the secret of charity, compassion and togetherness'[69]. He does not seem to acknowledge, however, that through this spirit, as Patrick O'Farrell has pointed out[70], they made an important contribution to the distinctive ethos which was coming to characterise the ongoing Australian conversation.

Patrick White's lessons are more sombre, perhaps. His main themes, in the words of Geoffrey Serle, are the 'solitariness of the individual and the view that men are self-destructive but redeemed by suffering'[71]. For White, however, ours is 'not a final and irrevocable state'. The 'love, simplicity, humility' which Serle points to as the principal virtues affirmed by White, the 'savage comedy' with which he scourges 'the socially pretentious' are not difficult to link with the egalitarianism to which Judith Wright has given a central place. Noel Rowe sees Serle's view of Patrick White's achievement as no more than partial. In his judgment, White was 'concerned to enact the process of vision itself', so that 'his images are more mythically inclined' than is generally recognised[72].

Both Judith Wright and Les Murray have spoken of the contribution we can make as a people to the conversation of the nations. Bruce Clunies Ross locates this contribution: 'in Australia, Europeans encountered a resistant environment, and two hundred years of engagement with this have exposed the limits of civilisation, just as they are becoming apparent everywhere else in the world'[73]. The wisdom we have been invited to find in our Australian experience is a wisdom the world as a whole must learn in the coming age. My colleague Tom Ryan has pointed to the distinct parallel that can be recognised between the Australian 'wisdom' I have been describing and the outlook expressed by the existentialist writer Albert Camus as he explores the limits of contemporary European civilisation[74]. Manning Clark speaks of his desire to make his history 'a celebration of life, a hymn in praise of life'. He gives expression to something of the wisdom he has found as an Australian when he says that this can only be done with authenticity by one who has looked into the heart of the 'darkness' that is the background to human existence, and 'has both a tenderness for everyone, and yet, paradoxically, a melancholy, a sadness, and a compassion because what matters most in life is never likely to happen'[75]. As I shall argue in the final chapter, what we have learned as Australians is not as distant as it may seem from wisdom of a higher kind.

[1]   'Some Religious Stuff I know about Australia', p.18, in D. Harris etc. (eds), *The Shape of Belief*, Homebush West (Lancer) N.S.W., 1982.
[2]   loc. cit.
[3]   Cited from *Clean Straw for Nothing* (1969) by Anthony J. Hassell, 'Quests', p.396, in *Penguin New Literary History of Australia*, L. Hergenhan (ed.).
[4]   'The Quest for an Australian Identity' (Inaugural Duhig Lecture), *The Catholic Leader*, 26 Aug 1979, p.3.
[5]   'Australia and the United States', p.396, in *Australia: The Daedalus Symposium*, S. Graubard (ed.).
[6]   'The Quest for an Australian Identity', loc. cit.
[7]   'Australia and the United States', p.397.
[8]   ibid., p.404.
[9]   *A Crucible of Prophets*, p.11.
[10]   'Heroes', p.60, in S. Graubard (ed.), *Australia: The Daedalus Symposium*.
[11]   Judith Wright, *Preoccupations in Autralian Poetry*, p.xix.
[12]   *Australia*, p.109.
[13]   'Quests', p.405, in *Penguin New Literary History of Australia*, L. Hergenhan (ed.).
[14]   'Quests', p.405.
[15]   *Voss*, p.447.
[16]   *The Creative Spirit in Australia*, p.65.
[17]   *Preoccupations in Australian Poetry*, p.73.
[18]   *The Creative Spirit in Australia*, p.65.
[19]   ibid., p.65.
[20]   'Literary Nationalism and the 1890s', *Aust. Literary Studies 5* (1971) pp.3–17.
[21]   1976 Boyer Lectures, p.15.
[22]   *The Creative Spirit in Australia*, p.65.
[23]   ibid., p.64.
[24]   'Realism and Documentary', p.247, in *Penguin New Literary History of Australia*, Hergenhan (ed.).
[25]   *Such Is Life*, p.95.
[26]   *Joseph Furphy*, in Series, *Australian Writers and Their Work*, Geoffrey Dutton (ed.), Melbourne, 1963, p.14.
[27]   Cited, McCarthy, *Gallipoli to the Somme*, pp.188–9.
[28]   ibid., p.191.
[29]   *Preoccupations in Australian Poetry*, p.73.

30   Sth Melbourne (Macmillan), 1978.
31   'Autobiography', p.564, in *Penguin New Literary History of Australia*, L. Hergenhan (ed.).
32   loc. cit.
33   *The Landscape of Australian Poetry*, Melbourne (Cheshire) 1967.
34   *Ideas for a Nation*, p.106.
35   *The Creative Spirit in Australia*, pp.110–11.
36   'Heroes', p.77, in S. Graubard (ed.), *Australia: The Daedalus Symposium*.
37   'Australian Humour', p.60.
38   P. O'Farrell, *The Irish in Australia*, pp.11–12.
39   Cantrell, *Writing of the 1890s*, p.12.
40   'Heroes', p.77 in S. Graubard (ed.), *Australia: The Daedalus Symposium*.
41   1976 Boyer Lectures, p.30.
42   loc. cit.
43   'Australian Humour', p.65.
44   *Kangaroo*, p.80.
45   Cited, McCarthy, *Gallipoli to the Somme*, p.147.
46   1976 Boyer Lectures, p.13.
47   'Australian Humour', p.66.
48   ibid., p.66.
49   loc. cit.
50   'Australian Humour', p.62.
51   ibid., p.63.
52   ibid., p.60.
53   ibid., p.74.
54   'Some Religious Stuff I Know about Australia', pp.16–17, in *The Shape of Belief*, D. Harris etc. (eds).
55   'Some Religious Stuff I Know about Australia', p.17.
56   loc. cit.
57   'Some Religious Stuff I Know about Australia', p.19.
58   *Preoccupations in Australian Poetry*, p.xvi.
59   *Voss*, p.446.
60   'Quests', p.393, in *Penguin New Literary History of Australia*, L. Hergenhan (ed.).
61   *Preoccupations in Australian Poetry*, p.xviii.
62   loc. cit.
63   ibid., p.xx.
64   ibid., p.xxi.
65   ibid., p.xxi.
66   ibid., pp.xxi–xxii.
67   ibid., p.xxii.
68   'The Quest for an Australian Identity', *The Catholic Leader*, 26 Aug 1979, p.3.
69   *A Short History of Australia*, p.77. He continues: 'They brought with them that charity of the poor towards each other, even when there was no claim to any relationship, and that compassion for the multitude they had learned from their holy faith'. Donald Horne makes a similar observation: 'the Irish, when they brought their faith, also brought the perception that the person who had compassion was to be preferred to the person who had gained the whole world' (*Ideas for a Nation*, p.72).
70   *The Irish in Australia*, pp.10–11.
71   *The Creative Spirit in Australia*, p.183.
72   In comments made to the writer.
73   'Literature and Culture', p.21, in *Penguin New Literary History of Australia*, L. Hergenhan (ed.).

⁷⁴ His comments are worth quoting at length: '1) There is a cosmic landscape devoid of "God", one that is harsh, at times malevolent (the Australian continent and North Africa). Nature is ambivalent in both: a source of suffering, yet a source of happiness once tamed or once contemplated and endured to the point of reconciliation. 2) The hero pits himself against impossible odds, where there is no triumph but only survival. 3) The hero is not of a noble stature that is flawed, so that he falls and rises above the fall, as in the classical tradition. Now he is part of common humanity. 4) They have heroes with modest claims: that the struggle is a value in itself... The best metaphor, then, is the humble bullock driver or the ordinary citizen doing his best against evil in the world (the plague in *La Peste*). 5) They envisage this struggle without reference to any absolute to vindicate or terminate it... 6) A crucial place is given to solidarity (Camus) or mateship (Australia). It is a trust in and need for other human beings as both necessary for survival, which results in a compassionate wisdom learned in adversity. 7) The hero is paradoxical and ironic. 8) The visions are primarily artistic rather than philosophical in form and content. Hence both points of view have the light and dark of art that involves ambiguity and irony. 9) There is a realistic lucidity in facing one's powerlessness in the face of destiny and circumstances one is unable to control (cf. Lawson). *They seem of differ, in that*: 10) Humour is more evident in the Australian hero's world... It is a healing, spiritualising form of humour... 11) There seems a stoic hope in both worlds... The fruits of that hope seem to be more optimistically grounded in the Australian hero's universe. 12) For Camus' hero solidarity has a more developed moral dimension which is embodied in a sense of social responsibility.'

⁷⁵ 1976 Boyer Lectures, p.12.

7.

THE LAND AS OUR ICON

To this point it is clear that the challenging environment presented by our island-continent has been the most potent factor in the ongoing experience of white Australians. I have already mentioned the overwhelming and quite unexpected impression made upon me the first time I saw the red heart of Australia, returning from overseas as a young man. Though unaware of it, I had already begun to form a relationship with the Australian continent which was fundamental to my identity as a human being. It is a relationship I share with other Australians. No doubt Carl Jung was right when he judged that our symbols and our myths spring from the earth in which we are nurtured.

It is one thing to acknowledge the fact of a relationship with the land, and another to understand the nature of this relationship. As we shall see, it is the outcome of a long and subtle cultural development.

1. Journey into the landscape

Making the landscape of the Australian continent our own has been a protracted and complex process. In his fine study *The Landscape of Australian Poetry* Brian Elliott traces this development as it is recorded in our literature. 'The long historical battle to grasp, absorb and express an environment so highly individual in itself', he writes, 'so defiant of all the traditional and established European expectations, provided a necessary education of the sensibilities in terms of local reality'[1]. It took many generations for Australians to make Australia their 'place' in the fullest meaning of that word.

Whether they clearly recognised the fact or not, Australia, as Judith Wright observes, meant 'something more to its new inhabitants than mere environment and mere land to be occupied, ploughed and brought into subjection'. From the first, it was 'the outer equivalent of an inner reality; first, and persistently, the reality of exile; second, though we now tend to forget this, the reality of newness and freedom'[2]. Following the course of this process can help us to understand ourselves more fully; it can also help those who are still coming to our shores in large numbers from other countries, as they seek to identify themselves with their adopted land.

The unfavourable impressions of those who glimpsed our continent before 1788 have often been quoted. 'The first prose poem about our country', writes Manning Clark, 'was possibly that sentence in which the Dutch summed up all their disenchantment and disappointment at what they had found: "He who would know this country must first walk over it"'[3]. Clark records the chorus of disappointment heard from those who first settled in the colony. 'From the coming of the First Fleet in January 1788 to the middle of the nineteenth century', he writes, 'most men of sensibility were dismayed when they first saw Australia'[4]. Bishop Broughton, for example, recorded in his diary the way his heart sank when in 1829 he first saw the 'dreary and cheerless' foreshores of Sydney harbour. Almost a century later, D. H. Lawrence's first impressions were similar. For Lawrence, the 'loveliest stretches of pale blue water' contrasted with the land which was 'so gloomy and lightless'; he was taken aback by 'the sun-refusing leaves of gum trees' which appeared to him 'like dark, hardened flakes of rubber'[5].

Bernard Smith's elaborately illustrated study *European Vision and the South Pacific 1768–1850*[6] provides abundant evidence of the extent to which perceptions of the antipodes were shaped by the models and conventions of European culture. As Geoffrey Dutton has put it in his poem on William Light, the designer of the city of Adelaide, the white pioneers of our land were strangers who 'came ashore, still looking over their shoulders'[7]. In 1788, Major Ross of the First Fleet wrote to friends in England, 'In the whole world there is not a worse country than what we have yet seen of this... here nature is reversed, and, if not so, she is nearly worn out'[8]. This idea of everything at the antipodes being turned about or reversed soon became a cliché which pre-empted the perceptions of the newcomers.

Barron Field, the author of the first book of verse printed in Australia whom I have already quoted, wrote 'Australia is a land of contraries, where the laws of nature seem reversed'[9]. A cultivated eccentric, Field gave expression to his bewilderment by describing in these poems the oddities of the antipodes with a sophisticated humour which was probably lost on most of his Australian contemporaries. His friend Charles Lamb, however, gave it an appreciative review in London. The kangaroo, one poem suggested, came from Nature 'on creation's holiday'; it is hailed, however, for redeeming Australia 'from utter failure'. Field described the Australian continent as a kind of 'after-birth' which 'emerged at the first sinning, / When the ground was therefore curst:— / And hence the barren wood'. The worrisome gum trees another observer at that time called 'nevergreens'[10]. Charles Darwin was certainly unimpressed, writing in his diary 'the climate is splendid and perfectly healthy; but to my mind its charms are lost by the uninviting aspects of the country'[11].

John Rickard considers the view 'that Europeans found the Australian environment hostile, alien, oppressive, and that they had great difficulty in coming to terms with it aesthetically' to be something of a myth; and he quotes in support of this view those who from the first found the climate 'salubrious' and 'enchanting'[12]. The words of Charles Darwin which I have just cited provide a clear response to this view. The climate, which he admires, is something very different from the impression of strangeness the continent had upon those who found themselves in this new environment, a strangeness completely at odds with the world of European culture which had formed them, and which Darwin found quite 'uninviting'.

Shortly before reading Rickard's comment I spent some weeks in New Zealand, where the distinction being made was very real in my experience. There I had no difficulty in admiring the scenery and the bush of remote parts of the country; at the same time I felt more than once positively oppressed by the primeval fern trees and windswept conifers. Their strangeness became profoundly disturbing for me as I tried to recapture the experience of New Zealand's isolated settlers in the nineteenth century.

It is certainly true, as we have seen, that European romanticism led early nineteenth century Australians to dwell upon the stranger features of their new environment. Even when they admired it, they were not at home with it as we are today. John Dunmore Lang's experience of Australia was similar in many ways to the New Zealand experience I have just described. He reacted vigorously to the suggestion 'that there is nothing like interesting scenery in New South Wales'. He had seen for himself 'natural scenery combining every variety of the beautiful, the picturesque, the wild, the sublime'. His enthusiasm was qualified, however. He admitted to a general monotony. The interior he found so oppressive that, echoing Field, he speaks of it as a place where 'the mind unavoidably partakes of the gloominess of nature; and the only idea that has forcibly hold of it is, that such must assuredly be the region on which the ancient primeval curse, to which the earth was subjected for the sin of man, has especially lighted'[13].

Lang was one of the nineteenth century observers who, as Patrick Morgan writes, 'treated Australia as though it were a blank page, on which any image they desired could be impressed'[14]. Exiles, they brought their frames of perception from the old world. Very important among these was European romanticism. Few descriptions of the Australian landscape have been so frequently quoted and commented upon as that of Marcus Clarke, published in the Preface he wrote to the *Poems* of Adam Lindsay Gordon (1833–70), of which mention has already been made. Clarke struggled to pay a fitting tribute to the land which, as an intelligent and sensitive observer who had spent most of his life in Australia, he knew it deserved. In fact, as Elliott has pointed out, Clarke's descriptive passage originated in pieces of art criticism which he wrote ten years earlier, when the romantic painters Louis Buvelot and Nicholas Chevalier exhibited their works in Melbourne[15]. The constraints of an essentially European perspective made it difficult for him to achieve his purpose.

The 'dominant note of Australian scenery' is, according to Clarke, that of Edgar Allan Poe's poetry, 'Weird Melancholy'. An 'airy', 'freshly happy' poem could not be written about it. The mountain forests, he said, are 'funereal, secret, stern'. 'Their solitude is desolation. They seem to stifle, in their black gorges, a story of sullen despair... The savage winds shout among the rock clefts'. The gums are 'melancholy'. The animal life of the 'frowning hills' he saw as 'grotesque or ghostly'. 'Hopeless explorers' have named the mountains, the 'frightful grandeur' of which fills the soul with 'their sentiment of defiant ferocity', so that it becomes 'steeped in bitterness'.

Having sounded all the notes dictated by the expectations of romanticism, Clarke attempted to convey to his English readers the strange attractiveness of the land in which Gordon's verses had been written. It has a grandeur, he wrote, which makes the 'lonely horseman' feel 'that the trim utilitarian civilisation which bred him shrinks into insignificance besides the contemptuous grandeur of forest and ranges'. There is a poetry to be found in the trees and flowers, but 'it differs from those of other countries'. Wanting to respond to old criticisms, Clarke came close to capturing something of the uniqueness of the Australian bush:

> In Australia alone is to be found the Grotesque, the Weird, the strange scribblings of nature learning how to write. Some see no beauty in our trees without shade, our flowers without perfume, our birds who cannot fly, and

our beasts who have not yet learned to walk on all fours. But the dweller in the wilderness acknowledges the subtle charm of this fantastic land of monstrosities. He becomes familiar with the beauty of loneliness. Whispered to by the myriad tongues of the wilderness, he learns the language of the barren and the uncouth, and can read the hieroglyphs of haggard gum trees, blown into odd shapes, distorted with fierce hot winds, or cramped with cold nights, when the Southern Cross freezes in a cloudless sky of icy blue. The phantasmagoria of that wild dreamland termed the Bush interprets itself, and the Poet of our desolation begins to comprehend why free Esau loved his heritage of desert sand better than all the bountiful richness of Egypt[16].

According to Brian Elliott, it was Gordon who 'found the key which opened the landscape to interpretation'[17]. In his judgment, Gordon 'is of the greatest importance as a landscapist, both for what he saw, and the way he saw it'[18]. Perhaps it was the very nonchalance with which Gordon looked on the land—an enforced exile, through personal circumstances, making the most of a bad lot, as it were—which enabled him to set aside the romantic seriousness of the times which hampered Clarke.

Gordon concentrates his attention upon the ordinary: he is most impressive, Elliott points out, not describing the splendours of sunset and dawn, but 'when he describes (or merely evokes) some other time of day: hours of sunshine, or glimpses of starlight'. His poetry is best 'when he is capturing routine impressions... when he records what everybody can see', and 'the fact that everyone does see just these things makes the experience memorable'. It is this 'common vision' which makes his poetry 'such a striking key to the colonial attitude to landscape'[19]. A frontier figure of the type to be glorified by Kipling, Gordon had immense appeal. For sixty years after his death in 1870 at the age of thirty-seven, Elliott tells us, 'he was regarded as Australia's principal poet'[20].

Analysing Gordon's portrayal of the landscape, Elliott finds it has certain constantly recurring features. Outstanding among these is his mastery of the effects of light — sometimes the subtleties of half-light, sometimes the brilliant light of a clear Australian day,

When the sky-line's blue burnished resistance, Makes deeper the dreamiest distance.

If he could not have the romance, beauty and history of the old world's landscape, Gordon had discovered that 'there was a living light in this landscape... new and not understood, but beautiful and appealing in its way'[21]. It is this same light which Tom Roberts and his companions of the Heidelberg School were soon to bring to clearer consciousness for their fellow Australians.

But what is most important about Gordon's landscape is the way it is always animated by a human presence: 'man's presence must be felt as an influence', Elliott writes, 'bushmen, his own real acquaintances'. Thus 'the landscape humanised when seen through a veil of tobacco smoke—for him an emblem of contemplative peace' becomes, with the pellucid sun, a symbol 'of more than ordinary importance' for Gordon. Sometimes this humanising of the environment is conveyed through the riding rhythm of his verse. Gordon's view of the landscape is fleeting, 'glimpses rather than views'. In this landscape he finds a capacity to respond naturally to bush birds and flowers[22].

Though he sees himself as an exile, Gordon is able to situate himself within the real Australian landscape and contribute to the building of a new cultural world which is firmly established in this landscape. Clarke, by way of contrast, though he has begun to love the same Australian landscape, is still standing apart with his English readers within another world. Elliott speaks of the other 'small voices' of Australian poetry which, at this time, took up the project of affirming an existence located first and foremost within the Australian environment. They were 'attempting to express the simple enjoyment of ordinary sensitive and perceptive people, living in a landscape which they were either born to, or had wholeheartedly accepted as their own; and which, they were convinced, lacked not beauty or splendour of its own kind, but only articulate voices to express it'[23].

Along with the small poetic voices Elliott has referred to were soon to be heard the more strident assertions of the literature associated with the *Bulletin*, unhesitatingly aligning themselves with Furphy's 'bias: aggressively Australian'. The *Bulletin* provided a forum for the celebrated debate between Henry Lawson and Banjo Paterson in 1892. Both men owned the Australian outback; the point at issue is whether it should be owned within the romantic framework adopted by Paterson, or not.

By the turn of the century the appropriation which Gordon had unreflectingly begun had become capable of a reflective awareness. H. H. Richardson is still mildly apologetic in her reference to 'the country's very shortcomings' as the starting point for the affectionate portrayal she gives in the opening paragraphs of the last part of her trilogy.

A. G. Stephens, writing in 1901, makes no apology. On the contrary he reacts sharply against the 'strangers' who 'foist upon us the English ideals' of bright colours: 'Verlaine's cult of Faded Things, extolling the hinted hue before gross colour, finds a natural home in Australia—in many aspects a land of Faded Things—of delicate purples, delicious greys, and dull, dreamy olives and ochres'. He stretches his point a little when he cites Morley Roberts who, having been raised among Australia's subtleties, found the colours of the English countryside 'unpleasant to the eye', even 'inartistic'. To see a gum tree touched by the breeze, writes Stephens, 'is to receive an aesthetic education'. He concludes with enthusiasm: 'In a word, let us look at our country... through clear Australian eyes, not through bias-bleared English spectacles, and there is no more beautiful country in the world. It will be the fault of the writers, not of the land, if Australian literature does not by-and-by become memorable'[24].

Victor Daley's poem 'Corregio Jones', of the same period, ridicules an imagined artist of this name, 'of pure Australian race', who found native subjects 'too common place'. He would prefer to paint 'Knights in mail or robbers in a camp'—'Grey gums', he cries 'and box-woods pale, / They give my genius cramp'[25]. In a more serious vein, Daley's poem 'The Muses of Australia' compares the 'Desert Muse' with the 'Muse of Streams' ('Kendall saw her face in dreams') and the 'Mountain Muse' ('Dead Gordon knew her well'). Men who follow the Desert Muse, he warns, may 'perish with their dreams':

In silence dread she walks apart—
Yet I have heard men say
The song that slumbers in her heart
Will wake the world some day[26].

The 'aggressively Australian' stance adopted by the provincial culture, as it owned 'an environment so highly individual in itself', was in danger, of course, of becoming what A. A. Phillips has called 'the Cultural Cringe Inverted': 'the attitude of the Blatant Blather-skite, the God's-own-country-and-I'm-a-better-man-than-you-are Australian Bore'[27]. It is a mark of Australia's culture having come to maturity that our major poets have achieved an unselfconscious capacity to make use of the imagery provided by Australia's very distinctive environment.

Elliott judges that Christopher Brennan was 'much more at one with his native land—and its landscape—than many are aware... The landscape is alive in his poetry, as it is in all the work of his contemporaries, and if it doesn't constantly appear that is because it has been assimilated'[28]. The gentle John Shaw Neilson's natural use of the Australian environment is such that, in the words of Judith Wright, there is evoked 'a new and different vision of a world no less real than our own, of the world as a parable, a tale invented to show men where the truth really lies'[29].

In Kenneth Slessor, Brian Elliott writes, we find 'a complete assimilation and functional application of landscape to consummate poetic ends'[30]. He instances Slessor's masterpiece 'Five Bells', in which the waters of Sydney Harbour provide a most natural and fertile matrix of images and symbolism in a completely unselfconscious way. James McAuley, in his poem 'The True Discovery of Australia', mocks the extravagances of the nationalistic school. His poem 'Envoi' is an unflinching look at contemporary Australia, where the 'people are hard-eyed, kindly, with nothing inside them ...independent, but you could not call them free'—yet the poet knows he is 'fitted to the land as the soul is to the body': its hard-won future will be also his. McAuley's 'Terra Australis' is a magnificent crafting of Australian images, literary memory and poetic imagination[31].

Judith Wright is a poet whose long association with and concern for our land finds a voice in much of her poetry. Her early poem, 'Bullocky', already discussed, is the work of a poet completely at home in the Australian environment, 'so highly individual in itself', able to call upon the fabric of that environment and the memories with which we have adorned it to provide themes and symbols which carry the reader to a deep meeting with what is ultimate in our common existence. The struggling, half-crazy old-timer is transformed as the poem progresses into a towering and strangely mystical character, a kind of father figure nourishing the nation from his grave.

Ivor Indyk says of Wright's poems 'they are clearly intended to have the force of myth, as if they were inaugurating a white Dreaming'[32]. Elliott makes the same point with regard to this poem: the old man becomes more than himself, he is 'also a symbol of the laborious, painful, dogged, slow yet somehow inspired conquest of the primitive landscape'. As 'all the old traditional animation-symbolism' is focused 'upon a single human figure', the half-crazy bullocky 'becomes a haunting spirit, much like one of the place-spirits of Aboriginal belief'[33].

Relationship to the environment is fundamental to the awareness of Les Murray. It holds him in a kind of reverence: all that has been achieved by his forebears in their New South Wales north coast valley 'amounts to a human breach in the silence'[34]. He is called back to read its secrets. 'It will be centuries / before men are truly at home in this country'[35]—either on the old farm ('the city will never quite hold me. I will be always / coming back here on the up-train, peering, leaning / out of the window to see'[36]) or on the way to the outback, 'to the outside country / where the sealed roads end / the far, still Centre'. He identifies with the 'plain young wife at the tankstand fetching water' who stands to 'gaze / at the mountains in wonderment / looking for a city'[37].

A similar process of identification has gone on among painters. In 1892 Arthur Streeton wrote to Tom Roberts, 'If I can raise the coin I intend to go straight inland (away from all polite society), and stay two or three years and create some things entirely new, and try to translate some of the great hidden poetry that I know is here, but have not seen or felt it'[38].

At that same time the poet G. E. Evans showed himself, in Elliott's words, 'the first to sense keenly the impact of the meta-physical landscape'. He wrote,

> Her song is silence; unto her
> Its mystery clings.
> Silence is the interpreter
> Of deeper things[39].

Half a century later, John Coburn's radiant paintings remind one of the serenity of John Shaw Neilson's contemplative poetry. Coburn tells us that he seeks the inner meaning of an environment which he took in as a child in North Queensland. 'I seek images that...I knew as a child, blackened tree trunks after a bushfire, a flight of screeching pink galahs over a dry creek bed'. His colours consciously mirror the browns and yellows and ochres of the soil.

Sidney Nolan, with his Ned Kelly series and other paintings, and Arthur Boyd, with such paintings as his 'Love, Marriage and Death of a Half Caste' series, have drawn on the environment to elaborate legendary themes in a way which parallels the mythical bullocky of Judith Wright and James McAuley's 'angophora' gum that 'preaches on the hillside / with the gestures of Moses'. Russell Drysdale depicts a landscape that challenges us, as the measure of our human existence—in the words of Bernard Smith 'a landscape alien to man, harsh, weird, spacious and vacant, given over to the oddities and whimsies of nature, fit only for heroes and clowns, saints, exiles and primitive men'[40].

2. Recognising another presence

The landscape is owned, becomes the ground upon which we can build our world, when we have *inhabited* it. But this land was inhabited long before the arrival of white colonists. If we have suppressed the memory of how we dispossessed its original inhabitants, we should not be surprised that our relationship with it has not been untroubled. It is significant that several of those quoted as exemplifying the final phase of our appropriation of the Australian landscape have drawn our attention once again to the Aboriginal presence. The poignant landscapes of Drysdale were, in fact, the first serious portrayals of the Aboriginal people for generations.

Ivor Indyk sees the poems of Mary Gilmore as conveying 'the empty landscapes and godless skies left by the destruction of aboriginal life'[41]. Perhaps the 'black gorges' and 'sullen despair' of the Australian bush described by Marcus Clarke in the passage already discussed were inspired by more than the conventions of romanticism and intimate something of the uneasiness I have spoken of. He refers, certainly, in his brief Preface, to the strange beliefs of the natives and to their 'dismal chant'.

The remarkable observations of D. H. Lawrence have a great importance in any discussion of the way in which the Australian landscape has been perceived. To quote Elliott, Lawrence 'displayed an extraordinary sensitivity in his appreciation of the Australian landscape image'; he 'reacted strongly to a persuasive mystical power in the Australian landscape, never before so accurately evaluated'[42]. During his brief stay in this country, Lawrence's intuitive genius achieved insights which touch on what is the key to the appropriation of the Australian landscape: the meaningfulness of a physical environment coming from its being seen as inhabited by a human presence.

In the novel *Kangaroo*, Lawrence grapples with his reactions to the unfamiliar Australian environment. In the opening pages of the book[43] he describes, through the character Somers, the frightening experience of a meeting with the 'spirit of the place' in the moonlight of the Western Australian bush. The bush 'scared him...so phantom-like, so ghostly, with its tall pale trees and many dead trees, like corpses, partly charred by bushfires'. It 'seemed to be hoarily waiting'; he wanted to 'penetrate its secret...What was it waiting for?' Under a 'huge electric moon' that made the tree trunks look 'like pale aborigines among the dark-soaked foliage', he became aware of a presence, 'big and aware and hidden'. Walking on among the 'tall, nude, dead trees', he was overcome by 'the terror of the bush'. He sensed again the presence among 'the weird, white, dead trees' and 'in the distances of the bush'. Turning back in fear he was unable to escape the 'horrid thing' he had encountered, which must surely be 'the spirit of the place'.

> He felt it was watching, and waiting. Following with certainty, just behind his back. It might have reached a long black arm and gripped him. But no, it wanted to wait. It was not tired of watching its victim. An alien people—a victim. It was biding its time with a terrible ageless watchfulness, waiting for a far-off end, watching the myriad intruding white men[44].

There is no escaping reference to a disquieting Aboriginal presence, a presence which seems to have left only ghostly memories, dead and charred corpses, foliage that has been soaked in blood, but which cannot be banished and waits patiently the moment when its dark arm will reach out and take revenge. On a later page, Lawrence once more makes the Aboriginal association explicit:

> ... they saw the magical range of Blue Mountains. And all this hoary space of bush between. The strange, as it were, *invisible* beauty of Australia, which is undeniably there, but which seems to lurk just beyond the range of our white vision. You feel you can't *see*—as if your eyes hadn't the vision in time to correspond with the outside landscape. For the landscape is so unimpressive, like a face with little or no features, a dark face. It is so aboriginal, out of our ken, and it hangs back aloof. Somers always felt he looked at it through a cleft in the atmosphere; as one looks at one of the... aborigines with his wonderful dark eyes that have such incomprehensible ancient shine in them, across gulfs of unbridged centuries[45].

Lawrence was unsettled and troubled in another way, as his perceptive genius recognised the tenuous nature of the foothold white Australians had established for themselves. Having banished the black presence, they had not established a substantial presence for themselves, and so they had rendered the Australian sky 'humanless', and the atmosphere 'unwritten'[46]. This sky does not have the impression of 'closing in' as the European sky does; the 'vacancy' that results is 'almost terrifying'. There is an 'absence of any inner meaning' together with a 'great sense of open spaces'[47].

Worse than this, Lawrence sensed that the white presence has been destructive and exploitative. More than once he was offended by a lack of respect for the place, by the way in which rubbish was discarded 'over the fence', as the saying went: 'this litter of bungalows and tin cans scattered for miles and miles'[48]. In *Kangaroo*, Somers's European wife observes to an Australian male that it 'feels as if no one has ever loved' this 'wonderful' land, whereas the other countries of the earth have 'been loved so passionately'. Without being loved, Australia could never be 'a happy country, a bride country—or a mother country'. She would love it if she were Australian, 'love the very earth of it—the very sand and dryness of it—more than anything'. The Australian grants that she is probably right. On reflection he thinks that 'most Australians come to hate the Australian earth a good bit before they're done with it'. If the land is a 'bride', he says, she is not the sort many want to take on: 'she drinks your sweat and your blood, and then as often as not lets you down, does you in'. The European visitor thinks it would take a 'lot of fierce love'. The Australian has the last word: 'They treat the country more like a woman they pick up in the streets than a bride to my way of thinking'[49].

Lawrence's perceptions were, of course, largely intuitive. In 1922 he almost certainly had no way of knowing that the Aboriginal attitude to the land had been one of reverence and love. Lawrence sensed the importance and power of the Aboriginal presence in the land; we may well ask ourselves what he would have made of Stanner's report, already cited, that he had seen an Aboriginal 'embrace the earth he walked on'.

Five years after *Kangaroo* was published, a new edition of Spencer and Gillen's pioneering study of Aboriginal life and customs aroused great interest in anthropological circles. Other studies, especially those of T. G. H. Strehlow, were soon to follow. The young South Australian poet Rex Ingamells (d.1955), taking his cue from Lawrence's imaginative insights, and benefiting from the new appreciation of Aboriginal culture—particularly its relationship to the physical environment—called Australians to a new awareness of the land. His initiatives gave rise to the Jindyworobak movement in Australian poetry. This movement signalled the fact that the relationship of white Australians to their country would never be the same again. If inhabitation makes the physical environment accessible, the fact that, prior to European settlement, Australia had been inhabited for countless generations through the Aboriginal Dreaming provided the basis for a remarkable expansion of white awareness.

Gordon's frontier horseman, with his early morning pipe, had inhabited the landscape and made it a place we could own. Beside the age-old, almost mystical, relationship of the Aboriginal people with every feature of the land, however, Gordon's device seems to be almost an empty contrivance, the momentary presence of lonely figures in a not unfriendly, but still strange landscape. Today, as Brian Elliott observes, even those writers who make no explicit reference to the Aboriginal presence would not repudiate it as a powerful new influence[50]. I have already referred to examples of this influence in the poetry of Judith Wright and the painting of Arthur Boyd.

As Elliott writes, 'the Jindyworobak programme introduced a new kind of place awareness', a new dimension of 'sheer spirituality' demanding recognition. This awareness 'had the effect of creating a large reservoir of romantic imagery and suggestion, partly of a landscape nature and partly tribal and totemic' to be drawn upon[51]. Thus white Australians have taken up the process of restoring the Aboriginal people to the landscape: 'they seemed to be so much part of the country', writes Elliott, 'that they could be supposed a permanent part of the landscape; and they gave symbolic significance to a national prospect, within which humanity itself—the spirit of man, including all men—took a new, bare essential, primitive, quasi-religious energy'[52].

The time was ripe for this development. Quite independently of the Jindyworobaks, it seems, Eleanor Dark adopted in her novel *The Timeless Land* (1941) an attitude to the land very similar to theirs. In telling the story of the beginnings of white settlement, largely from the point of view of the Aboriginal people, she adopted the recurring device of making the land a silent witness to the drama which was beginning to unfold. She shows Governor Phillip, for example, reflecting upon the attitude of the blacks, not exactly hostile nor really friendly, 'simply watchful'. 'He looked past them at the trees which clothed the hillside, and knew what it was. The land itself!... Neither welcoming nor repelling, neither genial nor inimical. Only watching out of some colossal past in whose arms they had rested so securely for so many ages that no change seemed possible... The watchful land, the watchful dark eyes' made the century of progress he was contemplating seem 'the hundredth part of a second'[53]. Rex Ingamells acknowledged the influence D. H. Lawrence had on the Jindyworobak movement. Reading this page of Eleanor Dark, it is hard to escape the impression that her inspiration came also from the passages of Lawrence we have just quoted.

The children's writer Patricia Wrightson has adopted a similar point of view. 'It is time we stopped trying to see elves and dragons and unicorns in Australia', she writes. 'They never belonged here, and no ingenuity can make them real'. Calling upon Aboriginal lore, she suggests to children 'another kind of magic, a kind that must have been shaped by the land itself at the edge of the Australian vision'[54].

This development reminds us once again of Bernard Smith's observation that our history is a challenge 'to become, and to remain human' in the concrete reality of the human situation. Literature is the register of a culture, articulating awarenesses which are present but often barely conscious in the life of a people. There can be little doubt that Australian consciousness as a whole has been profoundly affected by the discovery of the Aboriginal Dreaming as an age-old inhabitation of our strange continent. As we acknowledge this, we should recall Stanner's comment that we may well look upon ourselves as 'an affluent society enjoying the afterglow of an imagined past... reaching out for symbols and values that are not authentically its own but will do because it has none of its own that are equivalent'[55]. Without a proper reconciliation with the Aboriginal people, whom we have treated so unjustly in the past, our owning of their Dreaming could be something of a 'cheap grace' only compounding the moral compromise which has become a part of the identity of white Australians.

3. The inner landscape of the Australian soul

If ambiguities remain, the Australian landscape has left its imprint upon the depths of the Australian psyche. Few people, for instance, seem to be further from the thought of the outback than Barry Humphries as he satirises the foibles of Australian suburbia. Yet, as he told an interviewer at the time of the Australian bicentenary, the landscape of Australia's interior constitutes a determining symbol for him: he is 'always conscious of the desert inside Australia, of the vacuum in the heart of it'.

Although H. H. Richardson, author of what is generally considered Australia's greatest novel, left Australia permanently—apart from one brief visit—at the age of seventeen, the country remained in her bones. In the opening passage of the final part of her trilogy, *The Fortunes of Richard Mahony*, we meet a Mahony who 'could see less beauty than ever in' the country's 'dun and arid landscape'. 'It was left to a later generation to discover this', the writer continues, obviously speaking from her own experience, 'to those who, with their mother's milk drank in a love of sunlight and space, of inimitable blue distances and gentian-blue skies'. To them 'the country's very shortcomings were, in time, to grow dear': 'the scanty, ragged foliage', 'the unearthly stillness of the bush', the 'red roads running towards a steadily receding horizon', 'the colours in apparent colourlessness'. The exile who has come to know Australia, she writes, will be overcome by a 'rank nostalgia' for the smells of the bush, 'even for the sting and tang of countless miles of bush ablaze'.

Mahony's burial in the novel's final scene—within earshot of the surf of the Southern Ocean, that 'beyond a sandy ridge...breaks and booms eternally on the barren shore'—is portrayed as an ultimate reconciliation: 'On all sides the eye can range unhindered, to where the vast earth meets the infinitely vaster sky'; as his grave becomes no longer recognisable, the 'rich and kindly earth of his adopted country absorbed his perishable body, as the country had never contrived to make its own, his wayward, vagrant spirit'[56].

Christina Stead (d.1983), another Australian author, who spent over forty years away from her native land, wrote on her return in 1969 of the recovery of a childhood sense of the 'wide waters and skies', in a land where one is 'nearer to the planets'[57]. Eleanor Dark, whose views I have already referred to, concludes her novel *Tomorrow and Tomorrow* with the brief but telling sentence 'The earth remains'. Writing in 1911, C. E. W. Bean makes his point with a typical flourish. The Australian, he predicts, will always have a sense of the outback, where 'he comes in the end to the mysterious half-desert country where men have to live the lives of strong men'; 'the life of that mysterious country', he adds, 'will affect Australian imagination much as the life of the sea has affected that of the English'[58].

In the Australia of my youth, a number of Australian writers—Ion Idriess, Frank Clune and William Hatfield, for example—describing the continent and its history had become household names because of the appeal their works had for many Australians. Flora Eldershaw writes of these authors 'they give a romantic vision of a world with which many... secretly or openly want to identify themselves, the unique Australian world that is the possession and the kingdom of our imagination... They are wonder books... They are about *us*, even if we are townsmen, knowing no more of Australia than the face of the city in which we live'[59].

In his poem 'Strata', R. D. Fitzgerald declares that he has counted it a 'precious gift', that he has always been close to Australia's 'cliff, creek, ravine... red gravel of the ridge... some ledge neighbourly to the sun'; for his one inspiration in a changing world was

> that starved
> rock-mass to which one clung
> inwardly, where, wind-carved
> it woke leaf-shadowed, bird-sung.

Les Murray puts it more pithily in his 'Second Essay on Interest', in which he addresses the emu:

> my kinships, too, are immemorial and recent,
> like my country, which abstracts yours in words.

The novelist Randolf Stow, writing in 1961, said that Australia provided 'raw material' as 'an enormous symbol for the whole earth, at all times, both before and during the history of man'. Those who are seen against the Australian landscape, he suggested, are seen as if with the eyes of 'the newborn'[60]. The playwright Ray Matthew finds a similar symbolism in the landscape interiorised by Australians: ' "Australia" is not so much what a gum tree looks like as what a gum tree means'[61]. 'The imagined landscape at the heart of Australia', writes Bruce Clunies Ross, 'remains a compelling influence on Australian culture and a valid symbol, often endowed with the traditional associations of deserts, as places of visionary revelation or sterility and emptiness'[62]. Earlier pages have provided examples of these approaches.

The historian Geoffrey Blainey, reminding us of what we have seen concerning the formation of the Australian legend, sees this interior landscape as having taken shape through the interaction between Australia's 'creative artists' and the Australian people at large. 'For Australians of the coastal towns', he writes, 'the vision of who they are and what Australia is has been profoundly shaped by artists depicting in word and paint the life and landscape of that outback where the horizon is never reached'. He judges that no English creative writer, apart from Charles Dickens, has seized the imagination of Englishmen as Gordon, Lawson and Paterson seized the Australian imagination. In a similar way, he sees the painters Streeton, Roberts, Nolan, Drysdale and Williams as having possessed the public mind in a way which has no parallel in England[63].

Manning Clark's Australian is one who 'has had at least one great love in his life'—'the fragile beauty in our ancient continent'. He too is grateful for the superb way in which 'imaginative writers like D. H. Lawrence, Marcus Clarke and Patrick White' and 'painters like Sidney Nolan, Arthur Boyd and Russell Drysdale' have given us access to this beauty[64].

In the judgment of Judith Wright, 'there is a sense...in which the idea of Australia is a central, almost mystical, symbol in our literature'. The symbolic vision it provides can be one of a 'regenerative innocence' which brings 'a purification which is the result of hardship and endurance, of sacrifice of personal ease, sacrifice perhaps of life itself'[65].

These words bring to mind the diary in which Stan Arneil, the young Australian soldier, recorded the ordeal of his years as a prisoner of war in Changi and on the Thailand railway. It is a remarkable document from many points of view, not least of all being the way it makes it possible for all of us to meet this remarkable Australian[66]. Stan Arneil must have represented in many ways the young Australians of that time. As he yearns time and again for his homeland, the places which in recollection nourish his hopes come back like a refrain, giving us a kind of atlas of the Australia of his inner landscape: Sydney Harbour, particularly at night, St Mary's Cathedral and the domain, sunset over the Nepean River, the quiet of Penrith from the evening train, the paths of Katoomba. The most expansive entry of all[67] carries him back to happy days in the Megalong Valley, where he and a friend talked of Lawson, and to hitchhiking out on the Western Slopes, where he sat alone on the deserted verandah of an old bush school at sunset and sheltered in a deserted barn and watched the lightning over Mt Arthur.

Being Australian involves coming to terms at a very fundamental level with the physical environment of our continent. Human existence and identity, whether personal, political or cultural, is of its nature realised in and through relationships to a particular society and to the physical environment which shapes its culture. If being human is to become self-conscious and articulate, it must do so through a matrix of symbols, themes and story lines which have their reality within this concrete context. It is not difficult to recognise a relationship between the bush legend which has served

Australians in their search for an identity and the inner landscape
of the Australian soul.

As Bernard Smith observes, the 'vitality and capacity for survival'
of any moral system will depend upon the qualities 'it brings to the
solution of human problems during its emergence at a particular
time and place'. The ongoing 'struggle to be, and to remain human'
will call upon resources born of its own experience, and it must
continually test what it has achieved 'against the successive
challenges of its history'[68]. What Smith says has applications which
extend to all aspects of our attempts to build a world in which we
can have an authentic human existence. The deprivation suffered
by an exile or a refugee is radical and painful.

Those who first took up the conversation which has made white
Australia were exiles of one kind or another. The process whereby
we have come to own this continent as 'our place' has been a long
one and not always straightforward. Understanding this process
more completely can give us a better grasp of the symbolic function the Australian continent and its peculiar features have
assumed for us.

4. A cruel love

We live in a strange continent. Henry Lawson called it 'the worst
dried-up and God forsaken country'. Brian Elliott speaks more
soberly of 'an environment so highly individual'. Most people
coming to Australia, Craig McGregor remarks, 'expect it to feel
young'. To their surprise, they find a country where 'the bush
scrabbles across one of the oldest and flattest land masses in the
world, scoured and shaped and worn by the wind and rain for
aeons before even the aborigines arrived; there is a curious feeling
of age and permanence, of a people who have achieved some sort
of balance with a forbidding but neutral environment'[69]. He goes
on to quote Mary Gilmore:

> I'm old
> Botany Bay;
> Stiff in the joints,
> Little to say.

> Old Botany Bay
> Taking the sun
> From day to day.

It has sometimes been suggested that Australians today relate
more to the beach as an environment than to the bush. We have
heard C. E. W. Bean, early in the century, making the contrast and
warning that *true* Australians are nurtured in the bush, not among

'the sea-beaches and soft breezes' of the coast. As Richard White has pointed out, journalistic iconography has turned from the bush to the beach. Yet it seems that the disjunction is false. It was the island-continent as a whole which had begun to claim me when my first sight of its red interior filled me with such unexpected emotion in 1958. I expect that many Australians would share an experience in which the ocean margin has its full impact when one stands on a magnificent beach aware that it is the edge of the old continent Craig McGregor has described. The stillness of the interior is only taken in completely as one realises that the strangeness it bespeaks stretches in so many directions to the edge of vast empty oceans. I take it this is what Craig McGregor is ultimately referring to when he speaks of our beach resorts as being 'strangely melancholy'[70].

Having followed the course of the Murray to its mouth in South Australia, C. E. W. Bean's imagination is filled with an awareness of the continent as a whole. 'So this is the end. Sitting there, on a white sandhill, I can see them — the freshes from the Queensland hills, the snow of Kosciusko, the Macquarie marshes, the Darling lakes, the Anabranch, the Warrego, even the Paroo River when it is a river — sitting here I can see them all...'[71].

From a geological point of view, our continent is unique in many ways[72]. A large part of Western Australia constituted a section of Gondwanaland, the land mass from which the present lands of the southern hemisphere had their origin through the process of continental drift. Having been exposed above sea level for 2500 million years or more, it has one of the most weathered surfaces of the planet. Other parts of the continent acquired their present characteristics by being several times submerged by seas and lakes. They are bordered by sand dunes, a legacy of that past age, and have been left exceptionally dry and infertile. Yet when the irregular rains come, these great desert areas are capable of producing a miraculous abundance of flowers and ephemeral vegetation, the seeds of which lie dormant through the scorching heat of the subsequent dry period which may last for many years. Huge limestone deposits beneath the topsoil of the Nullarbor Plains on the southern rim of the continent were produced by a depositing of marine organisms when that area was under the sea.

A crescent of more fertile land on the south-eastern margin of the continent, where most of the population is concentrated, easily creates an illusion that Australia is well provided with forests. In fact only four per cent of the continent has forests and many of these are being depleted. The western slopes of the Great Dividing Range, where much of the nation's pastoral industry has been established, are particularly fragile. Prior to white settlement, only soft-pad footed animals grazed on the land, and the Aboriginal custom of burning off the ground cover for hunting purposes fostered the growth of delicate native grasses in the light, thin topsoil.

The Australian continent, therefore, did not have a capacity for development comparable with that of more fertile new world countries. Its physical reality imposed severe limitations which the settlers were slow to recognise. Flattened by aeons of weathering, surrounded by immense tracts of ocean, its climate is devastating in its extremes. Droughts, floods, bushfires as unpredictable and terrible as are to be found in any part of the world make agriculture in most parts of the continent uncertain and precarious. As Henry Lawson comments, beginning one of his yarns, agriculture in Australia is 'a game of chance. It depends mainly on the weather, and that, in New South Wales, depends on nothing'[73].

Having followed the fortunes of her forebears in New South Wales and Queensland, Judith Wright points out that 'very few farms or even large stations, in the early days of settlement remained in the same hands for more than a generation or two without some form of disaster overtaking the owners'[74]. Things have always been that way. Mary Durack quotes her grandfather, whose changing fortunes led him from New South Wales to Queensland and then across the continent to the Kimberleys: ' "Cattle Kings" ye call us, then we are kings in grass castles that may be blown away with a puff of wind...'. Numerous attempts to open up the land to small selectors and returned soldiers became disastrous and bitter experiences by reason of the unreliability of the Australian climate. Many of the itinerant workers who contributed to the bush legend of the 1890s had lost everything in this way. Joseph Furphy, Miles Franklin, Henry Lawson and later Steele Rudd have portrayed the pathos and heartbreak of their story.

Ignorance and impatience to make the fortune dreamt of in the decision to come to the colonies compounded these natural limitations. Fortunes were made when seasons were good and markets favourable, only to be lost within a year or two, the property being taken over by the mortgagees. Judith Wright describes her grandfather in central Queensland, digging sand from the waterholes in order to provide water for stock dying of thirst, and a short time later seeing miles of fencing swept away in a terrible flood.

The grasslands of the fragile inland plains were transformed by the introduction of stock. The hard hooves of sheep and cattle destroyed the natural habitat of the delicate local grasses. Once the Aboriginal custom of burning off the land ceased, the hardy shrubs which this burning had kept in check—giving much of the country a park-like appearance often noted in the early years of settlement—

took over the land in many regions. C. E. W. Bean, who showed a remarkable sensitivity to the damage being done to the ecology early in the century, commented in *On the Wool Track* upon the irony of government regulations requiring landholders to clear their properties as a condition of continued tenure, thus hastening the destruction of the fragile environment. Bean's capacity to identify essential issues is shown in his recognition of the problem of salinity which would derive from the irrigation being introduced early in the century[75].

Twenty years later, in 1930, Hancock's protest at the ruthlessness and greed which had 'violently disturbed the delicate balance of nature established for centuries in the most isolated of continents'[76] marked the beginnings of the first important provisions for ecological safeguards which were adopted in that decade. The introduction of the rabbit, the use of European farming methods quite unsuited to the light Australian soils, and the ringbarking of large areas of forest in the catchment areas of coastal streams all contributed to the immense damage done to the continent's meagre resources.

D. H. Lawrence, as we have seen, sensed the nature of the relationship white Australians had with their land. It had been violent and exploitative. The rubbish put 'over the fence' had parallels in many forms the length and breadth of the country. Judith Wright judges that our conflict with the land seemed to go deeper 'because there was in it so little of the heroic, so that we could not bolster up our self-esteem by boasting of our conquests; and because there was in it, too, so much of compromise... The real battle was of a different order, not so much for conquest as for survival, and in surviving we found ourselves, for many years, living on Australia's terms rather than our own'[77]. Perhaps our rubbish 'over the fence' was a subtle form of protest.

Yet it has become our land, the place of our existence. The struggle we had with it produced the 'central almost mystical symbol' of our national tradition, as Judith Wright has written: our struggle with the continent has brought 'a purification which is the result of hardship and endurance... sacrifice perhaps of life itself (Indeed, death is part of the legend; Australia has always been "the land where dead men lie")'[78]. As this same writer points out in a later essay, the discovery of the true nature of the continent and of its arid interior by Australian settlers 'came as a shock and frustration that may have darkened all our view. We came first as exiles, later as predators; love has come late, if ever, and by the time we began to understand a little of the land, we had already set a pattern of destruction'[79].

If 'love has come late', it is none the less real. It is not too late to go beyond the pattern of destruction. If our island-continent has been a cruel adversary which often overwhelmed and humiliated us, we have learned to love it. Lawson may call it 'the worst dried-up and God forsaken country'. But he tells us something of himself, and of us all, when he writes of the drover's wife: 'this bushwoman is used to the loneliness of it. As a girl-wife she hated it, but now she would feel strange away from it'[80].

Beneath the violence and exploitation, this strange love goes back a long way in the experience of white Australia. In his *Cooper's Creek*, Alan Moorehead recalls the love the early explorers have for the Australian desert, where they find 'a kind of exhilaration...a sense of freedom...perhaps even a spiritual regeneration, and no matter how much they are reduced by their hardship they return again and again'[81]. H. H. Richardson brackets the final part of her trilogy with a gesture of nostalgic affection. Mrs Aeneas Gunn, in the opening pages of *We of the Never Never*, speaks of 'that elusive land with an elusive name—a land of danger and hardship and privations, yet loved as few lands are loved—a land that bewitches her people with strange spells and mysteries, until they call sweet bitter and bitter sweet'. Manning Clark identifies himself with the 'man who has had the great good fortune to see the fragile beauty in our ancient continent, a man, that is, who has had at least one great love in his life'[82].

As I reflect upon my own experience and listen to the words of these various contributors to our Australian conversation, the image that comes to my imagination is that of an icon. Our land, the strange island-continent that we have come to love and venerate, has the qualities of an icon. For those who are still coming to know it, an icon has a character that makes it strangely different from other images, even forbidding and alienating. But as it reveals its secret, contemplation of its strange colours and cryptic symbolisms brings a blessing and gives access to a new order of things. The most venerable icons are old and worn, their origins lost in the mists of the past, fragile, crumbling with age; and they possess an aura bestowed upon them by the love of past generations possessed by their secret.

[1] *The Landscape of Australian Poetry*, Melbourne (Cheshire) 1967, p.302.
[2] *Preoccupations in Australian Poetry*, p.xi.
[3] 1976 Boyer Lectures, p.47.
[4] 1976 Boyer Lectures, p.18.
[5] *Kangaroo*, p.14.
[6] London, 1966.
[7] 'Theberton Hall', cited, Elliott, *The Landscape of Australian Poetry*, p.307.
[8] Cited, Elliott, *The Landscape of Australian Poetry*, p.14.
[9] ibid., p.17.
[10] Elliott, *The Landscape of Australian Poetry*, pp.17, 48–9.
[11] Cited, Elliott, *The Landscape of Australian Poetry*, p.20.

12   *Australia*, p.43.

13   Cited, Elliott, *The Landscape of Australian Poetry*, pp.20–2.

14   'Realism and Documentary', p.251, in *Penguin New Literary History of Australia*, L. Hergenhan (ed.).

15   Elliott, *The Landscape of Australian Poetry*, p.24.

16   Preface to *Poems by Adam Lindsay Gordon*, London, 1897, pp.ix–xi. Clarke is responding to the reversal theme so common in descriptions of the Australian environment, cf. Elliott, *The Landscape of Australian Poetry*, pp.22–3.

17   *The Landscape of Australian Poetry*, p.76.

18   ibid., p.77.

19   ibid., p.79.

20   ibid., p.77.

21   ibid., p.92.

22   ibid., pp.81, 84.

23   ibid., p.127.

24   Cited, Cantrell (ed.), *Writings of the 1890s*, pp.24–7.

25   Cantrell (ed.), *Writings of the 1890s*, pp.15–16.

26   ibid., pp.20–1.

27   *The Australian Tradition: Studies in a Colonial Culture*, Melbourne (Longman Cheshire) 1980, p.80.

28   *The Landscape of Australian Poetry*, p.276.

29   *Preoccupations in Australian Poetry*, pp.126–7.

30   *The Landscape of Australian Poetry*, p.295.

31   Elliott, *The Landscape of Australian Poetry*, p.532.

32   'The Pastoral Poets', p.361, in *Penguin New Literary History of Australia*, L. Hergenhan (ed.).

33   *The Landscape of Australian Poetry*, p.318.

34   *The Vernacular Republic: Poems 1961–1981*, Sydney (Angus and Robertson) 1984, p.5.

35   ibid., p.4.

36   ibid., p.5.

37   ibid., p.12.

38   Cited, Bernard Smith, *Australian Painting 1788–1970*, Melbourne, 1970, p.80.

39   *The Landscape of Australian Poetry*, p.81.

40   *Australian Painting*, p.251.

41   *The Pastoral Poets*, p.359, in *Penguin New Literary History of Australia*, L. Hergenhan (ed.).

42   *The Landscape of Australian Poetry*, p.237.

43   *Kanguroo*, pp.8–9.

44   Lawrence wrote to Katherine S. Prichard, whom he had met in Perth: 'It's a dark country, a sad country, underneath—like an abyss. Then, when the sky turns frail and blue again, the trees against the far-off sky stand out, the glamour, the unget-at-able glamour! A great fascination, but also a dismal grey terror, underneath' (Harry T. Moore, *The Priest of Love: A Life of D. H. Lawrence*, Penguin, 1980, p.448).

45   *Kangaroo*, p.73.

46   Cited, J. D. Pringle, *Australian Accent*, p.37.

47   *Kangaroo*, pp.21–2.

48   loc. cit.

49   *Kangaroo*, p.74.

50   *The Landscape of Australian Poetry*, p.239.

51   ibid., pp.40–1.

52   ibid., p.248.

53   *The Timeless Land*, Collins Fontana, 1985, pp.334–5.

[54]   *An Older Kind of Magic*, Penguin (Puffin), 1985, Epilogue, pp.150–1.
[55]   1968 Boyer Lectures, p.39.
[56]   *The Fortunes of Richard Mahony* (*Book III, Ultima Thule*), London, 1961, pp.585, 830–1.
[57]   Cited, Bruce Bennett, 'Perceptions 1965–1988', p.440, in *Penguin New Literary History of Australia*, L. Hergenhan (ed.).
[58]   *The Dreadnought of the Darling*, London, 1911, pp.317–18.
[59]   Cited, Serle, *The Creative Spirit in Australia*, pp.112–13.
[60]   Cited, Bruce Bennett, 'Perceptions 1968–1988', p.445, in *Penguin New Literary History of Australia*, L. Hergenhan (ed.).
[61]   Cited, Veronica Brady, *A Crucible of Prophets*, p.2.
[62]   'Literature and Culture', p.18, in *Penguin New Literary History of Australia*, L. Hergenhan (ed.).
[63]   'Australia: A Bird's-Eye View', p.9, in *Australia: The Daedalus Symposium*, S. Graubard (ed.).
[64]   1976 Boyer Lectures, pp.47–8.
[65]   *Preoccupations of Australian Poetry* (Sun Books) p.57.
[66]   *One Man's War*, Sth Melbourne, 1983.
[67]   ibid., p.200.
[68]   1980 Boyer Lectures, p.11.
[69]   *Profile of Australia*, London, 1967, p.20.
[70]   ibid., p.156.
[71]   Cited, McCarthy, *Gallipoli to the Somme*, p.73.
[72]   See Judith Wright's 'Landscape and Dreaming', in *Australia: The Daedalus Symposium*, S. Graubard (ed.), pp.29–56.
[73]   *On the Track and Over the Sliprails*, Sydney, 1945, p.36.
[74]   *Preoccupations in Australian Poetry*, p.51.
[75]   See McCarthy, *Gallipoli to the Somme*, p.73.
[76]   *Australia*, p.30.
[77]   *Preoccupations in Australian Poetry*, p.xvii.
[78]   ibid., p.57.
[79]   'Landscape and Dreaming', p.52, in *Australia: The Daedalus Symposium*, S. Graubard (ed.).
[80]   Cantrell (ed.), *Writing of the 1890s*, p.240.
[81]   London, 1963, p.10.
[82]   1976 Boyer Lectures, pp.48–9.

8.

AN

EMBARRASSING

SUBJECT

Robert Elegant, a *Newsweek* writer specialising in Asian affairs who recently revisited Australia, was led to conclude that the quality of life many of us share is 'probably still the best in the world'. He also warned, however, that our 'best days may be over'[1]. We Australians are going to face considerable challenges, making our way as a nation in a rapidly changing world. We must take stock of our resources, both material and spiritual.

It is a notorious fact that discussion of spiritual and religious issues—the subject of this final chapter—is a source of embarrassment within the Australian conversation. That state of affairs must have an important place in the exploration we are making. Components of the Australian ethos identified in the course of the previous chapters—the spirit of egalitarianism, the wisdom learned at the limits of human existence, and the symbolism we begin to recognise in the land in which we have carried on our struggle 'to be and to remain human'—have deep spiritual implications. If reluctance to take up the discussion of spiritual issues comes in part from the pragmatism which has been noted in the course of this study, it may also contain the seeds of something peculiarly Australian which is of great value.

Theologian Tony Kelly suggests that the silence of Australians concerning the ultimate dimensions of human existence points to something which, if it is explored and fostered, may prove to be an important resource. 'Silence or inarticulateness', he writes, do not necessarily mean 'an absence of spiritual depth'. They may indicate that Australians are waiting for 'the skill or opportunity to name what is most meaningful'; they may represent a reluctance to do so which is the beginning of wisdom.

Kelly suggests factors which may well have contributed to such attitudes. They remind us of some of the issues which have emerged already in our discussion: 'our antipodean isolation, the brutality of our historical origins...a general sense of something new struggling for expression in the harsh, raw world of Down Under'. The Australian experience has taken us onto a terrain 'in which the lush ideologies and cultural thinking of the old countries had to be denied before a new reality could be expressed'. If to this point the experience of being human has lacked a reflective expression in philosophy and theology, 'Grace kept on being grace' for the Australian experience 'in the silences that inherently resist all expression'[2].

1. Unsettled voices

In a clever flight of fancy, Douglas Stewart's poem 'Terra Australis' has Captain Quiros, the sixteenth century Portuguese explorer who sailed the Pacific in search of the Great South Land, and William Lane, the idealist who abandoned our southern continent at the end of the nineteenth century to build his utopian society in Paraguay, 'break the horizon / That shut the dead off in a wall of mist', and meet each other sailing in opposite directions—to their mutual consternation. Perhaps something of the hopes for Australia which were nurtured in the closing decades of the last century still smoulder in the Australian soul. Dame Leonie Kramer comments 'it is tempting to speculate that the great expectations directed towards Quiros's hoped for Australia del Espiritu Santo long before its discovery and settlement still haunt it, and that the impossibility of satisfying them is likely to sharpen, not blunt, a sense of failure to make the most of the "vision splendid"'[3].

Patrick White could hardly be described as a typical Australian. He made it clear, however, that his return to Australia at the age of thirty-six was a homecoming, insisting that he belonged here—'by reason of the generations of my family'—his forebears having been here since the 1820s. It was here that his life's work must be undertaken. In Veronica Brady's words, 'his return to Australia had a great deal to do with the descent into himself, the search for something of abiding value, stimulated by his experiences during the war and...the ruins he saw all round him in...post-war Europe'[4].

White set out to challenge the unreflecting pragmatism which tended, in Brady's words, 'to repose in political and economic solutions and, more fundamentally, the one dimensional sense of the world which that confidence presupposed'[5]. He recognised the magnitude of the challenge. 'In all directions', he wrote, 'stretched the Great Australian Emptiness in which the mind is the least of possessions, in which the rich man is the important man, in which the schoolmaster and the journalist rule what intellectual roost there is, in which beautiful youths and girls stare at life through blind, blue eyes... It was the exaltation of the average that made me panic most... the void I had to fill was so immense... I wanted to discover the extraordinary behind the ordinary, the mystery and poetry which alone could make bearable the lives of... (ordinary) people, and my own life since my return'[6].

It is not surprising that he provoked in many writers and critics of the realistic tradition an essentially hostile response. The fact that from the time he began to live and write in Australia Patrick White grew in stature in the eyes of fellow Australians, so that by the time of his death he had become an important national figure, is an indication that his challenging message was recognised as an important contribution to the Australian conversation.

Australia's best known historian Manning Clark has expressed concerns which have much in common with Patrick White's. Once again, the popular recognition his commentaries upon our history have received indicates that what he has had to say has awakened a genuine response in many Australians. Clark was a more congenial interlocutor than the testy novelist. He spoke in a familiar idiom; the questions he raised were asked from the midst of an experience shared with ordinary Australians; his voice was all the more engaging because he acknowledged that he had not found the answer to the questions he raised. But he refused, and he challenged us all to refuse, to settle for answers which are no answers at all.

If White was dismayed by the 'Great Australian Emptiness', Clark was tormented by the sense that Australian history has been in many ways a pilgrimage 'from the Kingdom of God to the Kingdom of Nothingness'[7], that we may find ourselves 'stripped bare of all faith... left comfortless on Bondi Beach'[8]. Concerned lest hedonism and consumerism should deprive Australians of that sense of suffering which is able to challenge them to face life's real questions, he listened sympathetically to the answers to his questions offered by the three great world-building systems which white Australians brought to these shores from the old world, those of the Enlightenment, of Protestant Christianity, and of Catholic Christendom. Yet he was unable to find in any of them the answer to his deepest need—so that they have left him grieving because it seemed, as he put it, that 'what is possible will probably never happen'.

In the seminal article I have already quoted[9], Les Murray

discusses at length the question of whether the Australian culture provides access to the transcendent. His approach is robust, his style 'take it or leave it', in a way which succeeds in avoiding preachiness. His basic assumption is enunciated without apology, however: 'Since the spiritual dimension universally exists in human beings, it has to be dealt with by them in some way or other'[10]. He tells Christians 'We are more widely judged on our own best terms than we think, and more insistently expected to be keepers of the dimension of depth than we find comfortable'[11].

Murray points to the 'sub-theological debate' which is aroused by the question of 'sacred treasures of the nation': from Aboriginal things to war memorials and the Barrier Reef—'no one slings off about' the Reef today, and 'only a few sub-cultures now eschew a fundamental respect' for things Aboriginal[12]. The implication is that our attitudes to these things place us on a threshold which leads to meeting with the ultimate questions of human existence.

We have already discussed the 'clown-icons' which Murray points out have developed in Australian culture, ritual symbols of derision which express a subtle self-mockery and in the end are a positive affirmation of our vision of human existence. He is critical of Barry Humphries, whom he sees as insensitive to this underlying wholesomeness, giving these things 'a flavour of class warfare' and turning them into a put-down[13]. In discussing Australian humour in an earlier chapter, I have already made reference to the 'wise and subtly ramified levity' which Murray sees as 'one of the great marks of our vernacular culture', and its relation to the 'underground traditions of working people's irony and fantastical peasant wit'[14].

Murray's comments upon Australian nationalism are interesting in the light of our earlier discussion: 'of course', he writes, 'any nation is a semi-criminal conspiracy'. Australia's sharing with the world at large whatever wisdom we have found in our 'new vision...new style...new tune for the world to enjoy and maybe whistle' may well be seen as 'a necessary work of atonement for stealing a continent and living well off the theft'[15].

Murray discusses other aspects of contemporary Australian life which in various ways involve the issue of self-transcendence. Taking up the phenomenon of the mass concert and the political rally—he notes that our spirit of 'proletarian evolution' gives us a healthy distrust of the latter—he analyses 'what we may call the liturgy of the rally', with its implications of the sharing of a secret and membership in a chosen company, substituting for the participants' 'lonely imagining something far more vivid and immanent, something which they can take with them into the dull world of bewilderment and dreary work or dreary unemployment'[16]. In the end, he suggests, political rallies are 'necessary problem-solving stuff and little more'.

The contemporary West's dilettantism in its search for spiritual meaning, which Murray calls the 'spiritual supermarket', he judges to be 'fairweather stuff, adjuncts to a prosperity which may now be vanishing'. If unbelief once seemed 'a daring and rather aristocratic gesture', it no longer serves today as a form of rebellion or protest. The same may be said, he observes, of 'sexual indulgence, pornography and the like'. In a world of aging populations it will be difficult to sustain 'the cult of unremitting youthfulness and physical beauty'. Today's 'liberal humanism', he suggests, is fragmented by dissension. Its most dedicated followers 'are often covertly uneasy at its lack of gentleness, its readiness to force the facts and its desolate this-worldliness'; they are daunted by the 'tragic complexity and strange intractability of the world'; and 'often when people who subscribe to' this view 'relax for a moment, their eyes are seen to contain an almost desperate appeal: prove us wrong, make us believe there is more to it than this, show us your God and that Grace you talk about'[17].

Of themselves, Murray argues, none of these attempts can succeed in breaking out of the constraints and limits we encounter through our being human, 'since what humans imagine to be their salvation can't logically be any greater than the human measure... there is impressive power in what we can imagine, but no transcendence... Political commitment, art, drugs and the like... may even mimic transcendence, but it is not the true otherness to which we are as it were keyed in the depth of our being'; 'without that transcendence' which is 'the only coin the soul recognises', humanity's frustrations give rise to enormities of false dedication and violence such as we have seen in the present century. We may change the world, 'but it remains the world'. 'All you have done', he writes, 'is to rearrange the pattern of joy and pain, bewilderment, disappointment and dominances. The hunger of the soul remains, even if we feed it on our very heart and mind and on the lives of millions of the innocent'[18].

'There is as yet no other vision abroad in our society', Murray is convinced, 'which commands the same authority as Christian faith does, the same sense of being the bottom line, the great resource to be called on in times of real need'[19].

What Les Murray has to say concerning the significance of the Anzac reality and the Anzac legend for Australians touches on a question which cannot be disregarded in any discussion of our Australian culture's openness to the transcendent, our attitude to death. Our national statistics are interesting. While these statistics show that in the course of the present century participation in all forms of institutional Christianity—Sunday attendance, baptism, marriages, etc.—has progressively declined, religious funerals are found to be an exception. Bruce Wilson judged in 1982 that ninety-seven to ninety-eight per cent of funerals were still conducted with religious rites[20].

The prospect of imminent death confronts men and women with the question of the ultimate significance of their human existence. Few have described the experience of facing death in more dramatic terms than that courageous Australian Douglas Mawson who, in the course of a heroic trek which he was forced to make alone in the Antarctic wastes, fell into a chasm and found himself dangling in his sledge harness:

> Exhausted, weak, and chilled (for my hands were bare and pounds of snow had got inside my clothing) I hung with the firm conviction that all was over except the passing. Below was a black chasm; it would be but the work of a moment to slip from the harness, then all the pain and toil would be over. It was a rare situation, a rare temptation—a chance to quit small things for great—to pass from the petty exploration of a planet to the contemplation of vaster worlds beyond. But there was all eternity for the last and, at its longest, the present would be but short. I felt the better for the thought[21].

The later legend has tended to transform the horror of Australian war casualties into something far removed from what was in the minds of the young Australians who went into battle facing the prospect of imminent death. The thought of vindicating Australia's national worth—the theme of newspaper editorials during the Gallipoli campaign: no doubt reflecting popular sentiment at home—was probably of some importance to them as they enlisted. However we may well presume that, with the course of time, the 'wise and subtly ramified levity' which Les Murray refers to would have tempered this view. He speaks, as we have seen, of Australians' 'ability to laugh at venerated things, and at awesome and deadly things', exemplified in the humour of World War I's *Anzac Book*, and in World War II by 'the infantrymen advancing into battle in North Africa singing "We're off to see the Wizard, the wonderful Wizard of Oz"'. This characteristically Australian humour he sees as something precious, as 'at bottom, a spiritual laughter, a mirth that puts tragedy, futility and vanity alike in their place'[22]. Facing death, the sentiments of the young Anzacs would rarely have risen to the cool heroism of a Douglas Mawson; it would have been more akin to Manning Clark's 'a whisper in the mind, and a shy hope in the heart'.

Bill Gammage judges that the realism of the Anzac experience was denied full expression in our national memory by the fact that

before the story of the Anzacs had been fully told—especially by
C. E. W. Bean, 'whose magnificent history was essentially about
the character of the men of the A.I.F.' and 'gave the Anzac
tradition substance and direction'[23]—the public issue had been
made 'whether a man was loyal to the Empire'[24]. His summary of
what he judges to be the attitudes of the Anzacs is worth quoting
for what it tells us of the 'shy hope in the heart' of these brave
Australians:

> They fought for their own prestige because that would
> probably be their last cause, they took greatest comfort
> from their mates because their mates were all they had,
> they accepted the sight and spectre of death because they
> were themselves to die, they adjusted to the daily routine
> of war because they did not expect to know another.
> They lived in a world apart, a new world, scarcely
> remembering their homes and country, and grieving little
> at the deaths of mates they loved more than anything on
> this earth, because they knew that only time kept them
> from the "great majority" who had already died, and they
> believed that fate would overtake time, and bring most of
> them to the last parade. So they continued, grim, mock-
> ing, defiant, brave and careless, free from common toils
> and woes, into a perpetual present, until they should
> meet the fate of so many who had marched before them
> down the great road of peace and sorrow into eternity[25].

Robin Gerster probably reflects a common reaction when he
speaks disapprovingly of 'a nostalgia for a time when patriotism
could propel men into an enterprise "larger than oneself"'[26].
There are ambiguities to be resolved here. For a closed Benthamite
utilitarianism, self-transcendence must be judged in the end as a
romantic folly or a refined self-indulgence. But for a view of
human existence which sees it as 'keyed' in its depths, to use Les
Murray's phrase, to the 'true otherness', self-transcendence is
essential to personal authenticity. For this latter view patriotism
and concern for the common interests of humanity must be
distinguished from the nationalism which Murray has described as
'a semi-criminal conspiracy', and the genuine self-transcendence of
one who gives his life for his fellows must be distinguished from
the lies of those who manipulate the course of human history for
the sake of some partisan gain.

These ambiguities have been compounded by a later rhetoric
which spoke of the 'sacrifices' made by young Australians 'for their
country'. Such language, as Richard Campbell points out, has often
made its appeal to 'religious motives' which 'are more reminiscent
of a Mithraic blood-sacrifice of immortal youth than of the

Cross'[27]. Murray makes the same point, describing such rhetoric as making the death of young Australians in the wars 'into a post-factum human sacrifice'[28]. He suggests that an authentic Christian consciousness would have saved us from such an enormity, recognising that in a fallible and all too often selfish world the story of Jesus of Nazareth shows that an ultimate self-transcendence for the sake of one's fellows is a real possibility for authentic human existence[29].

Some observers of the Australian scene who are concerned with the question of our culture's openness to spiritual values have adopted an approach in which they acknowledge an indebtedness to the late Bernard Lonergan's analysis of the ultimate dimensions of human inquiry. Through this analysis, Lonergan sought to establish a relationship between the resources of the Catholic tradition and contemporary Western culture's unprecedented exploration of human subjectivity, convinced that 'genuine objectivity is the fruit of an authentic subjectivity'[30]. For Lonergan, a wholesome subjectivity is grounded in the establishing and owning of the horizons of one's thought: intellectual, moral and religious. These horizons have their authenticity from the fact that they express a genuine response of the whole person to the experienced world. The decisions which establish these horizons, Lonergan notes, may call for 'conversions' in each of the three orders mentioned, because the horizons of which one first becomes aware are not fully deliberative and responsible: 'For the most part people merely drift into some contemporary horizon'[31].

The establishing of one's horizons calls for a clarification of where one places oneself, in the intellectual, moral and religious orders. This clarification takes place at the level of human subjectivity, 'on the level of deliberation, evaluation, decision'. It calls for a personal decision 'about whom and what you are for and, again, whom and what you are against'[32], a decision whereby one becomes 'fully conscious... about one's horizons, one's outlook, one's world-view'[33]. In fact, Lonergan is speaking about the same thing as Bernard Smith's struggle 'to be, and to remain human' in the concrete human situation in which one finds oneself.

Following Lonergan's lead, Frank Fletcher points out that an Australian must determine his or her horizons through a decision as to 'where one stands, or better, *with whom* one stands'[34] in Australian society. His experience in exploring whether, as a Christian, he has shared 'the meaning world of the majority of non-religious Australians', and the experience of his option to stand with the marginalised in Australian society, especially with the Aboriginal people, brings to mind in a vivid way Bernard Smith's reminder that morality is not realised by being owned in the abstract.

Another thinker who has followed Lonergan's lead is the theologian Tony Kelly. In his essay *A New Imagining: Towards an Australian Spirituality*[35], Kelly finds that the Lonergan-inspired approach which he has adopted makes important points of contact with Les Murray's thought, and he sets out to elaborate the implications of Murray's intuitive insights, adding much of his own thought that is original and creative.

Kelly quotes Les Murray's distinction, expressed in his inimitable vernacular style, between 'wholespeak' and 'narrowspeak'. The former, he says, is 'properly integrated poetic discourse' and 'embraces all good poetry, including that of religion'; the latter is 'based on the supposed primacy or indeed the exclusive primacy of daylight reason' and 'embraces most of administrative discourse by which the world is ruled from day to day, as well as most criticism'[36]. Murray's paradigm suggests to Kelly an approach which makes possible an owning of horizons, translating Lonergan's abstract analysis into something concrete and accessible. Poetry and 'imagination', in the fullest sense of a total, personal response to lived experience, provide a focus.

If personal integrity is grounded in the owning of authentic horizons, the shared experience of the Australian conversation has much to gain from a recognition of the inadequate horizons established by ideology and selfishness. We should learn, Kelly writes, to distinguish the 'common humanity' which we must strive for from 'a "standard humanity", a version of "mass man" in modern technological culture'[37]. Our consciousness must recognise the degree to which it 'is drenched with a flood of mass produced images as modern advertising... pollutes the symbols of the inner landscape of our feelings'[38]; we must dare to seek the large vision which lies beyond 'the monotony and timidity of our aspirations'[39]; we must find the courage to resist 'the dragooning forces of a culture addicted to wealth, power and technology'[40]; bold imagination must be preferred to 'mere respectability'[41].

The imagination which Kelly summons to the quest of authentic horizons and openness to a total objectivity, he identifies with the 'kind of permanent inner poem we carry within' which is Les Murray's refreshing description of what we call conscience[42]. Conscience, Murray suggests, 'shares with art an ability to be instantaneously and convincingly there and a total resistance to untruth'[43]. Kelly develops this analogy and its link with imagination. An authentic spirituality, he writes, dares in the light of this inner poem 'to imagine the world otherwise'[44]; it refuses 'to surrender to some lesser version of ourselves'[45]; it maintains 'a consistent protest against anything that would truncate our humanity'[46]; it 'projects us into the area of uncomfortable solidarity with others'[47]; it finds the courage to live by a spirit which 'demands forgiveness of past wrongs and self-forgetfulness in moving forward into a future from which no one may be excluded'[48]. Clearly, it is a program in which all upright Australians can find a genuine solidarity in openness to spiritual values.

If it is muted, the religious consciousness of Australians is still able to express itself, as the gifted interviewer Caroline Jones has made clear in her radio program 'The Search for Meaning'. This program has proved one of the most successful in the history of Australian broadcasting. In the judgment of Caroline Jones herself, 'The Search for Meaning' should 'lay to rest the myth of the inarticulate, irreligious Australian'[49]. The response it has had has given a new insight into the attitudes of the listening public.

We have already made reference to the renewed spiritual quest provoked in contemporary Australia by the spiritual void resulting from disillusionment—disillusionment with the ideologies which had been the bearers of traditional values in the formative period of Australian history. This quest has taken the forms of Christian fundamentalism and the 'New Age' movement.

Many of those seeking to respond to the ecological crisis rapidly developing in today's world are calling for a new sense of cosmic unity. An Australian Creation Spirituality Workshop held at La Trobe University in 1990 considered the contributions that Aboriginal spirituality, the mystical traditions of Christianity and the holistic understanding emerging in contemporary science can contribute to this awareness. It gave expression to a movement which speaks to the spiritual concerns of many Australians[50].

Addressing this conference, Veronica Brady spoke of an awakening of spiritual awareness which she linked with Australians' awareness of the land. 'Under the surface slickness of the consumer society we have become, of our absorption into the international media culture, there are signs of a longing for and an incipient awareness of the value of silence'. She went on to speak in terms which call to mind Tony Kelly's remarks about the reluctance of Australians to speak of spiritual things: 'The inarticulateness, the awkwardness of so many Australians, especially Australian men, may be the occasion of grace, the other side of a deep humility, of knowing one's place as someone finite and vulnerable, very small in contrast with the largeness of God, a largeness figured forth in the land itself'[51].

Speakers at this conference saw the wisdom of the Aboriginal culture and its relationship to the land as capable of speaking to this Australian silence. Elizabeth Cain quoted the Aboriginal artist Miriam Rose Ungunnmerr-Baumann. 'We are exploring a way of being that many of us know little about, although we may know some of the words. Our way of life does not easily let us enter into it. This way of being, the Australian Aboriginal artist and writer,

Miriam Rose, described as "Dadirri—the deep spring of inner, deep listening and quiet still awareness" that is within us all. As she sees it, this is the gift the Aboriginal people have for us if we are open to receive it'[52].

Another speaker, Kevin Treston, suggested that the worldwide concerns finding expression in the workshop registered an evolutionary leap taking place in the 'historical development of consciousness', as the Scientific or Industrial Age gave way to a Unitary Age, in which a shared vision 'will invite us into collaboration with others to preserve our planetary system, to combat divisive economic and social systems which are debilitating the quality of all life forms in the universe'[53].

It is too early to predict the impact which the presence of religious communities outside the Judeo-Christian tradition, such as Islam, will have upon the multicultural society which we are becoming. Perhaps Australia will see the beginnings of the great dialogue between the world religions which must take place in a world community which is rapidly becoming more unified.

If they have had a religious and spiritual awareness, the vast majority of Australians have derived this awareness from Christian traditions brought with them from Europe. It was an awareness far removed for the most part from the spiritual concerns I have just described. If we are to understand the Australian soul, we must follow the changing fortunes of this imported Christian tradition.

2. An inhibited Christian presence

The editors of the collection of historical and sociological essays entitled *The Shape of Belief: Christianity in Australia Today*, published in 1982[54], quoted with approval in their Introduction the judgment of one of their contributors that 'Christianity is still the great untried option in Australian culture'. On the other hand Bruce Wilson, their first contributor, notes that at the time the Australian nation was formed by the federation of the colonies, the overwhelming majority of Australians saw themselves as Christians. 'At the 1901 census less than one per cent of Australians described themselves as having no religion'[55]. At the heart of our national life there exists a remarkable paradox: while a large section of the Australian public have continued to identify themselves with a Christian outlook, the Christian point of view has remained an 'untried option' as far as the public discourse which reflects the formative influences in the mainstream of Australian culture is concerned.

Patrick O'Farrell's studies of the place of religion in Australian experience put us on our guard against neglecting its importance, despite the inhibitions to which I have referred. 'The relationship between the secular and the religious elements and tendencies in Australian culture and society', he writes, 'continues to be uncertain, complex, ambivalent. Or is it merely that the question of that relationship, being unpopular and foreign among the secularised intelligentsia, has remained neglected, unstudied? All the indicators are that religion—or the lack of it—can tell a great deal about the history and nature of Australian culture'[56].

Bruce Mansfield makes a similar point: indeed he is prepared to argue 'that (against almost all observers, secular historians and Christian hand-wringers alike)' the religious history of European Australia has been '—by and large—a success story'. Speaking as a Christian, he takes his stand on sound theological ground when he reminds his readers that according to the essential values of Christian faith, success is not to be identified with 'triumphalism'[57]. In the same vein, Michael Hogan's studies of Australian religious history lead him to the conclusion that if the Christian churches have not had a notable success in their declared goals, their 'efforts to overcome this disability have helped to shape the civil society in major and fundamental ways'[58].

Richard Campbell's article 'The Character of Australian Religion'[59], which makes a discerning analysis of aspects of this question, suggests that the disjunction between the endeavours of institutional Christianity and many of those who saw themselves as *real* Australians—'the emancipists, the larrikins, the battlers'—was already evident in the early nineteenth century. He cites the case of an uncultivated youth in the magistrate's court in about 1840 who when asked his religion replied 'I am a native'[60].

In the realm of more formal discourse, evidence is not hard to find. Writing in the first number of the *Victorian Review* in 1879, Marcus Clarke based the argument of his article 'Civilisation without Delusion' upon the premise—proposed as self-evident—that science has made the fundamental principles of religious belief an absurdity for enlightened nineteenth century Australians. He concluded, in a passage quoted in an earlier chapter, that 'discoveries of science' would displace 'churchmen's disputations' in popular concern. 'The progress of the world will be the sole care of its inhabitants; and the elevation of the race, the only religion of mankind'. He gave the last word to the *North American Review* which foretold that 'a twentieth century will see for the first time in the history of mankind a civilisation without an active and general delusion'[61].

At the turn of the century, Bernard O'Dowd and A. G. Stephens adopted a similar point of view. O'Dowd's 'Poetry Militant' has been discussed in an earlier chapter. Stephens's writings, from which I have already quoted, and his varied intellectual interests, show him to be in touch with the vital impulses of Western culture in his age. Writing in 1904, his comments on the prospects of religion in Australia were more measured, less doctrinaire, than those of Clarke and O'Dowd. He saw 'the spirit of Australia' as deriving from 'the habits of elder nations in older lands'. These old ways, their new environment has transformed: 'modifying, altering, increasing, or altogether destroying'. Stephens judged that this process was bringing 'destruction' to religious belief 'because with the spread of mental enlightenment the tendency is everywhere to decay in faith in outworn creeds'. He saw another factor working to undermine religion which was peculiarly Australian: 'there is in the developing Australian character a sceptical and utilitarian spirit that values the present hour and refuses to sacrifice the present for any visionary future lacking a rational guarantee'[62].

If we turn to the public discourse of Australian literature, we find that the religious dimension had little place in the work of novelists in the first half of the twentieth century. 'By and large', writes Veronica Brady, 'literature, like life in twentieth century Australia, has become increasingly indifferent to the question of God'. She notes, however, that poets are an exception to this generalisation. The work of such representative writers as Henry Handel Richardson, Katherine Susannah Prichard, Vance Palmer and Xavier Herbert do not take up the religious question in any direct way. Since the Second World War, Brady observes, there has been a renewal of interest in the issue on the part of a number of novelists, the most important of whom was Patrick White[63]. The mixed reception White's writings had in his own country, contrasting with reactions overseas, was probably due in part to his taking up of themes unfashionable in the prevailing naturalism of Australian writing.

In more recent times, those who can in no way identify with a religious point of view are much less assured in their taking of position. If thinkers such as Clarke, O'Dowd and Stephens can confidently foresee the demise of Christianity, Phillip Adams smiles at himself as he comments 'As a kid it seemed to me that by 1987 religion would be dead as the "dodo" but it's showing every sign of having a great revival'[64]. More recently, Adams has written that his 'I don't believe in God' stance means 'I don't believe in the God of my father ... or of my religious instruction teacher at East Kew State'. 'I believe', he went on to declare, 'that no human emotion, not even love, is as important as a sense of the numinous. It is the thing that links science and religion and the finest in literature ... it seems there's just a chance that our sense of the numinous (or, if you prefer, the transcendent) could be based in fact rather than dependent upon faith; that the two great streams of human thought, the mystic and the scientific, might escape their history of conflict and achieve the beginnings of harmony'[65].

Les Murray's *Anthology of Australian Religious Poetry*, published in 1986, provides evidence of a persistent religious concern running through Australian poetry. Perhaps this contrast between prose and poetry is related to the disjunction between personal concerns and public discourse, as far as religious expression is concerned, to which we have referred. After all, prose and poetry enter public discourse in different forms. The former is far closer to the prevailing idiom of public discourse; the latter, on the other hand, especially in its lyrical expression, assumes a form through which the reader is given a privileged access to what is essentially a personal statement.

The paradox of this disjunction needs to be carefully weighed. Ninety-nine per cent of Australians saw themselves at the time of federation as 'having a religion'. The churches played little or no part, however, in the public process which had led to the birth of the new nation. We have already made reference to the uninspiring language of the instrument whereby the Australian colonies entered into union as the Australian Commonwealth. The words with which the document of federation begins—'trusting in the help of Almighty God'—probably had the same mildly embarrassing connotations that prayers before parliament have today: as something which many politicians would gladly have done without, but which they dared not discard for fear of offending what they judged to be a widespread, if inarticulate, sentiment of the Australian public.

Not long before Marcus Clarke wrote his article 'Civilisation without Delusion', those who visited the goldfields were struck by the decorum with which the sabbath was observed. In the first years of the century, C. E. W. Bean found men lost in the outback counting the days in order to clean themselves up and 'spell' on Sundays. In the present century, statistics continue to give evidence of an enduring sense of Christian identity on the part of a large section of the Australian population. Even today, a sizeable percentage of Australians declare themselves to have been to a church service in the previous twelve months, apart from occasions such as christenings, weddings and funerals.

Trying to understand this disjunction, I am reminded of an observation of Cyril Halley, a sociologist who has been studying Australian society for many years. When I discussed this work with him in its early stages, he urged me not to neglect something to which I have already made reference in our discussion of Australian humour: the fact that the confident voices of thinkers and writers, and the too often overbearing voices of the media, express a secular humanist point of view somewhat different from that which shapes the lives of the men and women who make up the rank and file of society. By and large, these latter still wish to identify with the Christian tradition, though they would be embarrassed if they were asked to articulate what this implies.

Les Murray makes a similar point. If the articulate voices to which we refer are typically 'humanist', he writes, 'the religious tendency of what may be called majority Australia may best be described as Residual Christian, with side servings of such themes as stoicism, luck, heroism in the strict sense of survival through the memory of one's supreme achievement in approved fields, plus pieties of various kinds, for example towards the extended family, among country people especially, or towards dead comrades, among ex-servicemen'. Murray judges that this same majority identifies with 'the thousand-year effort to Christianise and civilise raw pride and... swagger'[66]. Describing attitudes which have established themselves deep in the Australian ethos, Murray's poem 'The Quality of Sprawl' makes the same point in a whimsical fashion, concluding:

> Sprawl leans on things. It is loose-limbed in its mind.
> Reprimanded and dismissed
> it listens with a grin and one boot up on the rail
> of possibility. It may have to leave the Earth.
> Being roughly Christian, it scratches the other cheek
> and thinks it's unlikely. Though people have been shot
> for sprawl[67].

Another of Murray's poems, 'An Absolutely Ordinary Rainbow'[68], describing the reactions provoked by a Christ-like 'fellow crying in Martin Place', captures the poignancy of the embarrassed silence we are discussing.

It is not difficult to recognise that this inhibition of public discussion of the religious dimension of human existence has inevitably had the effect of eroding and debilitating the religious commitment of Australians. With the haunting phrase which we have already quoted, Manning Clark describes the faith which is still a dimension of human existence for Australians as having 'dropped to a whisper in the mind, and a shy hope in the heart'[69].

Very obvious among historical influences which set this development in train is the fact that, in the originating moment of Australian experience, institutional Christianity was identified for many with the authorities maintaining order in the penal colony. As historians point out, these authorities looked to the clergy to help maintain order and discipline. The startling incident to which I have already referred, in which female convicts responded to the voice of officialdom by turning and exposing their posteriors, involved, it will be recalled, the Lieutenant-Governor and the chaplain.

Allan Grocott's historical study of the attitudes of convicts and ex-convicts towards the churches and the clergy in Australia during the first half of the nineteenth century[70] led him to conclude that there were 'several significant factors which intensified... anticlerical and anti-religious feelings'. He points to the residual contempt experienced by convicts who 'were forced to play the hypocrite in order to gain indulgences and shorten their sentences'. The official Anglican chaplains' 'participation in the repressive penal system' and their appointment as magistrates was most unfortunate. 'The clerical role of moral policemen', he writes, 'did nothing to help religion, as convicts saw them as sanctimonious spies of the government and puritanical "kill-joys"'. As time progressed, the tendency of the clergy to identify 'with the ruling class, the exclusionists, the "untainted", had very harmful consequences on their ministry'. The whole approach adopted by Australia's first clergymen, Grocott concludes, was doomed to failure:

> The evangelical and moralistic message of the Protestant Churches especially, was unappealing and unacceptable to the convict world. Many themes, such as a wrathful Jehovah, eternal damnation, subordination, resignation, patience, humility, diligence, rectitude, temperance, sabbatarianism, respect for those in authority, and a host of others, must have been particularly repelling to captive audiences. As far as the churches were concerned, almost everything smacked of 'the old country', and very little adjustment was able to be made in the colony, which was regarded as 'home' by most convicts and emancipists. Dean Inge once said that the church which marries the spirit of the age becomes a widow in the next. In Britain at that time, the 'Established' Church at least, by its identification with the State, its intimate association with the ruling class, and its belief in the existing social order being unquestionably God-ordained, had married the 'spirit of the age'. It paid dearly for it by becoming a 'widow' in the antipodes, so far as the great majority of convicts and ex-convicts were concerned[71].

Transposition to this new environment, as Grocott points out, faced the Church of England with an immense challenge of sociological adjustment. In the home country, the church was taken for granted as an essential part of the fabric of British civilisation. It would take generations to learn that not only could this state of affairs not be taken for granted in the emerging colonial society, but that it could prove a positive liability as the provincial culture sought to affirm its own identity. Having for a long time something of the character of the established church, it shared the fate of all such churches, of finding itself in a somewhat ambiguous relationship with a large number of nominal adherents[72]. The bitter attitudes which many Irish Catholics brought to this country and the antipathy which many Protestants had brought to Australia from Europe set up barriers of distrust which remained in place well into the present century.

Russel Ward sees the ballad 'My Religion', sent to Banjo Paterson and published by him in 1905, as expressing the attitude to organised religion that had established itself among bush workers sixty years earlier[73]. The ballad scorns the 'parsons and preachers', as 'all a mere joke'—they 'can't deceive God with their blarney'. A more credible 'doctrine' is argued for:

> To be upright and downright and act like a man.
> That's the religion for me...
> The heart that feels the woes of another.
> Oh, that's the religion for me.

The ballad is representative of an ethos which saw institutional Christianity as alienated from the difficulties and struggles of the Australian project, and as not speaking to the yearning for ideals which could make that project authentic and meaningful.

We are reminded of Joseph Furphy's rejection of 'ecclesiastical Christianity' as 'a failure of first magnitude'[74]. Furphy and O'Dowd must be representative of many Australians of their time who— ironically, through the teaching of the churches—caught an enthralling glimpse of what human existence should really be, and then turned away in disillusionment from the institutional Christianity of their day to day experience. Furphy's rejection is not made in the name of some secular gospel, but in that of 'the sunshiny Sermon on the Mount'[75], and of 'the grave truth, that the Light of the world, the God-in-man, the only God we can ever know, is by His own authority represented for all time by the poorest of the poor'[76].

A notable feature of the history of the churches during the nineteenth and early twentieth centuries was, certainly, the sectarian bitterness which characterised their relationships with one another[77]. Not only did this have the obvious effect of diverting and souring the energies of earnest Christians, but it brought to the Australian scene the age-old disputes and divisions of the old world. One of the most fundamental assumptions of the emerging Australian conversation, as I have suggested in an earlier chapter, was the conviction that Australians could build an unprecedented future because it was not burdened by such things: Australia, according to O'Dowd, was to be no 'drift Sargosso, where the West / In halcyon calm, rebuilds her fatal nest'[78].

The conversation which was intent on carrying forward the Australian project turned away from the bitter quarrels of the churches in disgust. Ironically, in more recent times, as the new atmosphere of ecumenism has led the churches to renounce sectarian dispute, their concern to find a neutral common ground from which they can make a concerted contribution to the ongoing Australian project has muted the Christian character of that contribution.

If Joseph Furphy reflects the mood of his time, his reaction is significant. In his study of Furphy, John Barnes sees the long essay on the division between Catholics and Protestants (inserted in parentheses in the course of his narrative concerning Rory O'Halloran) as reflecting the importance of the question for Furphy[79]. In the story, Rory O'Halloran, a Catholic friend of the bush philosopher Tom Collins, dramatises the curse of sectarianism, particularly in Rory's unhappy marriage. Collins resents the 'party spirit built into' the admirable if somewhat naive Irishman's being, which makes him skirt any discussion of religious questions 'because throughout every fibre of his moral nature there ran a conviction that the mere mention of Purgatory or Transubstantiation would be fatal to our friendship'[80]. 'O Catholic and Protestant slaves of dogma!' exclaims Furphy, somewhat pompously through Tom Collins, 'Fools all! ... fighting among yourselves, whilst the invincible legionaries of science advance confidently on your polluted Temple!'[81].

An appreciation of the way in which the development of ideological consensus shapes the outlook and securities of social groups can help us to a fuller understanding of how the Christian churches were alienated from one another and from the mainstream of social development in Australia. The rival Christian groups developed distinctive ideologies which set their members in bitter confrontation with each other. All too often they lived on slogans and prejudice rather than finding a spirit of Christian fellowship in which they could acknowledge all they shared in common, and a respectful relationship in which they could explore the nature of their differences in the light of the principles they shared. The real contribution they had to make to the Australian project, through the gospel message Furphy found so inspiring, tended to be lost in the clamour and bitterness of the tribal conflicts they brought to these shores from the old world. Meanwhile, the Australian conversation was carried forward, producing its own distinctive ideological presuppositions which expected no helpful contribution from a Christian point of view.

Richard Campbell makes an analysis which helps us to appreciate further the implications of this situation[82]. It contrasts in a striking way with that of the United States, where 'the most respected institution ... is not Congress, nor the Judiciary, nor the Presidency, but the church'[83]. He explains this in terms readily related to the ideological analysis we have been making: whereas the originating American experience, and the sense of national destiny which it inspired, took place within the framework of 'the traditional metaphysical and value systems in terms of which Christianity had been interpreted'[84], Australia had its beginnings at the very time this cultural construct was disintegrating. As a result, our beginnings were deprived of an 'idealistic framework' similar to that in which the American nation developed its sense of corporate destiny. Bruce Mansfield makes a similar point, observing that, at another level, the spirit of the Enlightenment had alienated our beginnings from the sacralised traditions which were the bearers of so many of Europe's religious values[85].

Campbell sees this as having contributed to our sense of 'disillusion (manifest in our distinctly sardonic humour)', and to our 'so-called pragmatism' and 'moralistic this-worldliness'[86], characteristics which A. G. Stephens commented upon early in the century. Campbell sums up: 'This fundamental shifting of intellectual ground was going on in Europe precisely during the time in which the cultural foundations of white Australia were being laid. Whereas America could think of itself—and still does—as formed by a rational and deliberate enactment, under Divine Providence, of a social contract between free, equal, and moral individuals, Australia never could. We knew too well how competitive is the struggle for survival, how equality is not a right received but a demand to be aggressively asserted...I cannot but feel that the timing and manner of our founding is reflected in the marginal position of religious doctrine in our national consciousness...'[87].

The disjunction between the project of institutional Christianity and the distinctive enterprise of the Australian people placed Christians in a difficult situation in which they were called to participate in two distinct ideological systems, to share in two quite different world-building processes.

There have been two kinds of reaction to this cultural disjunction. The first is an aggressive intrusion into the secular project in the name of Christian truth. The second is a seeking to be embraced by secular society through an identification with its status quo. It is not difficult to recognise that each of these responses runs the risk of distorting and compromising the Christian message.

The first reaction, of aggressive intrusion, is understandable. It is not surprising that the widespread disregard of accepted moral standards in the early days of the colony provoked stern denunciations on the part of the clergy. But when churchmen intervened in the national conversation to proclaim, for instance, that such things as the drought of 1825–27 or the economic collapse of 1840–43 were signs of 'the displeasure of Almighty God' for the sins, madness and folly of the colonial population, the possibility of a genuine meeting of minds was remote indeed. It is not difficult to see a link between this reaction and the 'wowserism' for which Australian Christians have been criticised.

The link is, it seems, more complex that is often assumed. Both Manning Clark and Richard Campbell speak of Protestant Puritanism and Catholic Jansenism finding common cause in this matter[88]. Patrick O'Farrell's research, however, leads him to the judgment that in the early nineteenth century Irish attitudes to sexuality were wholesome enough. They later came to be affected, he judges, by the prudery which characterised English Victorianism, as the Irish at home and overseas, both clergy and people, sought to measure up to the standards of acceptability set by the dominant culture[89].

David Millikin discusses the subtle relationship which existed between the spirit of 'wowserism' and Victorian middle class values. It may have served, he suggests, as a means whereby the middle class imposed a social control upon the working classes: 'keeping the masses well-washed and constrained in their social behaviour was a necessity for the proper workings' of a bourgeois society[90]. It may well be that the part played by the Protestant churches in the emergence of 'wowserism' had a complexity overlooked by the common stereotype attacked by the likes of Norman Lindsay.

The authentic Christian message presents itself as a gospel, *good news*, bringing affirmation and hope to what is deepest in us as human beings. In his own way, Joseph Furphy recognised this. His criticism of 'ecclesiastical Christianity' for failing to communicate this message was not without justification. A. G. Stephens who at the turn of the century took the Christianity of his time on its face value, saw it, in the comment I have already quoted, not as an affirmation of life, but as a call 'to sacrifice the present' for a 'visionary future lacking a rational guarantee'. If Christianity calls for a self-transcendence, this will only be credible to those called to accept its 'good news' if it brings with it a more authentic human existence.

Campbell points to the way in which the essential message of the Christian gospel has tended to become ideologically distorted as the Christian community reacted to a situation in which it found itself outside the mainstream of the Australian conversation and having to clamour for a hearing. There is, he writes, a 'pervasive theological mood' which may be detected 'right across the denominations'. His interpretation of this mood brings to light something of great moment for those who are trying to place the voice of Christianity within its broader Australian context. It is worth quoting his description in full:

It could be called 'fundamentalist', though by that I would not necessarily mean that set of doctrines associated with ultra-conservative Protestants, but rather the attitude which in a simplistic manner firms upon a few doctrines and practices and proclaims them as essential to salvation. It could be called 'positivistic', in the sense in which positive law is sometimes contrasted with natural law, if that term had not been pre-empted by an analogous scientific attitude. It could be called 'assertive', meaning by that the attitude which sees religion as needing to be asserted, projected into the society, rather than as a permeating structure simply there. It could be called 'conservative', if that term were not so vague and capable of meaning just a generous, accommodating sensitivity to evolving tradition. Other adjectives which come to mind are 'dogmatic', 'authoritarian' and 'confessional', but they are even more inadequate. If all these descriptions can be seen as arrows, each pointing towards an unnamed character which can yet be recognised in the different churches and church parties, my meaning will be conveyed[91].

In Campbell's judgment, this description fits all the major denominations in Australia — 'there is not much separating the sacred heart of Jesus from the old rugged cross', he remarks.

The 'assertive' self-expression of Australian Christianity which I have just described was satirised by Patrick White in his portrayal of the young evangelist who bounded into the final pages of *The Tree of Man*, jumping Stan Parker's fence and coming towards him 'stepping over beds rather than following paths, he was so convinced of achieving his mission by direct means and approaches'. Having reached Stan, he addressed his message concerning the 'glories of salvation' to 'the button of the old man's cap', quite incapable of sharing the old man's journey in what were, in fact, the final moments of his life. What he had to say was of no help to Stan.

White has also satirised the other reaction of a marginalised Christianity in Australia: that of identifying with that culture in a way which enlists the Christian message to support and validate its existing reality. Mr Bonner, for example, the merchant who provides financial support for Voss in return for the public recognition it brings him, is quite incapable of discovering what the explorer learns so painfully about authentic human existence: 'that the shell-less oyster is not more vulnerable than man', that spiritual freedom is found in the owning of one's limitations and vulnerability. Instead, Mr Bonner tries 'to calculate, for how much, and from whom, salvation might be bought, and, to ensure that his last entrance would be made through the right cedar door'; and so he had 'begun in secret to subscribe liberal sums to all denominations, including those of which he approved'[92].

Of course, Mr Bonner's religion was a dull, boring affair, of the sort well described by the sociologist, David Martin. 'There is a majority who believe in God, a certain public respect for Him and His advocates, but the activities associated with His name are regarded as simply boring or incomprehensible'[93]. Bruce Wilson quotes these words in making the point that for many in our society who have followed the path taken by Mr Bonner, the Christian religion has compromised its essential intentionality, becoming 'basically civic rather than transcendental in character'. Time and time again, in fact, the lessons of history show that institutional Christianity has identified itself with the wisdom of the status quo and a validation of the historical forms it has assumed—only to find that the embrace of acceptance proved suffocating to the breath of life it should bring to its age.

James McAuley's words in his 'A Letter to John Dryden' have a challenge for all of us:

> The puzzled sects have let their doctrines sag,
> Or melt like lollies in a bag,
> Until the Christian faith has seemed to mean
> Only: 'Be good, be kind, God save the Queen'.

If this tendency to call upon the Christian religion to uphold and validate Australia's existing secular order has been an obvious temptation for those denominations more identified with the Anglo-Saxon tradition, Catholicism has not escaped its own version of the same tendency. Frank Lewins comments, in discussing the challenge of Australia's emerging multicultural society, that the attitude to migrants of Roman Catholicism 'has been more Australian than Catholic', that 'the church has responded in the same way as other Australian institutions'[94], rather than as a community which sees itself as called to demonstrate the capacity of the gospel to overcome all barriers of race and culture.

It is interesting in this context to quote Patrick O'Farrell. 'The Victorian Land Convention of 1857, whose aim was restricted immigration, had an Irish president...and the huge number of Irish who joined it was widely noted'[95]. We would have to admit that this is true. In a similar way, our record in our relationships with the Aboriginal people has been shaped by prevailing attitudes, rather than by the gospel message.

The history of the Roman Catholic Church in Australia has owed a great deal to the energies generated by its position as a subculture which to some extent was, or saw itself as, discriminated against. The historian Patrick O'Farrell puts his finger on the challenge which it now faces when it can no longer see itself

as a disadvantaged minority: 'We have arrived. Equality of opportunity has more or less been achieved. So, where are we? We are
faced for the first time in our history with the need to approach
religious education, so to speak, without the impetus and support
formerly provided by our social situation...'[96].

In speaking of the relationship between the Christian faith and
the culture in which it must find expression, we touch on a question with such fundamental importance for contemporary religion
that it is worth exploring in its wider implications. Australian
Christianity shares with the whole Western world the challenge
brought by contemporary secularisation. It is understandable that
many Christians look upon this development with dismay. There
is emerging within Christian theology, however, a conviction
that secularisation may well prove an occasion of liberation and
increased self-awareness for the true genius of Christian faith[97].

Contemporary secularisation—the cultural movement identified
with the demand of 'modernity' for a legitimate autonomy for the
secular order—is a reversal of the process of *sacralisation* which
was basic to all previous civilisations. From the dawn of human
history until the emergence of modernity, the world-building
processes of cultural traditions which united human communities
were grounded in the assumption that they could only come to
terms with human existence and mundane reality by relating them
to the transcendent 'beyond' in which their being is ultimately
grounded. From the earliest human experience to which we have
access, religious concern has found expression through the mythology and ritual which were an attempt to break out of the framework of immediate experience, to pierce the 'beyond' and find the
transcendental order which explains the enigmas of the human
situation.

Whatever we may make of these attempts, they were the expressions of profound existential concern, that is, concern for
human well-being at its deepest level. Confronted by the questions
raised by the limited and precarious nature of personal and
mundane reality, these cultural traditions sought to satisfy humanity's deepest yearnings and needs through reference to the 'sacred'
realm in which this reality was grounded.

Any assessment of the religious dimension of the human project
must take into account the cultural achievements of the traditions
established upon this presupposition for, as historian Christopher Dawson writes, 'Religion is the key of history'. We cannot
understand the 'inner form' of any society of this kind 'unless we
understand its religion'. 'We cannot understand its cultural
achievements', he continues, 'unless we understand the religious
beliefs behind them. In all ages the first creative works of a culture
are due to religious inspiration and dedicated to a religious end.

The temples of the gods are the most enduring works of man. Religion stands at the threshold of all the great literatures of the world. Philosophy is its offspring and is a child which constantly returns to its parent'[98].

But for all the noble achievements of these sacralised traditions, we can recognise today that the cultural processes which produced them entailed ambiguities not fully recognised by those who shared in the world-views which they produced. They were the outcome of a human creativity producing symbolic forms which made a lived acknowledgment of the divine order fundamental to all spheres of human activity. Thus they created a situation in which it was impossible for individuals to share in the benefits of their cultural tradition without owning the religious interpretation with which it was so radically identified. More than that, the pre-reflexive manner in which these traditions developed gave rise, more often than not, to the illusion that the symbolic way of access to the divine which had in fact been devised by the culture was, indeed, divinely established.

Moreover, the enormous investment which the culture had made, in these pre-reflexive achievements and the coherent world they had established, caused these cultures to be strongly resistant to critical assessment and to all forms of dissent. The fact, moreover, that these sacralised traditions have often combined profound concerns and insights with what was distorted and even grotesque made them very vulnerable to the critical spirit of Western modernity.

The sacralised world-view, it must be acknowledged, conceived the relationship between mundane reality and the divine transcendent order in such a fashion that neither could be understood except in terms of the other and each was, in a sense, compromised. The divine mystery could not be recognised as unambiguously 'other' than the mundane, if it was seen as first and foremost the principle governing the functioning of the cosmos; the world could not be fully appropriated as having a worth in itself, if its essential function was seen to be the providing of a vehicle for divine agency and self-disclosure. In other words, the divine was deprived of its proper transcendence and the world was deprived of its proper autonomy.

The German theologian J. B. Metz describes the Hellenistic version of sacralisation. 'For the Greeks, the world always had a numinous side; there was always the dark beginning of God himself; all their horizons merged into a twilight of the gods'. For them, God was a 'world-principle', a 'cosmic reason and cosmic law', an 'immanent regulating principle of the universe' and as a consequence 'the divine was itself an element of their picture of the world'[99]. It has not been easy for the Christian tradition to recognise the essential challenge to this sacralised world-view which is at the heart of Judeo-Christian faith. As Metz writes, 'For a long time the classical view of the world', which found in divinised or numinised nature a fundamental avenue of access to the divine, 'persisted within the Western Christian world. Today it must be admitted that even the "classical" Middle Ages had a strong general quality of the pre-Christian world-view about them, and were dominated by a straightforward "divinism" (Y. Congar)'[100].

It was inevitable that such a view of mundane reality should come into conflict with the spirit of modernity and its affirmation of the proper autonomy of the secular order. Tragically, the history of the emergence of modernity has been, more often than not, a history of conflict with a Christian establishment which saw the call for a proper autonomy for the secular order—to replace the sacralised order which took shape in medieval Europe—as an attack on essential Christian principles. We are now in a position to recognise that this was far from being the case. In fact the Christian faith—which accepts as a basic principle that God has affirmed, through the incarnation of the Eternal Son, the inherent value of mundane reality—must acknowledge, in the words of Metz, that 'a genuinely Christian impulse is working itself out historically in this modern process of an increased secularisation of the world'[101]. Indeed, the essential genius of Christian faith is radically differentiated from the view of God which comes from the process of sacralisation whatever its form[102].

Today, theologians argue that, in the emergence of secularisation, Christianity is being offered the opportunity to recognise at a very radical level the fatal consequences of seeking the embrace of acceptance by identifying with existing cultural realities in a manner which has obscured the essential import of the Christian gospel. If Australia is 'the most secularised of all western cultures'[103], Christian concerns to participate more fully in our national conversation must be situated within this broader context.

As they do so, Christians should recognise that the challenge of secularisation—modernity's claiming of the secular order's proper autonomy—takes many forms in various parts of the Western world. European culture faces an acute problem by reason of the omnipresence of symbols produced by the long centuries of sacralised culture which produced the very identity of Europe. For these traditions, disengagement from the sacralisation of their past is a painful, often bitter and antagonistic experience. The cultural tradition of the United States is deeply linked with the religious stand taken by the founding fathers, a factor which one could say has given rise to a subtle dimension of sacralisation which profoundly complicates the process of secularisation. If this process is an obvious characteristic of our culture, there is a certain innocence with which the autonomy of the secular order has established itself in our national conversation which we must take into account as we face the challenges it brings.

If the Christian movement is to win a hearing in the secularised mood of the Australian conversation, its contribution must avoid each of the two extremes I have indicated. On the one hand, it will not be listened to by the majority of Australians if it is no more than an assertive voice, with the tone of a righteous intruder into the ongoing exchange shaping the Australian project, intent on putting Australians right. On the other hand, Christians know they have failed in making the contribution they are called to make to the endeavours of the Australian people if the message they bring is no more than a validation of the conventional wisdom of the existing culture.

3. Is there a Christian voice which is truly Australian?

Christian thinkers must acknowledge the fact that their concerns have remained on the margins of the public conversation of our nation. Their work has been, for the most part, a remote echo of the discussion of theologians working in other cultures. They face a considerable challenge if this situation is to be changed and they are to give expression to the vision of Christianity which speaks more effectively to Australian awareness, and makes a telling contribution to the national conversation.

The claims of Christian faith as they are proposed by contemporary theologians are exalted and challenging. 'In accord with the logic of love ... God enters into the life of the "other" and becomes human... Divinisation thus comes by means of a humanisation. All this may seem to the unbeliever nothing but myth or illusion, but it is the very object of faith and governs its design and structure' (M. D. Chenu). According to the Christian gospel, the revelation of God is given in the 'dazzling darkness' of an incomparable divine beauty made present to the world in Jesus of Nazareth, as 'God freely manifests himself... as a gift, as love and therewith as self-surrender... through the ineffable fact the God wills to be with me, for me and in me... (it is a) splendour which breaks forth from this love of God which gives itself without remainder and is poured forth in the form of worldly powerlessness'; for all its transcendent greatness, however, the gospel truth does not nullify the goodness and beauty of creation—rather, all that is deserving of love and admiration in our world of experience 'is drawn up into a relationship with this inexhaustible standard' (Hans Urs von Balthasar).

As the Christian movement has sought to give this gospel truth to the world, two models of evangelisation have emerged which have a recognisable relationship to the claims of Christian faith as they have just been described. One emphasises the divine self-giving which constitutes the ultimate objective content of the 'good news'; the other looks to human subjectivity as it is called by the gospel truth to an ultimate authenticity and fulfilment.

An analysis of their implications leads to the conclusion that these two models are of their nature complementary. They will prove inadequate and ineffectual if those who make use of them fail to recognise their complementarity and the dialectic that should bring about a vital interchange between them.

The gospel truth can only present itself as good news if it addresses humanity at the deepest level of personhood and need. The Second Vatican Council pointed to this aspect of evangelisation when it urged Christians to recognise that

> the Church has always had the duty of scrutinising the signs of the times and of interpreting them in the light of the gospel... We must therefore recognise and understand the world in which we live, its expectations, its longings, and its often dramatic characteristics... The people of God...labours to decipher authentic signs of God's presence and purpose in the happenings, needs, and desires in which this people has a part along with other men and women of our age[104].

On the other hand, if God has become present to the reality and struggles of human existence in Jesus of Nazareth, as the Christian gospel claims, the story of Jesus provides a final index through which the gracious presence of God in the story of humanity as a whole may be understood.

The emerging mood of Western culture makes it possible to look critically at the way in which the Christian tradition brought to this country from Europe has been articulated. As our secularised Western culture passes beyond the securities of a sacralised world-view, we sense the need to achieve a comprehensive, holistic understanding of the human situation. In this climate, Les Murray stresses the fundamental place his 'wholespeak' must have in our ongoing conversation. Tony Kelly's 'new imagining' seeks a response of the whole person to a total objectivity. Veronica Brady expresses something of this mood of our culture in the final paragraphs of her *A Crucible of Prophets*: 'The task of Australians, as of every individual and of every culture, is to come to terms with their memories, their bodies and their environment and then situate themselves as creatures within the mysterious, often painful but always worshipful cosmos'[105]. She is here concluding a study in which she has entered into a dialogue with the views of the human situation, in its relationship with God, registered in a series of Australian novels.

The 'story', we are coming to recognise, is of fundamental importance in the holistic view of human existence we are seeking. In the address which Alexander Solzhenitsen prepared at the time he received the Nobel Prize, he wrote of the manner in which great literature expresses a truth which is to be found in the lived reality of its own world: 'the convincingness of a true work of art is completely irrefutable', he writes, 'and it forces even an opposing heart to surrender'. Portrayals which manipulate or distort, he notes, do not endure; they end by convincing no one. But a true masterpiece 'bears within itself its own verification... those works of art which have scooped up the truth and presented it as a living force—they take hold of us, compel us, and nobody ever, not even in ages to come, will appear to refute them'[106].

Manning Clark has come to base his work as a historian upon a similar conviction. 'All the great stories of mankind', he writes, 'are told without any comment at all. Perhaps that is why they have outlived their generation, and said something to men at all times and places'[107]. Stories which live on in human memory, he notes, 'make a point about life; or, to extend this a little, they make us explicitly aware of what we had vaguely noticed before, of what life is like, of what will happen to us if in our folly or in some mad passion we defy the wisdom of humanity'[108]. The historian, he reflects, must endeavour to tell his story in a way that allows this truth to speak for itself.

The emerging mood of Western culture of which I speak has had important repercussions in Christian thought. A comparative historical view has made it possible to recognise that Christian awareness has been too much the captive of an analytical notion of truth derived from the intellectual tradition of the Greeks. This understanding of truth sees it as an *idea*, an eternal concept or proposition to be possessed by the mind. This intellectual approach—isolating the abstract, objective dimensions of the human encounter with reality—pointed the way towards the project of 'scientific' investigation, the critical spirit, so important and fruitful in the development of Western civilisation.

Valid within its own frame of reference, this analytical project is prone to reductionism, the mistake of confusing an understanding of the dismembered elements produced by its analysis with an understanding of the whole within which the parts have their proper reality. When it rules theology it easily judges that the task has been achieved when some doctrinal proposition has been clarified, and does not recognise that such propositions only live when they are in a relationship of vital dependence upon the total truth of Christian faith, given in the One who is the revelation of the divine mystery[109].

A review of the history of the Christian movement in Australia leads to an extension of this criticism. Not only was the Christian message proposed in abstract *doctrines*, but institutional Christianity was alienated from the mainstream of Australian experience because it assumed a form which was too heavily *ideological*: the group interests of the various denominations strongly influenced the way in which they shaped their presentation of the Christian message. The theological differences which split Christian Europe had established a partisan spirit among Protestants and Catholics which made the body of theological discussion distinctly ideological.

The polemical situation which had produced a stalemate in Europe was transported to Australia, with the result that too often protagonists on both sides were as much interested in countering the positions of their opponents as they were in giving to their age the substance of Christian truth. The fact that their assertive intrusions into the national conversation had no appeal to so many honest and upright Australians should have led them to ask themselves whether they were doing justice to the message they sought to share. One of the characteristics of an ideology as it establishes group solidarity is its resistance to criticism: the more beleaguered its adherents feel, the more they hold to the security it gives.

Many committed Christians, both Catholic and Protestant, will object, no doubt, that the teachings of their churches *did* bring them to a meeting with the gospel which has become the main support and inspiration of their lives. This has undoubtedly been so. Our criticism still stands. Ideologies, as the analysis made in earlier chapters should make clear, are not a *denial* of reality, but a selective presentation of reality, influenced by the historical needs of those who identify with them. Ideological presentations of the Christian message were not necessarily a denial of the gospel truth. Their selective emphases, however, did not allow that truth to be expressed with the clarity it deserved. While Protestant denominations presented Christian truth in a form which, to quote Richard Campbell's words, 'in a simplistic manner firms upon a few doctrines and practices and proclaims them as essential to salvation', and while Catholics reacted with a defensive and too wooden upholding of its traditional doctrinal positions, both sides to the debate failed to bring to light the true genius of the message they wished to communicate to their fellow Australians.

The doctrinal and ideological project taken up by the Christian movement, we can now recognise, was essentially derivative. Beyond it lies the realm of truth to which Solzhenitsen and Clark have referred, a truth much closer to ordinary life experience, a truth that is lived before it is told, the truth of Les Murray's 'permanent inner poem', the truth proclaimed in the silent witness of a selfless and dedicated life, the truth for which all men and women hunger in the depths of their existence.

As I have pointed out, the search for a holistic understanding of the human situation has led to a new appreciation of the importance of 'story'. The essential claim of the Judeo-Christian faith is that the story remembered in the record of the Scriptures discloses a truth about human existence which is universal[110].

The truth of what God would be for humankind is given to the world in the story of Jesus of Nazareth, a story which is lived before it is told. 'We preach Christ crucified', Paul declares, 'Christ the power of God and the wisdom of God. For the foolishness of God is wiser than men and the weakness of God is stronger than men' (1 Cor 1:23–25). The first followers of Jesus instinctively recognised that it was in the story, told in the end without interpretative comment and allowed to speak for itself, that the message of Christian faith finds its best expression. And so, by a kind of paradox, the name 'gospel' or 'good news' was given first and foremost, not to the Spirit-filled *interpretations* of what had been given to the world, which had been present in the church's preaching from the beginning, but to the *telling of the story*.

It must come as a challenging surprise to Australian Christians to learn that while they have been preoccupied with an expression of their faith in the derivative forms of doctrine and ideology, fellow Australians who stood apart from institutional Christianity were fascinated by the story of Jesus of Nazareth, making it the measure whereby they endeavoured to interpret our common existence.

If what Manning Clark called, with a surprising harshness (or was it irony?), 'that priest-ridden, sectarian-tainted, bigoted and superstitious corruption of Christianity that... emerged from centuries of poverty and oppression in Ireland' could hardly win his admiration, he praised Catholicism for 'preserving by some miracle the image of Christ and the Holy Mother of God'[111]. It is surprising that one who has reflected so deeply upon the function of 'story' for us all should speak of 'image'; he is certainly referring to what I have been discussing. In more recent times, the same thought came back. In a 1989 interview Clark said 'There is an important question we all have to answer. Who kept the image of Christ alive?... who kept alive the image that he said those things by the side of the waters of Galilee?...I think for all its faults and its corruption, wickedness, Rome did actually keep that alive'[112].

It is Dostoevski who provides the introductory quotation to the latest volume of Clark's autobiography: 'I want to be there when everyone suddenly understands what it has all been for'. One reviewer concluded that Clark's responsiveness to these words was related to his search for the transcendent ground of the better world for which he dared to hope. Once again it is the story of Christ that pointed the way: 'the whole of Christ and everything he said' was opposed to the doctrinal issues, which left him perplexed[113].

It is not surprising that Clark has expressed his profound admiration for Henry Lawson, recognising in him a kindred spirit as far as his fascination with the story of Christ is concerned. 'As a community', he said in the 1976 Boyer Lectures, 'we (Australians) are often divided between the "Banjo" Paterson and the Henry Lawson view of the world'[114]. He is referring, of course, to what emerged in the debate discussed earlier, in which romantic and realistic views of our Australian experience were set one against the other. Seeking his epic key, he related the two views to the meeting which each of these famous Australians had made with the gospel story. Paterson, as we have seen, had heard of Christ in 'a school which had prefects and a cadet corps', in one of 'those chapels where the emblems and trophies of war were displayed in a building dedicated to the teachings of the Galilean fisherman'. Lawson, on the other hand, 'was touched by the image of Christ, by all those wonderful remarks he made before he made the disastrous journey to Jerusalem'.

Manning Clark's biographical study *In Search of Henry Lawson* is a work filled with affection. In it he succeeds in bringing to light the fragile and pathetic greatness which lived on in the man, throughout a life torn in a tragic struggle between his extraordinary sensitivity and remarkable literary talent on the one hand, and a tyrannical alcoholism on the other. Clark sees the image of Christ and what he stood for as something which helps us to understand how Lawson carried on to the end, never completely losing sight of the vision which had inspired him.

Clark links this awareness of the gospel story with his early introduction to the works of Dickens by his mother. In his *The Life of Our Lord*, written for children in 1849, Dickens wrote 'No one ever lived, who was so good, so kind, so gentle, and so sorry for all people who did wrong, or were in any way ill or miserable, as he was... It is Christianity to be gentle, merciful and forgiving, and to keep these qualities quiet in our hearts...' Of young Lawson, Clark writes 'Like Dickens he was attracted to the idea that there had once been a man on earth who had not wanted to hurt anyone else, that there had once been a man who was not tormented by or enslaved by a cruel sensuality'[115].

It was the image of Christ which came to mind in later years as he tried to express the true spirit of mateship. 'He wanted human beings', Clark writes, 'to heed that new commandment given unto them, that they love one another'[116]. Like so many of the bushmen he described, Lawson had little sympathy for institutionalised Christianity. The poem 'The Shearers' begins:

No church-bell rings them from the track
No pulpit lights their blindness—
'Tis hardship, drought and loneliness
That teach these Bushmen kindness:
The mateship born of barren lands,
Of toil and thirst and danger—
The camp-fire for the stranger set,
The first place to the stranger.

And it ends with the jaunty lines we have already cited:

They tramp in mateship side by side—
The Protestant and 'Roman'—
They call no biped lord or 'sir'
And touch their hat to no man!

Lawson prophesied that words like 'mate' would never die, Clark writes, 'with the same fervour with which men of faith had hoped and prayed and believed that the Christ figure would never die, never disappear from the face of the earth'[117].

Sometimes Lawson made the link explicit. The story 'Send Round the Hat' is about a big bushman, nicknamed 'Giraffe', 'who would thrash a bully in a good-natured sort of way', and who quietly lent a hand to overworked bushwomen. For people in trouble it was Giraffe who would 'take round the hat', with a 'I hope I ain't disturbing yer, but there's a cove...' The strangers' friend, he considered, like Christ, that those who were despised and rejected were the ones needing help, the ones who could not manage life at all. He harboured no resentment. In Clark's words, 'he was one of nature's innocents, the fool in Christ of the Australian bush. Like Christ, he had sympathy for everyone'. 'Unlike Christ', he adds, 'he was not entirely at his ease when talking with women'[118].

The story tells of Giraffe 'taking round the hat' for some prostitutes the police are running out of town. One of them embarrasses him by asking him to kiss her. Thus, as Clark remarks, the story ends, not with a profound piece of wisdom, but with some bush clowning: 'For the bushman was both a clown, and a bearer of the image of Christ'. And he adds 'In Lawson's mind there was always somewhere in the Australian bush someone who was behaving in a Christ-like way'[119].

Another of Lawson's stories, 'Shall We Gather at the River', captures his affinity with the gospel and what it stood for. It describes Peter McLaughlin, a bush missionary of sorts. 'There was something, the reader is told', Clark writes, 'in his big dark-brown eyes that was scarcely misery, nor yet sadness—a sort of haunting sympathy'. Clark's summary of the preacher's message probably tells us as much about Clark himself as it does about Lawson and his subject. He had 'long since abandoned hope that either man or place could ever be different. He did not promise "better times" to a people whose crops were ruined by drought, to a people... starved off their selections and forced to work as hirelings for wages, leaving behind them a dusty patch in the scrub. He spoke to them about life as they knew it, about their secret longings for something better, and of how they would have to suffer before they could achieve anything in Australia. He told them there was beauty in their lives, yes and even in their harsh, uncouth land, if only they would look for it. He spoke to them about the evils of self-pity and not forgiving men their trespasses, and remaining hard of heart'[120]. Lawson concluded the preacher's service on a wry note, with the singing of the hymn 'Shall We Gather at the River'—all that remained of a watercourse thereabouts was 'a mudhole every mile or so, and dead beasts rotting and stinking every few yards'.

In the bush, Christ was Lawson's measure of true mateship. When he found himself in prison, it was the same. In the poem, 'One-hundred-and-three', composed in Darlinghurst Gaol, he wrote 'Yet the spirit of Christ is everywhere where the heart of man can dwell—/ It comes like tobacco in prison, or like news to a separate cell'[121]. Clark owes to Lawson his image of the incomparable moment when the eyes of mates meet over the rims of their first drink together. The painful irony of Lawson's yearning to share the true 'cup of loving kindness', and the alcoholism which time and again turned that splendid symbol into a destructive nightmare, runs like a tragic leitmotif through Clark's portrayal.

I have spoken more than once of the importance of the example and teaching of Christ for Joseph Furphy. His point of view is very similar to that of Lawson and Clark. In the words of Veronica Brady, 'the utopia he offers involves learning to live comfortably, even joyously, with the knowledge that an ideal society may not be possible in this world and that yet we must go on hoping and working for it'[122]. The ideal on which his eyes are steadily fixed is found in the gospel story. As we have seen, he judges 'there is nothing utopian...in the charter of that kingdom (preached by Jesus)—in the sunshiny Sermon on the Mount. It is no fanciful conception of an intangible order of things, but a practical, workable code of daily life adapted to any stage of civilisation'[123].

The challenge Australia faced in his day was not physical but the spiritual challenge of putting this code into practice. Like Lawson, his realism found in the teaching of Christ a call to identification with the marginalised: 'the Light of the world, the God-in-man, the only God we can ever know, is by His own authority represented for all time by the poorest of the poor'[124]. Veronica Brady says that Furphy's view of life is expressed in terms which at times remind us of a Pascal or a Kierkegaard, 'even if his tone is considerably more jokey than theirs'[125]. Like them, he is 'profoundly suspicious of systems and ideologies'[126]. His rejection of 'ecclesiastical Christianity' is a rejection of Kierkegaard's 'Christendom' (the sacralised Christian culture in all its unresolved ambiguities) in the name of a genuine 'Christianity'.

Too easily those wanting to share the Christian faith have taken for granted the story which haunted fellow Australians seeking the meaning of human existence. All too often boring preconceptions of what Christ is like, derived from elsewhere, pre-empted their awareness. The story of Pasolini's film *The Gospel According to Matthew* and the reaction of many Christians to his portrayal of Jesus well illustrates this. The film maker, who had little to do with the church, found himself stranded in a hotel room in Assisi because he had chosen to visit the town on the same day as John XXIII. To fill in time he took the Bible he found there and read the first of the gospels. The film that resulted he dedicated to John XXIII.

Thomas Merton comments on the reaction the film provoked: 'Many Christians who saw the film criticised it, not because it was unfaithful to the Gospel, but because it presented a picture of Christ that frightened them. The Christ of Pasolini, young, dark, splendidly aloof, dreadfully serious, was obviously not the sweet, indulgent Jesus of late nineteenth century art... The fact that so many Christians could be shocked by this is itself shocking, for the picture of Christ obviously rested on a very real and open-minded reading of St Matthew... The Christ of St Matthew can rigorously demand that men have mercy on one another as the only way to make them ready to receive mercy (cf. Mt 5:7; 21:31–46)'[127].

The story told in the gospels is so remarkable that Dostoevski, one of the greatest storytellers the world has ever seen, became almost obsessed with it in the later part of his life, making the New Testament his constant companion. It had so completely taken possession of him that he wrote 'If anyone could prove to me, that Christ was outside the truth, and if the truth really did exclude Christ, I should prefer to stay with Christ and not with the truth'[128].

Vincent Buckley—the late poet and professor of literature quoted in an earlier chapter—in an article published in 1970, 'The Strange Personality of Christ'[129], discussed the figure of Jesus in the gospel narratives from the point of view of a literary critic. He found 'a far stranger figure than is generally acknowledged', one who 'defeats all our expectations'. The one portrayed 'has power concentrated in his being'. Buckley has recourse to a category of the great authority on comparative religion, Mircea Eliade: Jesus is 'an hierophany and a creator of hierophanies' ('hierophany': a symbol which opens access to the sacred and the transcendent). The one portrayed, Buckley points out, has an astounding freedom and poise, he 'is wholly autonomous, and is the opposite of what Riesman called "other-directedness" '.

If we cease to take the Jesus story for granted, we can recognise how remarkable this last characteristic was. Jesus of Nazareth faced the world, and aroused a violent opposition that ultimately brought about his death, with no program, no slogans, no establishment with which he identified, no party machine of advisers and supporters who protected him when he was uncertain and the going was hard. If he identified with any group it was with the powerless and the marginalised. With astounding courage, unquestioned rectitude, and a childlike simplicity, he offered his friendship to those as diverse as the tax officers who were the detested friends of the occupying power and the revolutionary zealots bent on liberating their people; members of both groups became his followers. The story had to be told, even though the one remembered is in many respects bewildering and contradicts all stereotypes of a religious personage.

'Originality' is a term frequently used by those who have tried to describe the one portrayed in this story, which has no parallel in human experience. For the English biblical scholar, C. H. Dodd, the teachings of Jesus which are recorded provide a remarkable account of this originality. In touch with all that was going on around him, 'he must have enjoyed mixing with various types of people, showing an intense, unsentimental, absolutely honest interest in them'. Using the conventional thought forms of his age, he broke free from their limitations to bring a message that challenged those whom he addressed in the very depths of their being[130].

The mills of human wisdom grind laboriously and slowly; the person who can make some small contribution to the fund of that wisdom earns lasting fame. What Jesus has to give to humanity is of an entirely different order. 'No one', writes Karl Adam of his message, 'can make it straighter than it is'. It was this originality which captured the attention of Joseph Furphy, as he commended the 'sunshiny Sermon on the Mount' as 'a practical workable code of life, adapted to any stage of civilization'.

The great Swiss theologian Karl Barth expresses the challenge which the memory of the story of Jesus constitutes for all who share it: the life of this 'man...within our human history...this Stranger whom we cannot overlook or remove...because as such He is at home among us and like us and with us...this near neighbour...in all His otherness...is called light, revelation and word...this life...is a declaration...it is an address, promise and demand... Confronted and compared with His life, the life which we live or describe as such is only a vacuum and darkness'[131].

The German theologian Walter Kasper sums up the incomparable impression the story of Jesus made and still makes. 'In Jesus we finally come face to face with God. His life is the answer to the question, "Who is God?" Jesus does not fit into any category. Neither ancient nor modern, nor Old Testament categories are adequate to understand him. He is unique. He is and remains a mystery. He himself does little to illuminate this mystery. He is not interested in himself at all'[132].

Jesus gives an ultimate expression to the calling of humankind into God's rule of love. It is not long before he knows that men and women will not accept God's invitation. But God will have his way; love will have its way. The story of Jesus is indeed the greatest of his parables, overturning the world of false securities in which humanity is pleased to remain, and inviting all to a sharing in God's mystery and his ways of compassionate love.

The English writer Sebastian Moore quotes the remark of one almost reluctantly caught up in a meeting with God through the gospel story of Jesus: 'the reason why I can't get round the Gospels is that the mission of Jesus failed and the evangelists are at pains to emphasise that'. He comments 'Such trueness to *life* in a document concerned with *religion* is... simply uninventable. This to me is revelation, revelation into which I with all my worldly expectations must die... The early Church did not bypass the Cross. It did not pass from this bitter disappointment into another dream, the ecstasy of the hellenistic mysteries. It glorified in the Cross and found there the very coining of its mysteries. *This* is the process whereby Jesus becomes the meeting and oneing of the worlds and is believable as such'[133].

What Leonardo Boff, the Brazilian theologian, has to say about this story takes us to the heart of its meaningfulness for humanity, and helps us to understand the appeal it had for the Australian idealists I have mentioned. Most of the comments quoted to this point have drawn attention to what makes Jesus extraordinary, and leads us to an encounter with the 'otherness' of the divine mystery he brings into our midst. Probably the most powerful preconception which committed Christians bring to their hearing of the gospel story is one which sees Jesus as an otherworldly figure. Such a preconception prevents a meeting with the utter humanness of the one who is the ultimate revelation of the divine mystery. But, as Boff points out, we shall not appreciate the full import of the story unless we come to appreciate what he calls the 'ordinariness' of Jesus[134].

In this ordinariness we recognise that the one who leads us to a meeting with the divine mystery is anything but an otherworldly figure. It is this recognition which establishes the gospel truth in the midst of the world in which we have our existence. Henry Lawson's bush preacher had learned this lesson well, speaking to his people of 'life as they knew it, about their secret longings', and telling them 'there was beauty in their lives, yes and even in their harsh, uncouth land, if only they would look for it'.

Jesus stands in the midst of our history, not as one who would lead humanity into some sacred sphere of isolated piety and security, away from the struggle 'to be and to remain human', but as one who shows in his own being and life what authentic human existence is like, and who invites men and women to share that authenticity because it is there first and foremost that we shall find God. He shows himself, Boff writes, as 'someone liberated from the complications that people and a history of sin created'. The message he brings calls for nothing more or less than 'a radical and total liberation of the human condition from all its alienating elements'. He goes immediately to 'the essential things', knowing 'how to speak of them, briefly, concisely and with precision'; he speaks with 'an extraordinary good sense that surprised all about him'. Explaining what he has in mind, Boff reflects on the nature of this 'good sense': it is his ability to 'discover the core of things... related to the concrete knowledge of life... an unparalleled freshness pervades all that he does and says. God, human beings, society and nature are immediately present to him... his words bite into the concrete world until it is forced to make a decision before God'.

The 'originality' of Jesus, Boff suggests, means something far more than that he said and did unprecedented things. It means that he is one who 'is near to the origin and root of things' and who can lead others there with him. He can speak of these things with an 'absolute immediacy and superiority'; all that he says and does 'is translucent, crystal clear, and evident'. And people recognise this: 'All those in contact with Jesus encountered themselves and that which is best in them. All are led to discover their own root. Confrontation with this source generates a crisis: one is constrained to make a decision and either convert or install oneself in that which is derived, secondary, and part of the concrete situation'[135].

It is easy to recognise a link between what Boff is pointing out and the 'new imagining' to which Tony Kelly invites Australians. The genuine Christian will not enter into imagining what things might be like alone, but in the presence of the One who has shown us the way things should be. The link with Les Murray's 'permanent inner poem' is also easy to see. It is at the level of the fundamental presence to reality which the 'inner poem' represents that we are invited to meet Jesus of Nazareth. Murray expresses this admirably in the poem, 'Equanimity', published in the collection *The Vernacular Republic*:

> Whatever its variants of meat-cuisine, worship, divorce,
> human order has at heart
> an equanimity. Quite different from inertia, it's a place
> where the churchman's not defensive, the indignant
>   aren't on the qui vive,
> the loser has lost interest, the accountant is truant to remorse,
> where the farmer has done enough struggling-to-survive
>   for one day, and the artist rests from theory—
> where all are, in short, off the high comparative horse of
>   their identity.
> Almost beneath notice, as attainable as gravity, it is
> a continuous recovering moment. Pity the high madness
> that misses it continually, ranging without rest between
>   assertion and unconsciousness,
> the sort that makes hell seem a height of evolution.
> Through the peace beneath effort
> (even within effort: quiet air between the bars of our
>   attention)
> comes unpurchased lifelong plenishment;
> Christ spoke to people most often on this level
> especially when they chattered about kingship and the
>   Romans;
> all holiness speaks from it.

All this brings to mind Manning Clark's comment that his attempt as a historian to make his writings 'a celebration of life, a hymn of praise to life' leaves him with 'a melancholy, a sadness, and a compassion because what matters most in life is never likely to happen'[136]. As he sought the vision which could provide the key to the epic form he wished his celebration of life to take, the story of Jesus of Nazareth has constantly suggested itself to him as an ultimate point of reference.

4. The gospel story and the Australian story

If Christian faith is the possession of the divine truth, it is a truth which is found ultimately in the gospel story[137]. In introducing the last section reference was made to the two poles of the dialectic at the heart of an authentic evangelisation: the story of Jesus of Nazareth brings to light the deepest significance of our human story; at the same time, our deepest existential experiences help us to recognise the true meaning of the gospel story. The exploration of this dialectic is of basic importance for those who wish to make a witness to Christian faith an integral part of the Australian conversation. The gospel story should help them to enter into the unique experience they have shared as Australians. On the other hand, their experience can help them to enter more deeply into the real meaning of the gospel story.

In the previous chapters I have identified three themes which have had an importance in our Australian experience: the spirit of egalitarianism which would establish an Australian society free of the notions of inherited status and privilege; the hard lessons which the setbacks of our history have brought; and the land within which we have found ourselves as a people, and which has become a symbol of immense importance for us as we come to terms with the meaning of our human existence. Let us make use of these themes to explore the potentialities of the dialectic to which I have referred.

For all its ambiguities and blind spots, egalitarianism has established itself as a fundamental ideal in the Australian conversation. From a very early date, Judith Wright writes, a new attitude showed itself in the Australian experience in a 'sense that here something new could be made, some kind of new relationship between men was mistily becoming possible...'. 'The danger today', she continued in 1965, 'is that, in our present reaction against the often over-sentimentalised emphasis on "mateship" and the "Australian legend", we may lose the strength it gave us. For it did, in fact, form the basis of such real Australianity as we have'[138].

One of the remarkable things about the gospel story is the fact that whatever resources may be brought to a critical consideration of the man described in the story—and our age of suspicion is well provided with such resources—he is never 'found out'. As they recede into the historical past, the great figures of the human story are more and more revealed as being, in the end, creatures of their own time: playing their part upon the basis of presuppositions derived from the accepted wisdom of their age—presuppositions which we cannot entirely share, coloured as they are by the ideologies of the historical group to which they belonged. In particular, they are found to be blind for the most part to much that today we take for granted concerning a practical recognition of the dignity and freedom of the human person.

Certainly, Jesus of Nazareth was a man of his time, but the message he proclaimed is not something of the past. Today, as in every age, it stands before us, as a future which beckons us and constitutes a standard against which we must judge our struggles to make a society in which we can 'be human and remain human'.

The German scholar Erich Auerbach, in his pioneering study *Mimesis*[139], written in Istanbul during the Second World War, discusses the representation of human reality in Western literature.

The New Testament, he demonstrates, introduced a revolution in human consciousness which came to be reflected in the literature of the West. For the literature of the Hellenistic civilisation, the agents who shaped the course of history were the rulers and military commanders who stood at the centre of the stage. The common people were of no account, sometimes cluttering the stage as these great leaders proceeded to carry forward their projects, sometimes providing an audience which enabled them to explain their actions.

The gospel narrative completely reverses this situation. Auerbach illustrates this by comparing the story of Peter's denial of Jesus as it is narrated in Mark's gospel with the contemporaneous writings of Petronius and Tacitus[140]. In Mark's narrative, Auerbach writes, 'Peter is no accessory figure', as the lesser actors in the classical writers were. 'He is the image of man in the highest and deepest and most tragic sense'. This portrayal, Auerbach explains, derives not from some artistic purpose, shaped by the imagination of the writer: 'on the contrary, it was rooted from the beginning in the character of Jewish–Christian literature' which finds its ultimate inspiration in 'God's incarnation in a human being of the humblest social station, through his existence on earth amid humble everyday people and conditions, and through his Passion, which, judged by earthly standards, was ignominious'.

This gospel story, Auerbach goes on to point out, had 'a most decisive bearing upon man's concept of the tragic and the sublime'. Peter and the other actors in the story of his denial are of the humblest background and human qualification. 'A tragic figure from such a background, a hero of such weakness, who yet derives the highest force from his very weakness, such a to and fro of the pendulum' breaks out of the constraints of the 'sublime style of classical antique literature'. It arouses a sympathy and awareness in humanity, 'because it portrays something which neither the poets nor the historians of antiquity ever set out to portray: the birth of a spiritual movement in the depths of the common people, from within the everyday occurrences of contemporary life, which thus assumes an importance it could never have assumed in antique literature'. This incident, Auerbach observes, is representative of the whole New Testament. Taking up, as it does, the universal concerns of humanity it 'sets man's whole world astir...what we see here is a world which on the one hand is entirely real, average, identifiable as to place, time, and circumstances, but which on the other hand is shaken in its very foundations, is transforming and renewing itself before our eyes'.

The revolution initiated by Jesus placed the common man and woman in their rightful place at the centre of the stage of human history. It is a lesson which humanity has taken many centuries to assimilate fully. Australians who had little sympathy for institutionalised Christianity have been instinctively drawn to it, as they have tried to explore and validate the precious thing which emerged in our Australian experience as the egalitarian spirit of mateship. Manning Clark, for instance, in words which remind us of Auerbach's analysis, describes Henry Lawson's stories as 'draping a mantle of tragic grandeur over the lives of the previously despised barbarians of the Australian bush'[141]. In some ways they were more in touch with what the gospel story has to tell than institutionalised Christians were.

Our Australian experience can lead to a deeper appreciation of the stance adopted by Jesus as he identified with the common people of his world. At the same time, his remarkable attitude can help us to recognise the true value of the ethos we have come to share. In this way, the gospel story can help us to overcome the ambiguities and superficialities which the legend of mateship is in danger of assuming. These ambiguities must not be allowed to rob us of something of great significance as we stand on the threshold of a multicultural Australian community, something we could share with the broader world. The 'ordinariness' central to the Jesus-story invites us to make our ultimate meeting with him at the heart of our own Australian stories; it invites us to meet a truth which is not 'intrusive', but which is given to us as the truth with which we have all been wrestling in our struggles as Australian individuals and as an Australian people. In the words of Noel Rowe, in a comment made when this book was being discussed, in the Jesus-story we meet 'a deeper, rather than a higher, authority'.

The exploration of this dialectic leads us onto the terrain pointed to by Johann Baptist Metz when he insists upon the importance for humanity of 'the memory of suffering' as a key to the deepest resources in the traditions of the world's peoples[142]. In particular, this meeting demands of us a renewed concern to give a full share in our life together to those who in different ways have been pushed to the margin by the legend of mateship: the Aboriginal people, the women of Australia, and the stranger in our midst.

As Donald Horne points out, our consideration of the groups just mentioned should avoid a 'bias towards victimage': the role of the victim must not be seen 'as merely passive'[143]. If the first telling of our national story has been the work of the 'winners', when the stories behind that story are told the 'losers' will prove to be those who rescue the 'winners' from themselves.

The Aboriginal people have made it possible for us finally to inhabit this ancient continent; through the qualities they have exhibited in their ordeal, they are, for Caroline Jones, 'the steady beating heart at the centre of our Australian identity'[144]. The story of women in Australia, now beginning to be told, will liberate us from much that has hampered us in the past. Patrick O'Farrell makes us aware of the fundamental contribution Irish traditions have made to our Australian ethos. And Les Murray's identification, in his search for wisdom and grace, with the small farmers who refused to be beaten in their lonely struggle with the land puts beyond all doubt the continuing importance for us of the tradition of realism at the heart of our sense of kinship with the bush. The land itself was one of the great losers in our history; today, however, respect for the environment of our weathered continent promises to be one of the factors which will save us from our former foolishness. The gospel story of the victim who became the source of life and healing challenges us to explore more fully these paradoxes of our history, and to recognise why it is that God stands with the 'losers'.

The second theme we have identified is the wisdom which the Australian experience has been invited to learn, through the setbacks and failure which have been our constant companions, as we have come to terms with life on this oldest and most fragile of continents. It is not one to which we readily relate, caught up as we are in the maze of the consumer society created by our recent—perhaps passing—prosperity. Whatever our future material conditions may be, at a deeper level failure and adversity of different kinds are part of the lot of struggling humanity, rich and poor alike. They have been the source of some of our most precious gains. It is important therefore for those who tell the gospel story that they come to appreciate more fully the manner in which a meeting with that story can help Australians to enter more deeply into the lessons which are part of the heritage of their experience.

Auerbach, in the passage just quoted, notes the fact that Jesus identified with the suffering and failure that are the common lot of humanity. The gospel story invites those seeking an authentic human existence to an identification with the common experience of humankind as it opens up for us a renewed understanding of the tragic and sublime dimensions of our common story. Sebastian Moore, as we have seen, makes the same point: such trueness to *life* in a document concerned with *religion* shows itself as a revelation of God as the ultimate ground of our existence, a revelation in which we and all our worldly expectations must die as we recognise in Jesus 'the meeting and oneing of our worlds'.

Joseph Furphy leaves us in no doubt, in a passage quoted earlier, that it is to the gospel story that he makes appeal in his criticism of institutional Christianity. After he has found the dead swagman, Tom Collins muses:

> Few and feeble are his friends on earth; and the One
> who, like him, was wearied with his journey, and, like

him, had not where to lay His head, is gone, according to his own parable, into a far country. The swagman we have always with us—and comfortable ecclesiasticism marks the full stop there, blasphemously evading the completion of a sentence charged with grave truth, that the Light of the world, the God-in-man, the only God we can ever know, is by His own authority represented for all time by the poorest of the poor[145].

It seems true to say that doctrinal explanations of the mystery of the cross, in both the Catholic and the Protestant cultures brought to Australia, have failed to do full justice to the implications of the gospel story. As a consequence a man such as Albert Facey, who can surely be described as a kind of Christ-figure in our midst in the courage and unselfishness with which he embraced his 'fortunate life', could remain confused when facing the question of God[146].

It should serve as a challenge to confessing Christians to find Patrick White calling upon the tradition of the gospel story to provide the key he looked for as he set out to fill the Australian 'emptiness'. Voss, the explorer, takes his stand on a self-sufficiency nourished by the fashions of nineteenth century Europe and brought to Australia with him. It causes him no concern, he says, to think of 'his material body swallowed up by what he has named', for 'It was not possible really, that anyone could damage the Idea, however much they scratched it'[147]. Indeed, for Voss, as he sets out on his journey of discovery, the 'future is what you will make it. Future is will'[148]. He tells Laura, however, that he cannot be an atheist, for 'the God they have abandoned is of mean conception'. 'I do believe, you must realise', he protests, 'Even though I worship with pride ... My God is above humility'[149]. Even in this conversation, he is haunted by the words of the Moravian missionary he has met in the Moreton Bay district, who said to him in all simplicity 'Mr Voss, you have a contempt for God, because He is in your own image'[150].

As the story unfolds, Voss is gradually stripped of the suffocating conceptions in which he had imprisoned himself. It is the figure of Christ which he cannot escape until he has found true wisdom, the 'true knowledge' which, as Laura says in the novel's concluding pages, 'only comes of death by torture in the country of the mind'[151].

Even on the 'lovely morning' of the expedition's departure, an image of the Christ figure intimates the coming struggle. 'No one would be crucified on any such amiable trees as those pressed along the northern shore' of Sydney Harbour as the ship sails[152]. The confrontation begins in a subtle way: Voss feels isolated by the rapport established immediately between Palfreyman, the ornithologist who is a sincere Christian, and Judd the ex-convict, as they 'gratefully sensed that they were equal in each other's eyes'[153]. 'Rocks will not gash him deeper, nor sun cauterise more searingly than human kindness', comments the farewelling squatter's wife as she observes Voss's discomfort[154]. When Palfreyman comes to admire the strong Judd's 'almost Christlike humility'[155], Voss protests, 'I detest humility... sin is less ugly'. When Judd suggests observing Christmas Day, Voss calls a halt, but he spits out his disdain for those who want 'to drag in the miserable fetish that this man has insisted on! Of Jesus Christ!'[156]. Almost immediately he is overcome, however, by a horrible image of 'racked flesh' that 'had begun to suppurate', and he is startled in his reverie by the flapping wings of a swooping hawk which seemed for a moment like an emerging soul.

As his struggle intensifies, a mysterious kinship of spirits develops between Voss and Laura, though they are a thousand miles apart. And they begin to explore together the 'country of the mind' which is becoming Voss's real challenge. He confesses to learning the beginnings of humility, even though he protests it still seems weakness to him[157]. She for her part wants to say to him 'I believe I have begun to understand this great country, which we have been presumptuous enough to call *ours*, and with which I shall be content to grow... Do you know that a country does not develop through the prosperity of a few landowners and merchants, but out of the suffering of the humble? I could now lay my head on the ugliest rock in the land and feel at rest'[158].

The companions of Voss, in their various ways, confront him with the Christ-image until, in a terrifying confrontation with hostile blacks, 'All remembered the face of Christ that they had seen at some point of their lives'[159]. Palfreyman, who takes upon himself to parley with the blacks, becomes a living Christ image as he is speared, and dies calling upon the Lord he thinks he has failed: 'Ah Lord, if I had been stronger'[160]. (There is an ambiguity, it must be acknowledged, in White's portrayal of Palfreyman, which we Christians would do well to ponder: it seems to involve a subtle parody of sentimental Christianity which seems out of place in the group.)

Though he is gradually learning to admit to himself his moral frailty[161], it is only the sight of the sore on his horse 'which had crept out from under the pommel of the saddle' which brings Voss 'at last openly' to 'wear his own sores that he had kept hidden'[162]. To the boy, whose loyalty to him had made him so exult with pride that he seemed in possession of the whole firmament, he now says 'I am no longer your Lord, Harry'[163], and he admits that he has always been frightened[164]. Asked what his plan is, he replies 'I have no plan, but will trust to God'[165].

Laura and Voss are linked in a common discovery: 'Dear Christ', she prays, 'now at least I understand your suffering... not that he is humble... when man is truly humbled, when he has learned that he is not God, then he is nearest to becoming so. In the end he may ascend'[166]. Facing his approaching death, Voss is brought to the threshold of faith and cries out in the language of his childhood 'O *Jesus, rette mich nur*! *Du lieber*!' Haunted by the poem of one of his companions which speaks of God with a spear in his side, he is overcome by a delirious fear 'of the arms, or sticks, reaching down from the eternal tree, and tears of blood, and candle wax, of the great legend becoming truth'[167]. As he looked into the night sky for the last time, 'there were the nails of the Cross still eating into it'[168].

The final pages of the novel point to the meaning that had been offered. After Laura has spoken of 'death by torture in the country of the mind', it is suggested that 'our inherent mediocrity as a people... is not a final and irrevocable state; rather it is a creative source of endless variety and subtlety... If only we will explore them'[169]. The future which is offered by God may become present: 'Every moment that we live and breathe, and love, and suffer, and die'[170]. Laura is convinced 'that Voss had in him a little of Christ, like other men'[171]. She too has struggled to be true to the lesson which was offered her, being 'willing to give up so much to prove that human truths are also divine. This is the meaning of Christ'[172].

I have detailed the Christ motif of White's novel—and many other references could have been given—to make clear that it is essential to the author's sustained effort to explore what human existence might be for those who share in the experience of life on our Australian continent. In order to achieve his purpose, White could find no other ultimate measure than that of the gospel story. And it cannot be denied that he has evoked something of the mystery of the divine 'foolishness' of which the gospel story tells. In his peculiar style, he has made a statement which has much in common with those of the other writers I have discussed. This fact constitutes a great challenge to those who see themselves as the bearers of the gospel message: these pioneers in our search for an authentic Australian existence have pointed out a way which leads to a genuine hope close to the experience which has shaped Australia. Perhaps those who have Christian hope have failed to recognise that finding that way and courageously travelling it themselves is the best way to witness to Christian faith[173].

We have seen three writers representative of Australian experience coming to an acceptance of the fact that a perfect order of things is, in this present world, an unattainable goal—one however which we cannot lose sight of without betraying our humanity. As Manning Clark puts it, 'I realised... that the hungers of the human heart were never likely to be satisfied, but I also felt that if you accepted this you had a richer life'. Lawson's preacher has long since abandoned hope that either people or places could ever be any different, but he points to the beauty that is in his people's lives, even in their failures. The same sense that his vision of what Australia could be like will never be fulfilled runs through the musings of Furphy's storyteller in *Such Is Life*. Veronica Brady sees Furphy's attitude as having much in common with that of 'the true wayfaring Christian'[174]. The same could be said of Manning Clark and Henry Lawson.

The third theme identified is our relationship with the unique island-continent which is the place of our human existence. This relationship provides the basic symbol through which we are reminded of what it is to be 'mates'. The land becomes a kind of icon, the repository which preserves for us the wisdom we have found in our Australian experience. As Bernard Smith has reminded us, morality—the struggle 'to be and to remain human'—is not realised in the owning of disembodied propositions and codes, however exalted or authoritative they may be, but in the values and ideals which are owned in concrete human existence in a particular time and place. Our successes and our failures, and what we have made ourselves through them, are identified with our inhabiting of the face of this strange continent. 'The prevailing tone', which has emerged in the literature which celebrates our Australian experience, Cantwell has reminded us, is 'an uneasy acceptance of a world which seems to offer more than it can give'. Joseph Furphy's passing remark 'a long term of self-communion in the back country will never leave a man as it found him. Outside his daily avocation, he becomes a fool or a philosopher' points to the 'disturbing depths of bush experience' and the need to find 'a defence against the bush and its emptiness'[175].

It was necessary for us, as Brian Elliott said in an earlier chapter, to overcome the seeming emptiness, to 'inhabit' the land, and to recognise finally that it had been inhabited and cherished for long ages by black fellow-Australians who had a prior claim to it, before we could finally make it 'our place'. This owning of the land brings a subtle identification through which we are no longer exiles putting up with the hardship of frontier life for our various reasons, and we are able to give ourselves completely to the project of 'being human and remaining human' here in Australia.

The land comes to meet us, as it were, and its strange and beautiful greatness provides the symbolic 'inner landscape' which so many reflective Australians have recognised as essential to their personhood. A. D. Hope expects that 'still from the deserts the prophets come'. Laura, the friend who shares in Voss's struggle to come to terms with his existence through a journey into the

Australian interior, finds this identification, when she has 'begun to understand this great country, which we have been presumptuous to call *ours*'. The struggle to be human, for her, takes place in 'the country of the mind'. As Veronica Brady writes of White's novel: 'God reveals himself precisely where he seems to imaginations nurtured by the Enlightenment's notions of God to be absent, in the physical necessity which presses so urgently in the landscape and in the spiritual desert inhabited by so many Australians, victims of misfortune, of subjection and impersonal fate'[176].

Once more, confessing Christians must ask themselves to what degree their faith awareness and the form in which they have preached the gospel message have been nurtured by theological systems which obscured the manner in which this Australian experience was ready for a meeting with the good news of God given to us in the gospel. The Jesus who reveals the ways of God in the gospel does so first and foremost by inviting us to a testing of the limits and boundaries of the human situation in which we find ourselves. He invites us to recognise for what they are the smug worlds our self-interest and timidity make for us, and to join him in the new order of his Father's 'kingdom'. And having set out upon this journey, he proclaims in his Beatitudes the ultimate paradox of our human struggle: he calls those fortunate who are taken beyond the point at which they are still self-sufficient—those 'who are poor', 'who are hungry now', 'who are weeping now' (Lk 6:20–210)—because this experience may lead them to a genuine meeting with the one who alone can take up their cause, and the ways of his rule of love.

The wonder of the gospel story is that it shows that his words were not an empty exhortation, but expressed his own human existence. In the folly of love which identifies with the beloved, he made his own the words of the psalmist 'The poor man cried and the Lord heard him'. He plunged into the deepest darkness of a foolish and selfish world and made his own the experience which is the common lot of humanity: suffering, mental anguish, alienation, failure and death. He made himself powerless and utterly vulnerable, 'taking the form of a slave' (Phil 2:7).

These themes have been proclaimed so many times; they have been the subject of countless sermons; but how many Christians have seen their relationship to our Australian experience, as Henry Lawson's preacher did in his faltering way when he refused to promise his people that times would get better, or as Patrick White did in the strange story of Voss? Once again, only a witness that resonates with a personal discovery which has been made at the limits of human existence will win a hearing.

The Australian experience of the limits of existence is inseparable from the land and the struggles and setbacks which we have known here. Our land is a kind of icon which in its peculiar way leads us to a meeting with what is ultimate in our human existence, confronting us with our successes and our tragic failures, in our struggle 'to be and to remain human'.

The man who is remembered in the gospel story is not an otherworldly figure; he is very much at home here—'Like a sapling he grew up before him, like a root in arid ground' (Is 53:2). He has much to teach us, if only he is recognised as he really is. Too often, one is tempted to suggest, he is decked out in paraphernalia which tends to prevent a meeting with the divinely simple truth he brings.

---

[1] *Weekend Australian*, 28 March 1990, taken from *Pacific Destiny*, Penguin, 1990.

[2] *A New Imagining: Towards an Australian Spirituality*, Melbourne (Collins Dove) 1990, pp.13–14.

[3] 'The Media, Society and Culture', p.308, in *Australia: The Daedalus Symposium*, S. Graudard (ed.).

[4] *A Crucible of Prophets*, p.70.

[5] loc. cit.

[6] 'The Prodigal Son', *Australian Letters*, vol.1, n.3, 1958.

[7] Conclusion to 1976 Boyer Lectures.

[8] Conclusion to *A Short History of Australia*.

[9] 'Some Religious Stuff I Know about Australia', in *The Shape of Belief*, D. Harris etc. (eds).

[10] ibid., p.14.

[11] ibid., p.26.

[12] ibid., p.16.

[13] ibid., p.17.

[14] loc. cit.

[15] ibid., p.18.

[16] ibid., p.20.

[17] ibid., p.26.

[18] ibid., p.21.

[19] ibid., p.26.

[20] 'The Church in a Secular Society', p.3, in *The Shape of Belief*, D. Harris etc. (eds).

[21] Cited, Serle, *The Creative Spirit in Australia*, p.149, from *The Home of the Blizzard*.

[22] 'Some Religious Stuff I Know about Australia', p.17, in *The Shape of Belief*, D. Harris etc. (eds).

[23] 'Anzac', p.63, in John Carroll (ed.), *Intruders in the Bush*.

[24] ibid., p.62.

[25] ibid., p.55.

[26] 'War Literature', p.350, in *Penguin New Literary History of Australia*, L. Herganhan (ed.).

[27] 'The Character of Australian Religion', *Meanjin*, 36 (1977) p.182.

[28] 'Some Religious Stuff I Know about Australia', p.15, in *The Shape of Belief*, D. Harris etc. (eds).

[29] loc. cit.

[30] *Method in Theology*, London (Darton, Longman and Todd) 1972, p.292.

[31] ibid., p.269.

[32]   ibid., p.268.

[33]   loc. cit.

[34]   'Drink from the Wells of Oz', p.59, in *Discovering an Australian Theology*, Peter Malone (coordinator).

[35]   Melbourne (Collins Dove), 1990.

[36]   *A New Imagining*, p.18.

[37]   p.2. Cf. *Habits of the Heart*, R. Bellah etc. (eds), pp.279 and 294, for comments upon the 'discouraging situation' created in contemporary Western culture by the 'mass media'.

[38]   Kelly, op. cit., p.19.

[39]   ibid., p.13.

[40]   ibid., p.7.

[41]   ibid., p.46.

[42]   ibid., p.37.

[43]   Cited, p.37. In a recent interview Murray declared 'I am interested in one thing and one thing only, and that is grace. I found this instrument called poetry and I was going to play it to see how good I'd get. I do it over and over again to bring to myself and others the experience of grace. There are only two ways to come to that. One is prayer, the other is art. They are both evocations and I tend to get more out of the one called art—although I get important returns out of the one called prayer' (*Weekend Australian*, 'Review' Section, p.2, 4–5 May 1991).

[44]   Kelly, op. cit., p.6.

[45]   ibid., p.8.

[46]   ibid., p.18.

[47]   ibid., p.36.

[48]   ibid., p.57.

[49]   *The Search for Meaning*, Crows Nest (A. B. C.-Dove) 1989, p.7.

[50]   For an account of this workshop see Matthew Fox etc., *Creation Spirituality and the Dreamtime* (ed. Catherine Hammond), Newtown, N.S.W. (Millennium Books) 1991.

[51]   *Creation Spirituality and the Dreamtime*, p.47.

[52]   ibid., pp.83–4.

[53]   ibid., pp.54, 70.

[54]   *The Shape of Belief*, D. Harris, D. Hynd, D. Millikan (eds), Homebush West, N.S.W. (Lancer) 1982.

[55]   'The Church in a Secular Society', p.1.

[56]   'The Cultural Ambivalence of Australian Religion', p.13, in *Australian Cultural History*, S. L. Goldberg and F. B. Smith (eds); cf. also 'Spurious Divorce? Religion and Australian Culture', *Jour. Rel. Hist.*, 15 (1989) pp.519–24.

[57]   'Thinking about Australian Religious History', *Jour. Rel. Hist*, 15 (1989) pp.331, 337.

[58]   *The Sectarian Strand*, Penguin, 1987, p.293.

[59]   *Meanjin* 36 (1977) pp.178–88.

[60]   ibid., p.180.

[61]   Cf. M. Hogan, *The Sectarian Strand*, p.155: 'One of the most talented politicians of the age, Victoria's George Higginbotham, gave respectability to the search for a non-religious basis of social morality, as in a lecture in 1883 when he was a judge of the Supreme Court, soon to become Chief Justice: "I take it to be an indisputable fact that at the end of the Nineteenth Century of the so-called Christian dispensation a very large number of the most cultivated, the most thoughtful, the most sober-minded and the most upright men in all the world, are really unable to determine whether good and sufficient reasons can be found for belief in the existence of God, and whether there is any basis for morality other than supposed personal interest or utility".'

[62]   Cited, Veronica Brady, *A Crucible of Prophets*, p.1.

[63]   *A Crucible of Prophets*, p.69.

[64]   In an interview with Caroline Jones, *The Search for Meaning*, Crow's Nest, N.S.W., 1989, p.84.

[65]   *Weekend Australian*, 'Review' Section, p.2, 23–4 Feb. 1991.

[66]   'Some Religious Stuff I Know about Australia', p.24, in *The Shape of Belief*, D. Harris etc. (eds).

[67]   *Anthology of Australian Religious Poetry*, p.52, L. Murray (ed.), Melbourne (Collins Dove) 1991.

[68]   *Anthology of Australian Religious Poetry*, p.100.

[69]   'Heroes', p.77, in *Australia: The Daedalus Symposium*, S. Graubard (ed.).

[70]   *Convicts, Clergymen and Churches*, Sydney U.P., 1980.

[71]   ibid., p.284.

[72]   Cf. David Hilliard, 'Anglicanism', pp.15–32 in *Australian Cultural History*, S. L. Goldberg and F. B. Smith (eds).

[73]   *The Australian Legend*, p.183.

[74]   *Such Is Life*, p.111.

[75]   ibid., p.112.

[76]   ibid., p.107.

[77]   For a comprehensive treatment of the complex history of sectarianism in Australia, cf. Michael Hogan, *The Sectarian Strand*, Penguin, 1987; 'Whatever Happened to Australian Sectarianism?', *Jour. Rel. Hist.*, 13 (1984) pp.83–91.

[78]   'Australia', in L. Cantrell (ed.), *Writing of the 1890s*, p.86.

[79]   *Joseph Furphy* (Series, *Australian Writers and Their Work*, Geoffrey Dutton (ed.), p.27.

[80]   *Such Is Life*, p.71.

[81]   ibid., p.74.

[82]   In the article to which reference has already been made, 'The Character of Australian Religion', *Meanjin*, 36 (1977) pp.178–88.

[83]   ibid., p.182.

[84]   ibid., p.185.

[85]   'Thinking about Australian Religious History', *Jour. Rel. Hist.*, 15 (1989) p.331.

[86]   Campbell, op. cit., p.184.

[87]   ibid., pp.185–6.

[88]   Cf. 1976 Boyer Lectures, p.30; 'The Character of Australian Religion', pp. 182–3.

[89]   *The Catholic Church and Community in Australia: A History*, West Melbourne (Nelson) 1977, pp.375–376; *The Irish in Australia*, pp.84, 153, 165.

[90]   'Christianity and Australian Identity', p.35, in *The Shape of Belief in Australia*, D. Harris etc. (eds). M. Hogan, in *The Sectarian Strand*, pp.74, 135–9, 154, provides support for this judgment.

[91]   Campbell, op. cit., p.183.

[92]   *Voss*, p.349.

[93]   Cited, Bruce Wilson, 'The Church in a Secular Society', p.10, in *The Shape of Belief*, D. Harris etc. (eds).

[94]   'The Multicultural Challenge', p.90, in *The Shape of Belief*, D. Harris etc. (eds).

[95]   *The Irish in Australia*, p.88.

[96]   Quote from a public lecture by Andrew Hamilton, *What's Been Happening in R.E. in Australia?*, Blackburn, Vic., 1981, p.20.

[97]   Cf. the writer's *Christian Mystery in the Secular Age: The Foundation and Task of Theology*, Westminster, Md. (Christian Classics) 1991, pp.3–31.

[98]   *Religion and Culture*, London (Sheed and Ward) 1949, p.50.

[99]   *Theology of the World* New York (Herder and Herder) 1971, p.34.

[100]   ibid., p.35.

[101]   Metz, *Theology of the World*, p.39.

[102]   Cf. M. D. Chenu, 'The Need for a Theology of the World', in *Great Ideas Today 1967*, R. Hutchins and M. Adler (eds) Chicago (Britannica), pp.53–68; J. Thornhill, 'Is Religion the Enemy of Faith?', *Theological Studies*, 45 (1984) pp.254–74, for further discussion of this question. It goes without saying that the secularisation which is in accord with Christian principle must be distinguished from a closed secularism which denies any openness to the transcendent in human existence.

[103]   Professor Colin Williams, Dean of the School of Theology at Yale University, cited, D. Millikan, 'Christianity and Australian Identity', p.39, in *The Shape of Belief*, D. Harris etc. (eds).

[104]   Pastoral Constitution on the Church in the Modern World (*Gaudium et spes*), nn.3–4, 11.

[105]   Brady, op. cit., p.112.

[106]   Text given in the *Sydney Morning Herald*, 2 Sept. 1972.

[107]   1976 Boyer Lectures, p.50.

[108]   ibid., p.52.

[109]   In the judgment of Bruce Mansfield, 'Australian Christianity belongs to a stage in the history of Christianity where, however important the cult and personal piety may be, faith has to be put in statements, for acceptance or rejection. The well-known contention by Broughton Knox, "Propositional Revelation, the Only Revelation", may be debatable theologically, but historically it provides a clue to the place of Christianity in Western society in what I might call the Australian period and, therefore, in Australia itself', ('Thinking about Australian Religious History', *Jour. Rel. Hist.* 15 (1989) p.334). In what follows we shall argue that such doctrinal reductionism makes the mistake of not recognising that doctrine is a derivative and inadequate expression of the truth of the gospel.

[110]   Cf. T. R. Wright, *Theology and Literature*, p.84.

[111]   *A Short History of Australia*, p.109.

[112]   *Sydney Morning Herald: Good Weekend Magazine*, 23 Sept. 1989, p.76.

[113]   Review of *The Quest for Grace*, *Sydney Morning Herald*, 29 Sept. 1990.

[114]   1976 Boyer Lectures, p.15.

[115]   *In Search of Henry Lawson*, 1978, p.17.

[116]   ibid., p.67.

[117]   ibid., p.67.

[118]   ibid., p.95.

[119]   ibid., p.97.

[120]   ibid., p.97.

[121]   ibid., p.109.

[122]   *A Crucible of Prophets*, p.46.

[123]   *Such Is Life*, pp.111–12.

[124]   ibid., p.107.

[125]   *A Crucible of Prophets*, p.48.

[126]   ibid., p.50.

[127]   *Opening the Bible*, London (Geo Allen and Unwin) 1972, pp.30–1.

[128]   Cf. Hans Kung, *On Being a Christian*, New York, 1978, pp.138, 142.

[129]   *Quadrant*, Sept, 1970, pp.11–25.

[130]   *The Founder of Christianity*, London, 1970, ch. 3.

[131]   *Church Dogmatics*, IV/3, pp.55, 83–4.

[132]   *Jesus the Christ*, London (Burns and Oates) 1977, p.70.

[133]   'The Secular Implications of the Liturgy', in *The Christian Priesthood*, N. Lash and J. Rhymer (eds), London (Darton, Longman and Todd) 1970, pp.218–19.

[134]   *Jesus Christ Liberator*, London, 1980, pp.81–2.

[135]   ibid., pp.95–6.

[136] 1976 Boyer Lectures, p.12.

[137] In an address to which reference has already been made, Kevin Treston writes 'The search of scholars for the historical Jesus has distracted us from the exploration of what the cosmic Christ means for Christian faith' (*Creation Spirituality and the Dreamtime*, ed. C. Hammond, p.68). The point is an important one—provided that the distinction is not made into an opposition or a substitution. It is through the truth that is lived before it is told in the story of Jesus that Christian faith must find the true greatness of the cosmic Christ.

[138] *Preoccupations in Australian Poetry*, pp.xix, xxi.

[139] *Mimesis: The Representation of Reality in Western Literature*, Princeton, N.J.

[140] ibid., pp.41–2.

[141] *The Search for Henry Lawson*, p.63.

[142] Cf. *Faith in History and Society*, New York (Herder and Herder) 1980, chs.6 and 8. Reference to the 'memory of suffering' calls to mind another of Rowe's observations: he sees the Christian story as having a 'comic' rather than a 'tragic' ending. The point is an important one, opening up a perspective much neglected in Christian thought. Perhaps we should say that the story is at once comic and tragic—since, in the end, the life-giving dialectic of our meeting with the gospel touches all dimensions of our human existence.

[143] Cf. *Ideas for a Nation*, p.259.

[144] *The Search for Meaning*, p.17.

[145] *Such Is Life*, p.107. See also Furphy's letter to the *Bulletin*, 'The Teaching of Christ', reproduced in *Joseph Furphy*, John Barnes (ed.). St Lucia (University of Queensland Press) 1981, pp.399–400.

[146] Cf. *A Fortunate Life*, Penguin, 1988, p.314.

[147] *Voss*, p.44.

[148] ibid., p.68.

[149] ibid., p.89.

[150] ibid., p.50.

[151] ibid., p.446.

[152] ibid., p.93.

[153] ibid., p.138.

[154] ibid., p.139.

[155] ibid., p.151.

[156] ibid., p.197.

[157] ibid., p.215.

[158] ibid., p.239—cf. p.271.

[159] ibid., p.342.

[160] ibid., p.343.

[161] ibid., p.285.

[162] ibid., p.363.

[163] ibid., p.379.

[164] ibid., p.390.

[165] ibid., p.379.

[166] ibid., pp.386–7.

[167] ibid., p.390.

[168] ibid., p.391.

[169] ibid., p.447.

[170] ibid., p.448.

[171] ibid., p.445.

[172] ibid., p.371.

[173] See Gordon Dicker, 'Kerygma and Australian Culture', in *Toward Theology in an Australian Context*, Victor C. Hayes (ed.), Bedford Park, S. A.,

1979, pp.46–52, esp. pp.48–52, 'The Aussie Battler Image', for reflections along the lines we are suggesting.

[174] *A Crucible of Prophets*, p.46.
[175] John Barnes, *Joseph Furphy*, p.14.
[176] *A Crucible of Prophets*, pp.82–3.

CONCLUSION

Australia is a young country. I undertook this study convinced that it is important for us, as we enter a new and challenging multi-cultural phase of our history, to take stock of the way of life we have shared. My expectations were modest, but I soon found that the reluctance we Australians have to embark upon the path of self-aggrandisement points to something in our shared ethos which is a strength. As my study has progressed I have been overtaken by a sense of discovery and gratitude. The resources we bring to the challenges we face are unique and remarkable. It is important that we own them more consciously and work to overcome their ambiguities. We have something which deserves to be shared with the broader world.

The characteristics of our Australian ethos I have singled out are those which have caught the attention of one observer. Others suggest themselves which are equally deserving of attention. The resourcefulness which became necessary to ensure survival in the challenging environment of our continent has emerged as a remarkable Australian characteristic. This trait, no more than touched upon in our discussion of the bush legend, deserves fuller consideration. So too does the part sport has played in our national ethos. Both of these themes have a distinct relevance to the concerns of the final chapter, since, as sociologist Peter Berger points out, the hope which inspires human resourcefulness in the face of difficulty, and the joy which is the ultimate intention of all play are 'signals of transcendence' in the midst of life.

In an article published in the *Sydney Morning Herald* on the second day of our bicentennial year, one of our leading journalists, Craig McGregor, took an honest look at our country as it began its year of celebration. He pointed to the challenges we face in the 'post-modern' world, in the midst of a disillusionment which has 'shattered in a million fragments' the 'key myths and ideologies of Western culture for almost a century': 'the Master Narratives of our (past) time—Marxism, Socialism, Freudianism, even the utopian myth of Progress which has been the motor behind Western development since the 19th century'. In a society in which the old Master Narratives are no longer convincing, McGregor puts his hope in the 'spectrum of movements, groups, institutions and individuals committed to changing' our Australian project for the better, by way of 'minuscule, incremental steps'.

It is significant that in this wide-ranging article McGregor makes no mention of the contribution the Christian message may make to our country's future. As a Christian thinker I recognise the challenge this silence implies. The 'intrusive' voice of the church has seldom found a sympathetic hearing in the public conversation of our country. The most effective contribution Christians can bring to that conversation, it would seem, must be at the grassroots level to which McGregor refers. It is at this level that those who would make this contribution must explore the truth of Les Murray's observations, cited in the course of our discussion: 'There is as yet no other vision abroad in our society which commands the same authority as ours does, the same sense of being the bottom line, the great reserve to be called on in times of real need... We are more widely judged on our own best terms than we think, and more insistently expected to be the keepers of the dimension of depth than we find comfortable'.

INDEX OF NAMES

INDEX OF SUBJECTS